Debating Orientalization

Monographs in Mediterranean Archaeology

Series Editor: A. Bernard Knapp

Editorial Board
Dr John Baines, Oriental Institute, Oxford University
Dr Piotr Bienkowski, Manchester Museum, University of Manchester
Professor Robert Chapman, University of Reading
Professor John F. Cherry, Brown University
Professor Andrew G. Sherratt†, University of Sheffield
Susan Sherratt, University of Sheffield
Dr Simon Stoddart, Cambridge University
Dr Peter van Dommelen, University of Glasgow

Aimed at the international archaeological community, *Monographs in Mediterranean Archaeology* (*MMA*) seeks significant new contributions from the multicultural world of Mediterranean archaeology. In general, we publish problem-oriented studies that present a solid, extensive corpus of archaeological data within a sound theoretical and/or methodological framework. *MMA* volumes will deal with major archaeological issues related to the islands and lands or regions that border (or have had a demonstrable impact on) the Mediterranean Sea. No constraints are placed on the period of focus, from Palaeolithic through early Modern. We encourage contributions that treat the social, politico-economic and ideological aspects of local or regional production and development; issues related to social interaction and change or exchange; or more specific and contemporary issues such as gender, agency, identity, representation, phenomenology and landscape, etc.

MMA volumes might include, in addition to original case studies: revised PhD dissertations, well-structured and coherently interpreted final excavation or survey reports, tightly-edited conference proceedings or other collections of high quality and general interest. Purely descriptive excavation reports or survey results will not be considered.

Published:
Mortuary Ritual and Society in Bronze Age Cyprus
(Volume 9)
Priscilla Keswani

Rural Landscapes of the Punic World
(Volume 11)
Peter van Dommelen and Carlos Gómez Bellard

The Power of Technology in the Bronze Age Eastern Mediterranean
The Case of the Painted Plaster
(Volume 12)
Ann Brysbaert

Forthcoming:
Understanding Cypriote Cult
Potnios Theron and the Search for a Principal Male Divinity in Iron Age Cyprus
(Volume 13)
Derek B. Counts

Monumental Architecture, Place and Social Interaction in Late Bronze Age Cyprus
(Volume 14)
Kevin D. Fisher

Material and Landscape in Early Bronze Age Anatolia
Innovation, Opportunism and Conflict
(Volume 15)
Christoph Bachhuber

Monographs in Mediterranean Archaeology 10

Debating Orientalization

Multidisciplinary Approaches to Change in the Ancient Mediterranean

Edited by

Corinna Riva and Nicholas C. Vella

General Editor for this volume

John F. Cherry

LONDON • OAKVILLE

Published by

Equinox Publishing Ltd.
UK: 1 Chelsea Manor Studios, Flood Street, London SW3 5SR
USA: DBBC, 28 Main Street, Oakville, CT 06779

www.equinoxpub.com

First published in hardback 2006. This paperback edition published 2010.

© Corinna Riva, Nicholas C. Vella and contributors 2006

All rights reserved. No part of this publication may be reproduced or transmitted in any form or by any means, electronic or mechanical, including photocopying, recording or any information storage or retrieval system, without prior permission in writing from the publishers.

British Library Cataloguing-in-Publication Data

A catalogue record for this book is available from the British Library.

ISBN   978 1 84553 891 0   (paperback)

Library of Congress Cataloging-in-Publication Data **(I have left this in as a placeholder - Iain)**

Debating orientalization : multidisciplinary approaches to
change in the ancient Mediterranean / edited by Corinna Riva and
Nicholas C. Vella.
       p. cm. -- (Monographs in Mediterranean archaeology)
  Includes bibliographical references and index.
  ISBN 1-84553-192-2 (hb)
  1. Mediterranean Region--Civilization. 2. Mediterranean
Region--Civilization--Middle Eastern influences. I. Riva, Corinna. II.
Vella, Nicholas C. III. Monographs in Mediterranean archaeology (Equinox
Pub.)
  DE59.D43 2006
  930.09'822--dc22
                              2005032073

Typeset by ISB Typesetting, Sheffield
www.sheffieldtypesetting.com
Printed and bound in Great Britain by

Contents

	List of Contributors	vii
	List of Figures	ix
1	Introduction Corinna Riva and Nicholas C. Vella	1
2	Orientalizing: Five Historical Questions Nicholas Purcell	21
3	Approaching Ancient Orientalization via Modern Europe David Wengrow	31
4	Orientalization and Prehistoric Cyprus: The Social Life of Oriental Goods A. Bernard Knapp	48
5	The View from East Greece: Miletus, Samos and Ephesus Sarah P. Morris	66
6	Notes on the Phoenician Component of the Orientalizing Horizon Eric Gubel	85
7	On the Organization of the Phoenician Colonial System in Iberia Maria Eugenia Aubet	94
8	The Orientalizing Period in Etruria: Sophisticated Communities Corinna Riva	110
9	The Orientalizing Phenomenon: Hybridity and Material Culture in the Western Mediterranean Peter van Dommelen	135
10	W(h)ither Orientalization Robin Osborne	153
Index		159

List of Contributors

Maria Eugenia Aubet is Professor of Prehistory at Universidad Pompeu Fabra in Barcelona, and director of the excavations at the Phoenician sites of Tyre (Al-Bass) and Malaga.

Eric Gubel received his PhD from the Free University of Brussels where he now teaches, besides being Senior Keeper of the Antiquity Department, Royal Museums of Art and History. His research has concentrated on Phoenician art and iconography, the interaction of Mediterranean cultures, glyptic studies and the publication of the results of his excavations in Lebanon and Syria. Besides numerous articles published in different journals and the recent catalogue of Phoenician sculpture in the Louvre, he is at present preparing a reference catalogue of Phoenician seals in the Bibliothèque nationale de France.

A. Bernard Knapp is Professor of Mediterranean Archaeology in the Department of Archaeology, University of Glasgow. Research interests include archaeological theory, regional survey archaeology and the archaeologies of landscape, gender and social identity, island archaeology and insularity, and the prehistory of the Mediterranean, in particular that of Neolithic-Bronze Age Cyprus. He co-edits the *Journal of Mediterranean Archaeology* (with John F. Cherry) and edits the series *Monographs in Mediterranean Archaeology* (both published by Equinox, London). His most recent monograph, co-authored with Michael Given, is entitled *The Sydney Cyprus Survey Project: Social Approaches to Regional Archaeological Survey*. Monumenta Archaeologica 21. 2003, Los Angeles: Cotsen Institute of Archaeology, UCLA.

Sarah Morris is Steinmetz Professor of Classical Archaeology and Material Culture at the Department of Classics and the Cotsen Institute of Archaeology at UCLA. Her teaching and research interests include early Greek literature, Greek religion, prehistoric and early Greek archaeology, ceramics, Greek architecture and landscape studies, and Near Eastern influence on Greek art and culture. She has excavated in Israel, Turkey and Greece, and is currently co-director of a new project in Albania. She is the author of *Daidalos and the Origins of Greek Art* (1992) and has co-edited a volume of essays entitled *The Age of Homer* (1998). Her particular interest remains the interaction of Greek culture with neighbouring civilizations as traced in art, archaeology and literature.

Robin Osborne is Professor of Ancient History at the University of Cambridge. His work ranges over ancient history, archaeology and the history of art. His monographs include *Greece in the Making c. 1200–479 BC* (1996), *Archaic and Classical Greek Art* (1998) and *Greek History* (2004), and he has recently edited (with Barry Cunliffe) *Mediterranean Urbanization 800–600 BC* (2005). He is on the editorial board of *World Archaeology* and the *American Journal of Archaeology*.

Nicholas Purcell is Fellow and Tutor in Ancient History at St John's College, Oxford, and University Lecturer in Ancient History. His interests in Greek and Roman social, cultural and economic history have led him to investigate the problems of how to do Mediterranean history on large chronological and geographical scales.

Corinna Riva holds a MA degree in Mediterranean Archaeology from the University of Bristol and a PhD degree in Etruscan Archaeology from the University of Cambridge. She was a Junior Research Fellow in Archaeology at St John's College, Oxford, before taking up a temporary lectureship in Mediterranean Archaeology at the University of Glasgow in 2006. Her research is focused on Etruscan archaeology and pre-Roman Italy, but her interests cover the Archaic Mediterranean as a whole. Her fieldwork is in east central Italy where she is co-director of the Upper Esino Valley Survey.

Peter van Dommelen holds MA and PhD degrees in archaeology and classics from Leiden University (the Netherlands) and has been a lecturer in the Department of Archaeology at the University of Glasgow since 1997. His research interests involve postcolonial approaches to ancient and early modern colonialism as well as survey and rural archaeology in the late prehistoric and early historical western Mediterranean. He has a particular interest in Punic and Roman Republican rural organization. His fieldwork is focused on Sardinia, where he co-directed the *Riu Mannu* field survey between 1991 and 1999. He presently directs the Terralba Rural Settlement Project.

Nicholas C. Vella is Senior Lecturer in the Department of Classics and Archaeology at the University of Malta. His research interests include later Mediterranean prehistory, landscape archaeology with an emphasis on the study of spatial perceptions in antiquity, and the development of archaeological traditions in Malta. He has been Assistant Director of the University of Malta excavations at the site of the Phoenician sanctuary at Tas-Silg in Malta since 2000.

David Wengrow is a Lecturer at the Institute of Archaeology, University College London. His research addresses the nature of early social transformations in Egypt and Iraq, and the role of the remote past in the formation of modern political identities. Recent publications include: 'The Intellectual Adventure of Henri Frankfort: a missing chapter in the history of archaeological thought' *(American Journal of Archaeology* 103, 1999) and 'Landscapes of Knowledge, Idioms of Power: the African origins of Egyptian civilization reconsidered' (2003, *Ancient Egypt in Africa,* D. O'Connor and A. Reid eds., UCL Press).

List of Figures

1.1 Pallottino's map depicting the area of diffusion of Orientalizing culture prepared for his entry to the *Encyclopedia of World Art* published in 1965.

3.1 Bronze medallion commemorating the publication of *Description de l'Égypte*, 1826. After Curl 1994:133, fig.81.

3.2 *La Musée Charles-X en 1863*. Engraving by A.Régis. After Andreu *et al.* 1997:23, fig.6.

3.3 The origin of Britain according to John Bale, Bishop of Ossory (d.1563). After Kendrick 1950:68.

3.4 Detail from Pieter Coecke van Aelst, *Procession of Sultan Süleyman II through the Atmedan*, woodcut from *Ces Moeurs et fachons de faire de Turcz*, 1533. After Jardine and Brotton 2000:151, illus.62 (note obelisk, top left).

5.1 Hittite bowl from Hattusas with graffito of Aegean (?) warrior. Photo by author after Kurt Bittel *Revue Archéologique* 1976, 11, fig. 3.

5.2 North Syrian horse frontlet, bronze, from Samos. DAI Samos 88/1022.

7.1 The Phoenician colonies in the West.
7.2 The island of Cerro del Villar, near Málaga (reconstruction).
7.3 Phoenician dwellings at Morro de Mezquitilla (after Schubart).
7.4 Alabaster urn from Almuñecar with inscription of pharaoh Apophis.
7.5 The central area at Toscanos and plan of the warehouse.
7.6 The market street at Cerro del Villar.
7.7 Cerro del Villar: reconstruction of the market street.
7.8 8th century pottery kilns at Cerro del Villar.

8.1 Tomba delle Statue, Ceri near Cerveteri.
8.2 Hut-shaped urn, Monterozzi, Arcatelle necropolis, Tarquinia (Scavi comunali 27/II-4/III).
8.3 Interior space, Tomba degli Animali Dipinti I, Caere.
8.4 Tintinnabulum, Tomba degli Ori, Bologna.
8.5 Verucchio throne and engraved scenes.

9.1 Map of southern Sardinia showing the main Phoenician-Punic settlements and other relevant sites mentioned in the text. Legend: 1: Genna Maria—Villanovaforru; 2: Su Mulinu—Villanovafranca; 3: Monte Prama—Cabras.
9.2 Selection of three oil-lamps of Hellenistic date from the ritual deposit at Genna Maria (Villanovaforru). No. 1 is hand-made of the so-called 'boat-shaped' type and nos 2 and 3 are mould-made Black Glaze specimens imported from North Africa (2) and central Italy (3) (after Lilliu 1993: plates I and IV).
9.3 Iron Age bronzetto figurine of a warrior-chief found in Uta (SE Sardinia) (photo Museo Nazionale Cagliari).
9.4 Examples of so-called 'geometric' (1) and 'sub-geometric' (2) pottery from early Orientalizing contexts at nuraghe Piscu (Suelli) (after Santoni 1991:figs 7 and 8).
9.5 Reconstruction of one of the warrior statues from Monte Prama (after Bernardini and Tronchetti 1990:fig. 204).

In memory of Roger Moorey and Andrew Sherratt,

inspirations to many people

1 Introduction

Corinna Riva and Nicholas C. Vella

On the weekend of the 7th and 8th September 2002, scholars gathered at St John's College in Oxford to debate the theme of ancient Orientalization. The idea to organize a symposium on this topic occurred to us while we were researching cultural interaction and change in Etruria and in Sardinia. It became clear that the 'Orient' was often brought in by scholars intent on explaining change in both places, a veritable metaphorical bazaar, with its opulence and sophistication, that purportedly had a lasting impact on western Mediterranean communities. Challenged by what we thought were limitations in the literature to explore more closely Orientalizing—invariably described as a phenomenon (Pallottino 1965:784), revolution (Boardman 1999:47 n. 7), or movement (Niemeyer 2003:201)—and stimulated by the comments to debunk Orientalizing (Osborne 1993), we asked a select group of scholars the following questions: whether they felt that Orientalization was a valid heuristic term for interpreting dynamics of cultural contact and change within the ancient Mediterranean, and whether they felt that the term was simply a construct of modern historiography or of art history to the point that the terms Orientalization or Orientalizing could no longer be maintained.

We were aware that there had been other successful gatherings of scholars that discussed the theme of ancient interaction—notoriously East-West—in the Mediterranean, even those that did not restrict debate to the 8th and 7th centuries BC (e.g. Fischer-Hansen 1988; Kopcke and Tokumaru 1992; Prayon and Röllig 2000; Stampolidis and Karageorghis 2003), the era with which the Orientalizing period is normally identified. We therefore thought that an alternative way to explore the theme of ancient Orientalization would be to bring together speakers with diverse backgrounds, training, and approaches, even at the risk of providing a narrative that excluded several micro-regions in the Mediterranean and of having opinions that could ultimately refuse to gel together and a consensus not reached: prehistorians working in different areas of southern Europe and the Mediterranean (M.E. Aubet, A.B. Knapp, K. Kristiansen, P. van Dommelen, D. Wengrow), classical archaeologists (S. Morris, A. Naso, C. Riva [who replaced M. Cuozzo, unfortunately indisposed at the very last minute], M. Shanks), a curator/archaeologist (E. Gubel). Papers were delivered in four sessions for which a number of scholars, again from diverse backgrounds and training, kindly agreed to act as chairpersons and respondents respectively to papers that had been circulated in advance: Historiography (N. Purcell); the Late Bronze Age (A. Sherratt, S. Sherratt); the Iron Age (O. Murray, S. Dalley, A. Naso); Anthropology and Culture History (R. Osborne, C. Gosden). The ensuing discussion was taped and transcribed and distributed to the speakers who were asked to take the critical discussion into consideration when they provided us with the final version of their papers for publication.

We have decided to place what started off as a response to Wengrow's paper first in this volume, immediately following this introduction, for it became apparent during the course of the symposium that Purcell's intervention based on five historical questions provided much food for thought and provoked several speakers to return to the implications involved in maintaining the term Orientalizing which not only supposes an Oriental origin for whatever culture process is being studied, but which masks the profound regional differences and the plurality of the recipients at a time, the first half of the first millennium BC, when the Mediterranean was an entangled web of people, things, skills and ideas. Wengrow, who was asked to consider Orientalization as a process of concrete cultural interaction from the perspective of historiography, brought to the discussion Edward Said's concept of Orientalism, the fashioning of a self-image predicated upon distance from an exotic 'Other'. Making a plea for rooting in cultural memory any attempt to evaluate ancient Orientalization, Wengrow shifts from century to century to illustrate how dynasts and popes, archaeologists and sociologists, used images, material remains and observations of the manners and customs of Orientals to set European values and institutions against the social orders of ancient times.

We felt that the chronological boundaries usually set for Orientalizing ought to be broken down to consider the earlier Late Bronze Age, when trade networks had already brought different regions of Asia, Europe and the Mediterranean together (Bietti Sestieri 1997; Giardino 1995; Mederos Martín 1997). Knapp presented evidence from Cyprus—traditionally a metal-bearing nodal zone of the Late Bronze Age eastern Mediterranean—to argue that for Cypriot elites intent on affirming their political authority, the distant Orient provided them with the source of royal sumptuousness and cultured erudition to do so. Knapp grounds his narrative in anthropological theory and argues that the phenomenon of acquiring goods from the 'primary' Asian states is *ancient* (in contrast to *modern* Saidian) Orientalism, a term he coins: a process whereby Cypriot political elites acquired the Orient ideologically and economically as a commodity and through this commodity affirmed their own political authority at home. If Cyprus is often taken to be part of the monolithic Levant, Knapp's stance provides an alternative, placing emphasis on the cultural ideals of an elite that tried to come to terms with geographically distant places, people and ideas.

Kristiansen made a case for the European Late Bronze Age dimension of the Orientalizing process, particularly with reference to the later impact of Levantine, Greek and Etruscan trade and lifestyle on the development of the aristocratic courts in central Europe. Unfortunately, his contribution could not be published, but we refer to previous work where he has explored similar issues in a different context elsewhere (Kristiansen 1994).

Morris's view is from East Greece and, in particular, from the 'golden triangle' of the region of Ionia in Asia Minor:Samos, Miletus and Ephesus and their sanctuaries. She focuses on relations among native Anatolian and Greek communities and the Levant, and, perhaps in contrast to Knapp's optimistic stance on the concepts and ideas that objects may convey and signify, deals with the invisibility of certain types of exchange in the imported objects, their imitations and the wider context of use of what we call *exotica*. Some of these, such as soft commodities or even mobile people such as mercenary soldiers, can only be glimpsed at through textual evidence which Morris lays out and compares to the artefacts themselves which, we presume, underlay these types of exchange. These invisible relations, she argues, did not appear in an empty vacuum but were the results of contacts stemming back to the Bronze Age, and this leads Morris to see Orientalizing, which she defines as East-West exchange, in a dilated form throughout antiquity. The problem with this, she argues, is that the crucial movers of this exchange and a whole series of borrowings from the East, that is, mobile people, remain invisible to us. The Phoenicians may be some of these invisible movers, yet Morris sees them at the centre of Orientalizing, or even Phoenicianizing, an ancient concept of Orientalizing.

Two scholars were asked to talk specifically about the Phoenicians, the maritime culture for which several saw a solution for the Orientalizing dilemma during the discussion at the symposium despite Purcell's caution. Gubel was invited to talk about the relationship between the Phoenicians and Orientalization from a Mediterranean-wide perspective. In choosing to study typologies of artefacts and distribution of objects he presented new data and explored regional differences for a culture presumed all too often to be a homogenous entity. Gubel's innovative contribution lies in the fact that he considers Phoenician (and more specifically, Sidonian) art as contributing to, rather than be equated with (see below), the Orientalizing artistic horizon.

Aubet, on the other hand, considers the Orientalization of Iberia not by concentrating on the ubiquitous theme of the Phoenician effect on the Tartessian hinterland but by studying the internal dynamics of Phoenician foundations in the farthest reaches of the Mediterranean in the light of new archaeological evidence and settlement history. She relates Orientalizing to economic practices and social processes, encapsulated in the coming together of rich Phoenician merchants and indigenous elites at market places on Phoenician settlements.

Indigenous elites are also prominent in discussions of Orientalizing in 7th-century Etruria. Riva's contribution explores the archaeological evidence on Etruria from a fresh angle which attempts to debunk the notion of Orientalizing Etruria as a princely culture, and explain the funerary sophistication achieved through Orientalizing goods as expression of a variety of power negotiations within indigenous communities.

Van Dommelen and Shanks were asked to bring a theoretical approach to the study of Orientalization. In view of earlier publications on Sardinia that explored settlement history from a postcolonial perspective, van Dommelen was asked to consider whether the concept of hybridization would explain the Orientalizing phenomenon of the island during the Iron Age. Whereas the author is happy to consider hybridity at work in later Punic Sardinia, when foreign cultural elements are reworked by the locals for ultimate deposition in ritual contexts, he argues against the concept of hybridity to explain the use made by local elites of foreign objects brought to Sardinia by the Phoenician settlers. In presenting a clear case about the social processes that the impact of the complex exchange of Phoenician objects must have entailed in the diverse regions where they are known archaeologically, van Dommelen starts filling the gap left by iconographic studies like Gubel's.

Shanks, who could not submit his paper for publication, was invited to explore alternative ways to interpret iconographic motifs within a narrative that is socially and historically informed. His plea—made through a set of pre-circulated notes and in his presentation—was to stop seeking the origins of stylistic repertoires inherent in the very use of the term *Orientalizing* and in the art-historical approach preferred by others (including Gubel), and to concentrate instead on cycles of production and consumption—a veritable lifecycle of an object, as he called it—where the manipulation of components takes a central role in a contextual study of artefacts and the motifs which decorate them. As on other occasions (cf. Shanks 1995 with comments), the anthropologically informed approach stirred debate, even in view of Purcell's suggestion that studying consumption is a more profitable undertaking.

We invited Robin Osborne to sum up the two-day proceedings at the symposium. There and here, he upholds the use of the term 'Orientalizing' and advocates the role of active transformation and re-working of cultural goods from the east in western, primarily Greek, contexts. Here, the re-working, namely Orientalizing, bears the baggage of Orientalism which has little to do with colonial relations but which still carries different forms of power strategies.

In what follows in this introduction we trace the archaeological discoveries which led to the conception of the Orientalizing period in ancient (Greek) art history. We shall show how the periodization proposed by archaeologists went hand-in-hand with the classification that was required for the displays of those museums in Europe that were acquiring artefacts excavated in the Levant. The story starts, however, with discoveries not in the East where a race was on between French, British and German savants and enthusiasts (cf. Reinach 1888:1–12) to reveal to Europe the world of Oriental manners and customs, both ancient and modern, but in the central Mediterranean. We shall return to the explanation that archaeologists sought to give to the artefacts, an explanation that departs from classification and typology to view Orientalizing more in terms of social transformations and lifestyles. In our attempt to give an overview of the changes in approach and the intellectual developments we realize that many scholars, sites and finds have been left out. We believe, however, that the outline we provide will allow readers to place the individual contributions that follow this introduction in a historical perspective.

Periodization and the Orient: metal bowls and art history

The application of the term 'Orientalizing' to designate a style in the art of the ancient Greeks came from the classical scholar Alexander Conze in 1870, a date that has been called a landmark in the study of Greek art (Demargne 1964:270). Conze, professor at the University of Vienna, thought that the term would define the style of the painted vases that had been discovered in Etruscan tombs in Italy in the first half of the nineteenth century (Conze 1870). He argued that the Orientalizing stylistic group had evolved out of a style with linear patterns having no relation to nature, hence Geometric, until then only apparent from a few discoveries in Greece. The swirling floral motifs and representations of wild beasts and fantastic monsters were held to be reminiscences of the Orient, Egypt in particular, by the archaeologists who worked in central Italy in the years preceding the remarkable discoveries in Assyria from 1845 onward. At Cerveteri, the ancient Agylla or Caere, two associates Vincenzo Galassi and Alessandro Regolini, army general the first, archpriest of Cerveteri the second, made a great discovery on an estate in the parish on 22 April 1836. From two chambers within a burial mound distant about 4 km distant from the cemetery of the Banditaccia, their workmen recovered an array of extraordinary gold artefacts, mostly jewellery, and metalwork. Amongst the objects found, bracelets, a pectoral, fibulae, and pendants were ornamented in repoussé, with lions and birds, winged sphinxes and winged genii, flowers and palmettes, in rows or curves or concentric circles. Two bronze cauldrons, one decorated with lion heads and the other with griffin heads turned inwards, and four shallow silver bowls decorated with pictorial scenes were also recovered. The tomb became known as the Regolini-Galassi following the acquisition, in 1838, by the Vatican of the collection for its newly inaugurated Museo Gregoriano Etrusco where the objects were displayed according to type and material (cf. Pareti 1947; Buranelli 2000:512–13). This discovery, especially the silver bowls, was to be the first in a series of archaeological finds that induced archaeologists working in Italy and Greece to look to the Orient for a source of this art work. By 1847, when the first Assyrian museum in the world was inaugurated at the Louvre to house Paul-Émile Botta's extraordinary finds at Khorsabad, a source of production was sought for the Caere examples by the French savant D. Raoul-Rochette, the superintendent of antiquities in the Bibliothéque in Paris.

On 5 January 1849, on his second archaeological expedition to Assyria, this time on behalf of the British Museum, a young Austen Henry Layard discovered a hoard of bronze bowls during his excavations in Room AB (the 'Room of the Bronzes') of the North-West Palace at Nimrud, 40 km south of Mosul. Layard described a selection of them in his *Discoveries in the Ruins of Nineveh and Babylon* (1853a:182–91) and had engravings made of several (1853b:pls 59c, 60, 62b, 63, 64). He remarked upon the Egyptian character of the hairstyle, dress and jewellery worn by the figures; lion or leopard, winged griffin, ibex, gazelle, ram and the bull were of Assyrian character, 'designed with considerable spirit' he held. Layard noticed the resemblance between the mythical animals and the ornaments portrayed on the Nimrud bowls and plates and the painted pottery and metal artefacts found in Etruria, especially in the Regolini-Galassi tomb as they appeared in Grifi's *Monumenti di Cere Antica* (1841). 'They forcibly call to mind the early remains of Greece' he remarked but argued that whilst the character of the designs on the bowls was Egyptian, the 'minute and curious' workmanship, 'peculiar' subjects and mode of treatment were Assyrian rather than Egyptian. Layard sought the origins of certain artistic traits and elegant ornaments in Assyria itself, noting in a characteristic ethnographic mode that the tiny floral motifs could be compared to the bright scarlet tulips which abound in early spring on the plains and meadows of the country (1853a:184; cf. 1858:55). He believed, however, that the artist 'either copied from Egyptian models, or was a native of a country under the influence of the arts and taste of Egypt' (1853a:192). Using Homeric references to renowned Sidonian metalwork, Layard concluded that the Nimrud vessels could be the work of artists hailing from the Phoenician homeland, a geographic position—between Egypt and Assyria—that could have harboured the 'mixed art'. This would also be confirmed by the fact that one bowl depicting a series of vultures devouring a hare (Layard 1953a:188 cat. no. 6; 1953b: pl. 62b) had an inscription in the Phoenician cursive script below the rim. The tin needed to manufacture the bowls may have been brought over by the Phoenicians from the British Isles, whilst the artefacts could have ended in Assyria as tribute from Tyre or with captive craftsmen.

As a footnote, and to prove a Phoenician origin for the metalwork, Layard cited two shallow gilded silver bowls that had just been found in Cyprus, historically known to have been a Phoenician outpost. The bowls were found in 1849 together with another eight or ten during illicit excavations at Ambelliri, the western acropolis of Idalion. According to Adrien de Longpérier (1855:411), who went on to publish the catalogue of the Louvre Asiatic collection that went by the name of *Musée Napoléon III* (1868–74) and meant to serve as a historical tool for the appreciation of eastern and western art, the two bowls were rescued from a furnace in Larnaca by two French gentlemen who purchased them; by 1855 they were in the Louvre. One depicts a four-winged figure slaying a lion and a youth slaying a griffin, each separated by a stylized palmette, together with a military procession of horsemen and foot soldiers led by a king in his chariot followed by three bowmen; the other depicts an Egyptian king wearing a crown who is threatening to strike a group of suppliant enemy captives surrounded by a register of combat scenes between humans, lions and griffins. De Longpérier (1855:416) believed that Raoul-Rochette was vindicated by Layard's exceptional discoveries; such bowls could be seen being held by Assyrian kings on the bas-reliefs excavated from Nimrud and the Kuyunjik mound (ancient Niniveh). He also noted that the animals which appeared on the silver bowls also occurred on pottery that had been found at Corinth in Greece, on some of the Aegean islands and in Etruria (1855:418). Acknowledging the indebtedness to Egyptian artistic forms, de Longpérier was convinced that the style was borrowed from the East, through direct contact with the Phoenicians and the Assyrians.

Knowledge of the ambivalent art style was enlarged as new metal objects were found depicting the same themes and mixture of Egyptian and Assyrian motifs. The method of investigation was one that rested on inferences drawn from a juxtaposition of visual parallels. When the German archaeologist Wolfgang Helbig of the Deutsches Archäologisches Institut in Rome published his essay *Cenni sopra l'arte fenicia* addressed to Giovanni Spano in 1876, spurred by the wish to define the artistic style of objects recovered in Phoenician tombs in Sardinia, he listed the discovery of a silver bowl from a rifled tomb in Amathus in Cyprus announced by Luigi Palma di Cesnola (Myres 1933; Markoe 1985: cat. no. Cy4), and a silver bowl that formed part of a treasure found in Kourion by the same Cesnola who supplied Helbig with a hitherto unpublished photograph of it (Marquand 1888; Markoe 1985: cat. no. Cy8). Besides listing the finds from the Regolini-Galassi tomb, Helbig also included a description of a bowl found in the ancient necropolis of Praeneste near Palestrina by Prince Barberini in 1855 (Helbig 1876:203 cat. no. X; Markoe 1985: cat. no. E5) and three bowls excavated from a tomb in the Frollano estate in Palestrina by the Bernardini brothers in 1876 (Helbig 1876:203 cat. nos XI-XIII; Markoe 1985: cat. no. E1-E3). On one of these bowls, in the medallion just above the wing of a falcon that hovers over the figure smiting enemy captives, is a Phoenician inscription. Helbig argued at length that the style was an amalgam of Egyptian and Assyrian traits but maintained that the bowls were of Phoenician origin. Despite the fact that no such metal bowls were known from the Phoenician homeland, Helbig referred to the results of Ernest Renan's survey work in Phoenicia undertaken for Napoleon III (Renan 1864), recalling that the characteristic admixture of styles was also present on architectural fragments recovered from sites there.

Debates about the origin of the silver bowls and hence of the identification of the Levantine prototypes of Greek Orientalizing art became a major concern of academics and curators employed in universities and museums respectively. Whereas Georges Perrot and Charles Chipiez championed the Phoenician origin of the bowls in their oft-cited work *Histoire de l'Art de l'Antiquité* (1885:338–73), Heinrich Brunn's view expressed in his *Dei Kunst bei Homer* (1868) was that the Cypriot and Caeretan bowls were the product of an incipient Greek industry. The discoveries of Heinrich Schliemann at Mycenae after 1874 (Schliemann 1878), those at Olympia from 1875 on (Furtwängler 1879), and especially those at the Idaean Cave in Crete in 1884 (Orsi 1888) raised the problem of establishing the aesthetic and chronological relations between Mycenaean, Geometric and Orientalizing art. While some insisted that the Orientalizing style grew directly out of Mycenaen art, others held that the remarkable enrichment of the iconography that transformed an austere and formal Greek art was owed to a source from outside Greece. In a review of Schliemann's volume on his excavations at Mycenae, the Keeper of Greek and Roman Antiquities of the British Museum,

Charles Newton, concluded that the period when the 'rude untaught instincts of the Hellenic artist were stimulated and developed by the importation of foreign works, the product of a more advanced civilisation' ought to be called Graeco-Phoenician (Newton 1880:289). He set its lower limits to the fall of Niniveh, the source of the style and subject in the metallic art of places so wide apart as Nimrud and Cerveteri. Setting the upper limit meant giving a date to the Homeric poems and the Heroic Age that Schliemann associated with the Mycenaean palaces, a controversial issue that was raging at the time (e.g. Ridgeway 1896; cf. Morris 1997a:106–11). Newton remarked that no metal bowls were found in the Mycenaean tombs that were decorated with the battle and hunting scenes that Phoenician craftsmen excelled in and celebrated in the Homeric poems. The art of Mycenae with representations of animal art characterized by 'a feebleness of execution, the result of barbaric ignorance' and representations of life which Newton could hardly rate 'much higher than the work of New Zealanders and other savages' had to be pre-Homeric in date. The debate had obvious repercussions on the pre-Classical chronology of Italy (Montelius 1897 with discussion by A.J. Evans and J.L. Myres).

The amount of archaeological evidence that had accumulated by the close of the nineteenth century had made it clear to Newton and other scholars that the Orient—Assyria, Phoenicia, Egypt—held the key to Greek (e.g. Collignon 1886:28; Harrison 1885) and Etruscan (e.g. Martha 1889:114–6) art history. It also made it possible for the art historian and theorist Alois Riegl to write his seminal history of ornament by considering the development of vegetal motifs from Egypt onwards for several centuries (Riegl 1893). Doubts, however, on the periodization of early Greece persisted and the extent of Oriental influence in the Aegean before the 7th century remained unclear. An Orientalizing period is missing from Gardner's *A Grammar of Greek Art* (1905) which relegates a discussion of Levantine iconographic motifs on Greek pottery to a Geometric period dated to 900–700 BC. The *Guide to the Greek and Roman antiquities in the British Museum* (1899) compiled by A.H. Smith, assistant at the museum, talks of a 'period of strong Oriental influence' for the small ceramic vases of the 7th century BC when he describes the First Vase room at the museum. Della Seta (1922) accepted the idea of 'Orientalizing art' in his manual on Italian art history and so did Ducati (1927:ch. 3) in his history of Etruscan art. Gisela Richter, the Metropolitan's first woman curator, was unambiguous in her handbook to the Classical collection of the museum (Richter 1927) probably because by then Frederik Poulsen (1912) had made a clear-cut case for the indebtedness of Greek art towards the Orient:she dates some of the objects in the Second Room of the museum to the 'Period of Orientalizing influence' to 700–500 BC so that the period formed an integral part of the 'Early Greek Period' that goes from 1100 to 550 BC. For her, in this period of Oriental influence, the Greeks who had grown accustomed to seeing Oriental goods brought to them by Phoenician traders, gradually awoke to new ideas and energies. Creative innovations were a product of superior Greek artists who were able to transform the gaudiness of Phoenician luxury items which no longer appealed to the refined tastes of the Greek or Etruscan aristocracy from the 7th century onwards; stylistic diffusion was stopped in its tracks when the Orient was losing its fascination (cf. Brown 1960:28, 46).

Discoveries in southern Spain since 1890 ensured that the furthest reaches of the Mediterranean came to be engulfed in the wave of cultural diffusion from the Orient through Phoenician and apparently Etruscan intermediaries, and an Orientalizing artistic style

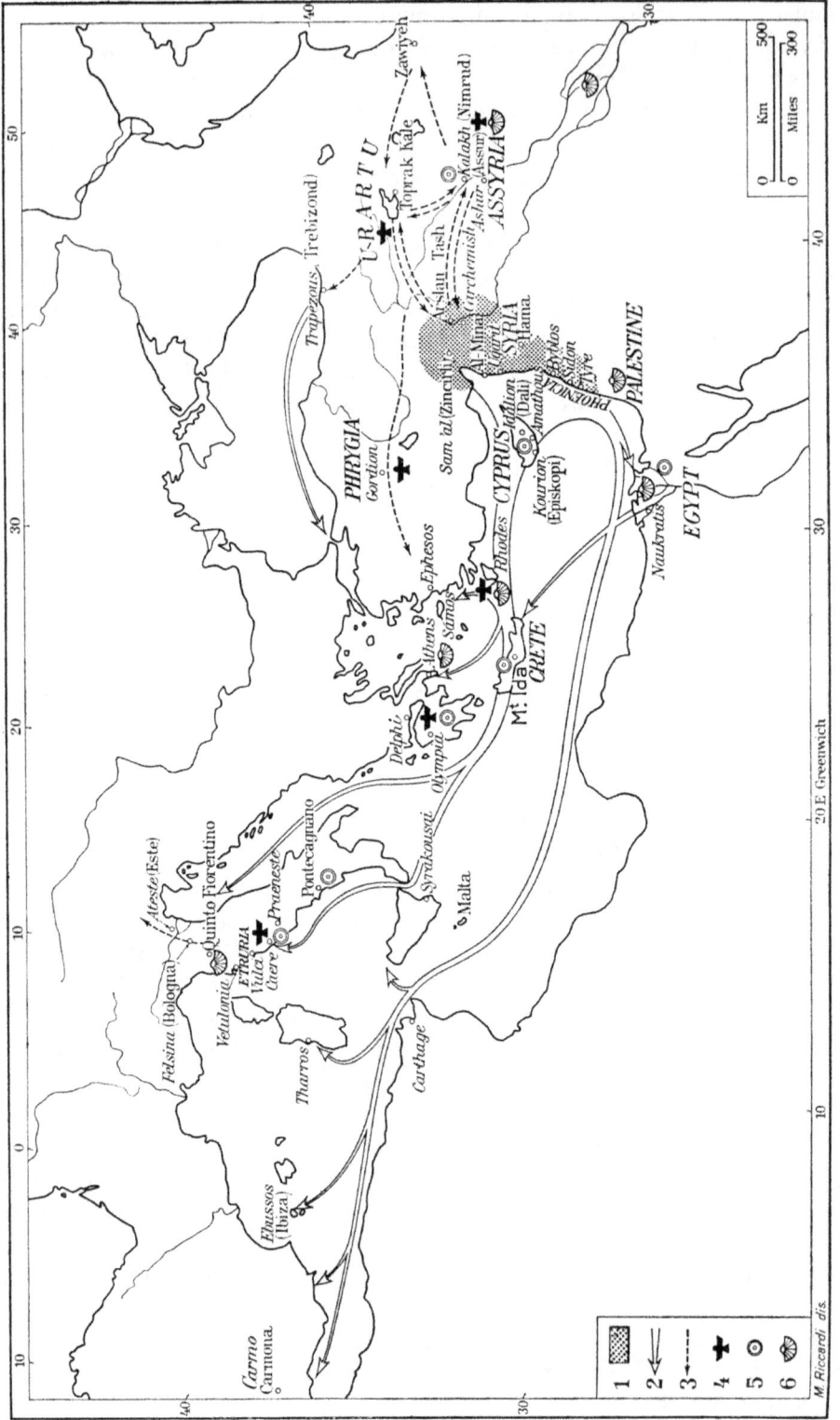

Area of diffusion of Orientalizing culture: (1) Primary area of development of a composite Eastern art; (2) principal routes of maritime commerce; (3) probable overland routes of transmission and direction of cultural contacts. Distribution of some typical classes of Orientalizing objects: (4) "Sirens"; (5) metal pateras with embossed decoration; (6) decorated Tridacna shells and their imitations.

Figure 1.1   Pallottino's map depicting the area of diffusion of Orientalizing culture prepared for his entry to the *Encyclopedia of World Art* published in 1965.

and historical period were acknowledged and made to herald the changes that Tartessian aristocratic society underwent (Almagro Gorbea 1991; Aubet 1984; Gran-Aymerich and du Puytison-Lagarce 1995; Harrison 1988: ch. 4).

While arrows of diffusion are clearly drawn to traverse maps of the Mediterranean westwards from a variegated Orient (Figure 1.1), the tradition of reinterpreting the imagery depicted on the old discoveries (e.g. Aubet 1971; Botto 1993; Cristofani Martelli 1973; Hopkins 1965; Markoe 1985: ch. 4), classifying new finds (e.g. Canciani 1979; d'Agostino 1977a; Maggiani 1973; Winter 1994), mapping the distribution of particular classes of objects (e.g. Grau-Zimmermann 1978; Franz 1998–99), seeking out Oriental prototypes and sourcing iconographic motifs—lions, griffins, sirens, winged bulls, birds (e.g. Bisi 1965; Brown 1960; Goldman 1960; Muscarella 1962, 1970; Shefton 1988)—has continued to characterize scholarship over the years (also Strøm 1971). Several have also tried to understand the structure and format of the narrative on the metalwork (e.g. Güterbock 1957:69–70; Markoe 1985: ch. 3; Myres 1933; Rathje 1980), mostly in an effort to show that this was no mere hodgepodge of motifs. More interesting, perhaps, were the attempts to explore mythological attributions and contextual meanings:the essay by the French diplomat and orientalist, Clermont-Ganneau (1880) on the Palestrina bowl, remains a significant excursus, with its suggestion that works of art like this and similar ones from Cyprus provided the Greeks with an incentive to invent their own mythology. This was a line of investigation that was given an impetus in the late-19th century by classical scholars of the likes of Jane Harrison who combined anthropology and sociology in order to explore the ritual origins of the institutions of Greek culture (Harrison 1912; Ridgeway 1901–31).

The favourite theme for investigation, however, had to remain the vexed question of origins, with a focus on new places in the Orient as artistic styles and production centres associated with regions beyond the traditional Phoenician homeland were identified, Urartian and North Syrian especially (Karo 1920; Pallottino 1958; Winter 1988), while the traditional all-encompassing label "Phoenician" given to such objects as the Nimrud ivories excavated by Layard came under review (Barnett 1948; Winter 1976, 1981). Moreover, a Cypro-Phoenician label became an alternative tag to describe cultural assimilations on an island long held to be at the crossroads of Orient and Occident with its spectacular aristocratic and warrior burials that recall the world of Homer (Markoe 1985; Karageorghis 2002). If the iconographic motif or object type lacked a 'homeland', particularly in the relatively unknown Iron Age archaeological levels in Lebanon, a centre of manufacture or workshop—like Rhodes—was sought to accommodate itinerant skilled Levantine craftsmen long suspected to explicate the distribution of luxury objects in copper-rich Cyprus, silver-rich Etruria and Iberia (Poulsen 1912:64; Barnett 1948:2; Burkert 1992), an explanation that builds on a historical model proposed for the earlier Late Bronze age (Giardino 1995; Zaccagnini 1983). This explanation remains popular (Markoe 2003) and would seem not to be invalidated by the apparent paucity of data in the Phoenician homeland (but see Gubel, this volume). For as Niemeyer (2003:204 n. 4) has recently recalled, more than a century of excavation in about 3000 tombs at Carthage has failed to recover similar luxury items clearly meant not for local (Phoenician) consumption but for diplomatic and commercial ventures abroad. But phantom itinerant or residential craftsmen—Phoenicians or Orientals—are not popular (see Lemnos 2003 and discussion), and the identity of the intermediaries responsible for cultural diffusion or stimulus—Phoenicians, Euboeans, Corinthians—is as elusive as ever (Kopcke

1992; Markoe 1996; Niemeyer 2004; Ridgway 2004), a stark reminder perhaps that it is context rather that origins that will get us out of a quandary that sees no signs of abating (see Osborne, this volume).

Manners and customs: the Orient as lifestyle

Interpreting the phenomenon of a mixed art purely in terms of stylistic borrowings from prototypes was soon deemed as a first step towards understanding a far more complex relationship with the Orient. During the end of the 19th and the beginning of the 20th centuries, whilst some historians held eastern contacts and influence in Greece as a material, external phenomenon deserving no other explanation (Burckhardt 1998: ch. 3, 136), archaeologists attributed Greek civilization of the Homeric age with Oriental manners and customs. In his *Das Homerische Epos* of 1887, Helbig stated that to a spectator's eyes life at the eastern courts of Nineveh would be indistinguishable from that in a Greek *megaron* (Helbig 1887:426). Curiously, Helbig's emphasis on eastern objects underlying certain manners bore some resemblance to what historians and archaeologists would have made of Orientalizing a century later or so:that in the 7th century people throughout the Mediterranean used objects coming from somewhere east in ways that were Orientalizing, a process of becoming Oriental via material objects (Osborne 1993:235; 1996:166–7). To most scholars of Helbig's generation, however, the Heroic age of Homer spanned a long time that included the palatial period of Mycene and ended with the Archaic age of Greek history: a viewpoint which was held by Homerists since the 18th century, for whom the Homeric age began with the remotest past of Greece and ended with the beginning of the Olympiad (Morris 1997a:100). It was only after the 1950s, following the discovery of Linear B, that Homer was placed in the post-Mycenean Dark Age, a stepping stone for the periodization of early Greek history and for the Mediterranean as a whole, and that Orientalizing was situated within a more discrete phase. At the same time, through the work of Moses Finley, the Homeric world gleamed through a fangled socio-cultural lens that was later to stimulate scholars working on Archaic Greece (Finley 1962). Yet, the world of Odysseus, which Finley placed in the 10th and 9th centuries, was to become more and more the world of the 8th century (Morris 1986), and in time, with new archaeological discoveries most notably at Lefkandi (Popham 1994, 1995; Popham *et al.* 1980, 1987, 1993; Popham and Lemos 1995, 1996) but also at less spectacular sites such as Nikoria (Coulson 1983a, 1983b; Mazarakis Ainias 1997:174–80), what used to be known as the Dark Age has no longer been quite so.

That the Dark Age is more a historiographical construct than a historical reality of a specific time period is a given amongst prehistorians of the central Mediterranean where a continuity of activity from the end of the Bronze Age is known from the archaeological visibility of settlements, exploitation of metal sources, and trade links between east and west Mediterranean, particularly at Cyprus (Knapp 1990; Lo Schiavo 1990, 1992, 1996; Lo Schiavo *et al.* 1985; Lo Schiavo and Ridgway 1987). It is surprising that such evidence from the central Mediterranean has hardly been used by scholars to engage with debates on the supposed darkness of the Aegean. Even now there is a certain apprehension in making explicit cross-Mediterranean links that are, by contrast, presupposed for the first millennium BC. That the Phoenicians were responsible for the continuity of these links from the end of the Bronze Age may have something to do with maintaining this circumspection, both in the ways in which Phoenician 'activity' is elusive and difficult to detect accurately in the Late Bronze Age and in later periods in a kaleidoscopic Mediterranean (Purcell, this volume), and in the ways in which we tend to resist the prospect of abandoning comfortable notions of ethnic identity with which we like to associate artefacts and artistic styles.

The consequence of these recent studies and finds has been that, for the centuries between the end of the Bronze Age and the Archaic period (10th to 7th centuries BC), what looked like a time run by a discontinuous set of events is now increasingly being appreciated as a filamentous concatenation of change, and this has had a fundamental impact on views of Orientalizing in the Greek world as in other Mediterranean regions. Lefkandi, for example, has convinced us that parts of Greece were already Orientalizing by the 10th century (Morris 1997b), or to put it differently, that what we perceive as dramatic changes from the 8th century were in fact the tip of the iceberg of a web of contacts that are now visible, at least in Euboea. This picture is expanding at a strikingly fast pace as new finds from Iberia are also strongly imposing a picture of continuity of contacts with the eastern Mediterranean and elsewhere from the end of the 10th century (Gonzalez de Canales *et al.* 2004). At the same time, the Homeric epic is no longer appreciated as recounting a Dark Age or the end of the era (Murray 1993:35-54), but rather a mixed account where the 8th century features prominently (Morris 1986). At one extreme viewpoint, Orientalizing is viewed as a dimension rather than a phase of Greek civilization (Morris 1992:130 and in this volume). One may argue in these terms for the Mediterranean as a whole, especially now that we find ourselves increasingly encouraged to think of Mediterranean history as connectivity or slopes of connectivity (Horden and Purcell 2000; Purcell 2003; see Harris 2005 and articles therein by Harris and Horden and Purcell for a latest review on Mediterranean history). Yet, to most scholars, the 8th and 7th centuries indeed represent an era of intense contact with the East, and hence, are ascribable to a discreet moment in time (Burkert 1992; Murray 1993; Osborne 1993). Even to those who reject the term Orientalizing *tout court* and question the existence of an East/Orient recognize that the first half of the first millennium BC is a period of profound change coinciding with an upsurge of Mediterranean connectivity (Purcell, this volume). The 8th and 7th centuries shine through as a changing world, sparkled by large-scale and long-distance contacts, both via the movement of Phoenicians along a myriad of routes and through a heightened mobility of the Aegean world outwards. 'Uses of the Oriental' (Osborne 1996:167) are a symptom of these contacts, and disclose cultural associations with the East that are displayed through particular objects. Even if we refuse to endorse the existence of an Orient, there is still a case to be upheld for the visibility of materials and representations that we associate with the eastern Mediterranean of previous ages in other, more westwards regions of the Mediterranean— what Purcell calls the westward-pointing signposts (Purcell, this volume). And this is precisely the process of Orientalizing that today historians and archaeologists alike have largely come to endorse. Furthermore, it is the active transformation by certain people in non-eastern contexts of eastern objects and cultural goods that is relevant and is what we may also define as Orientalizing (Osborne, this volume).

Yet 'becoming Oriental' may not necessarily imply a conscious desire of emulation on the part of the consumer or producer (Osborne, this volume), and there is a case for arguing that the value in retaining the notion of Orientalizing is precisely the ambiguity in using and consuming objects that Orientalize without necessarily indicating an intention or desire to emulate. It is useful to state this distinction between a 'detached' form of Orientalizing without intention, and a form of conscious desire for and emulation of things East. The quality of ambiguity and vagueness, however, is what makes the concept of Orientalizing hard to accept for some because it can also be seen as negative and malign to the kind of history we produce (Purcell, this volume). Yet, the question that remains is the following: how easily can we make this distinction in the material and representations at our disposal?

This dilemma is what historians and archaeologists working in the Greek world today largely recognize, and the debate is nowhere near reaching a consensus as the papers contained in this volume purport to demonstrate. On the other hand, scholars working in other regions, particularly central Italy and Etruria as well as further west in Spain, share a deep-rooted outlook on Orientalizing precisely as a conscious desire of imitating the East (Cristofani and Martelli 1994; Delpino and Flourentzos 2000; Delpino and Bartoloni 2000; Naso 2000a, 2000b; Rathje 1979, 1980, 1984, 1988; Ruiz Delgado 1989; Riva, this volume). Alternatively, as in the specific case of Iberia, Orientalizing is sometimes deemed as homologous with the settling of Phoenicians along coastal sites (Aubet, this volume).

Since Pallottino's (1965) formulation of Orientalizing, a desire for the East has been held as an aristocratic pursuit and very much restricted to the elite groups of the central and west Mediterranean regions (Dore *et al.* 2000; Karageorghis 2003; Riva 2005). The archaeological evidence from these regions indeed seems to uphold this picture. In fact, this view developed along with, and is encapsulated by, the concept of the princely burial, following the excavation and publication of wealthy tomb-groups in central Italy, Cyprus and Iberia since the late 19th century (cf. Ruby 1999; see the contributions of the *table ronde* held in 1984 and published that same year in *Opus* 3(2)). Further excavation of non-funerary sites, namely those that have been defined as 'palaces' or *regiae* in Italy and in Iberia (Torelli 1992, 2000; Guerrero 1991), have done nothing but enhance the aristocratic nature of Orientalizing to scholarly eyes. Nowadays, the phrase 'Orientalizing phenomenon' or 'movement' is widely used and well understood to imply precisely all this. In fact, knowledge of these non-funerary contexts have encouraged a particular consideration of aristocratic emulation that has now become the new orthodoxy amongst scholars working in the central Mediterranean: by imitating the East through material objects, aristocratic elites espoused a certain lifestyle that closely corresponded to manners and customs of those societies from which the objects originate (Naso 2000a). In other words, use of certain objects, whether imports or local imitations of the imports, implied the practice of certain ways of living that were themselves imitated. The objects are seen as material correlates of the customs that were adopted: uses of writing, wine drinking and the reclined banquet. In particular, wine drinking and banqueting have been thoroughly examined not simply as straight Oriental borrowings, but the social context in which these manners were practised and their meaning re-elaborated has been a significant venue of analysis (Rathje 1983, 1990, 1991, 1995). We find, in this approach to Orientalizing, a striking resemblance to attempts by earlier historians and archaeologists to disentangle the complex relation that the Homeric epoch—that is, the Aegean as 'west'—had with the Orient, a resemblance made all the more explicit by the fact that the Homeric epic is today taken as a textual record of the lifestyle of Orientalizing elites throughout the Mediterranean (d'Agostino 1977b; Rathje 1990; Ampolo 2000; Riva 2005). Untangling the lattice of this relation now largely involves an analytical, painstaking examination of the artefacts, their stylistic and typological characteristics, and the relation between their context of use and their context of origin in an attempt to understand how these customs and manners were adopted and adapted. Although detecting any direction of influence or indeed any single influence in the movement and/or findspots of artefacts is deemed to be an impossible if not irrelevant exercise (Purcell, this volume), this is by far the most widely recognized approach to Orientalizing today in the areas further west of the Aegean. On the other hand, attempts at unravelling Orientalizing in the central Mediterranean in some new light lay emphasis on novel modes of representation and symbolic language that are expressed through material objects (Riva, this volume).

Although the notion of 'princely burial' appeared in the first half of the 20th century, it was not until the 1970s when the excavation of tomb-groups from central Italy allowed wide comparative studies of the grave-goods of similar assemblages, that scholars began to perceive Orientalizing as a way of life. The publication of the *tombe principesche* from Pontecagnano in Italy represents a benchmark (d'Agostino 1977a), after which followed a whole stream of publications on single themes, most conspicuously wine drinking (Rathje 1983, 1990, 1995). At that time, one perceived a cautious mood in the ways in which the term *principi* was used in inverted commas, and analysis of the material revolved around culture, ideology and taste (d'Agostino 1977a:61). Today, 'princely' has become synonymous with the use of the hackneyed phrase 'way of life', which is often adopted untranslated in non-English-speaking scholarship (Naso 2000a:227).

Although what we may define as the 'lifestyle approach' has found most fertile grounds in the central and west Mediterranean, it shares an important element of analysis which forms the core of how archaeologists and historians working elsewhere in the Mediterranean understand Orientalizing:consumption. This is perhaps the one and only concept that is common to geographically and conceptually different areas of scholarship today. It is a theme of analysis that could throw fresh insight into the research of the central and west Mediterranean so far described:consuming rather than adapting and/or adopting way(s) of life may be a wholly new and fruitful angle of interpreting a rather unique phenomenon common to the Italic and Iberian peninsulas where Orientalizing is most strongly detected in funerary contexts. It has also been a central theme of recent research on the Greek world of this and later periods (Foxhall 1998), and is also an attractive perspective to those who reject the term Orientalizing but admit to the 8th and 7th centuries BC as a distinctive chapter of interaction and change in Mediterranean history (Purcell, this volume). More interestingly, as we perceive a growing concern with breaking down the straitjacket imposed by the periodization of the 1st millennium BC and as new discoveries invite us to recognize the end of the Bronze Age as yet another fruitless barrier, emphasis on consumption also allows us to explore the junctures and seams of a history of the Mediterranean that perceives period labels as historical cop-outs (Purcell, this volume). Studies on consumption in later periods, for example, show us how this is not only possible, but is also vital for discerning the 8th and 7th centuries less as outburst or indeed renaissance (Hägg 1983) and more as thickened flow of interaction and change that spills into the 6th century (Foxhall 1998).

In all of this, the Phoenicians play a key role. Absence of cultural homogeneity, and indeed of a fixed form of ethnicity (cf. Garnand 2002), let alone of a corpus of direct written sources have prompted historians and archaeologists to conceptualize the Phoenicians in terms of 'activity' or 'vectors' through the material objects with which we identify them. Indeed, we often think of Phoenicians as objects rather than people to the point that diffusionism and the aura of vagueness that this model imposes has become a way of seeing the Phoenicians at home and abroad. Semitic-speaking elites in Cadiz, Levantine travellers settling down at Sulcis and Carthaginians had probably less in common with one another than those 'Phoenicians', 'Greeks' and 'Etruscans' meeting on Pithekoussai in the 770s. What we think of as objects carried by and identified with Phoenicians had very little to do with them by the time they were consumed in indigenous rituals of the living and the dead, away from home, in copper-rich Cyprus, northern Etruria and southern Iberia. Bringing to the same discussion table two scholars working on very different areas of Levantine archaeology, both geographically and conceptually, has opened our eyes to the urgency for a plurality of scholarship on what we still uniformly call Phoenician archaeology (Gubel, Aubet, this volume). Only during encounters such as this are we able to recognize that two scholars studying Phoenician settlements in the Iberian peninsula and Phoenician art across the Mediterranean have as much to share as an Etruscan specialist and Greek archaeologist do. What there is to share and to debate is plenty as the symposium and the publication of this volume demonstrate.

Acknowledgments

The symposium was made possible by the generous help and sponsorship received from various institutions and committees which we would like to thank:St John's College, Oxford, The British Academy, the University of Malta, the Istituto Italiano di Cultura in London; at the University of Oxford:the Craven Committee, the Meyerstein Fund—School of Archaeology, the Astor Travel Fund, and the New Faculty Board of Classics.

We would like to especially thank for their advice, support and stimulus throughout the symposium: Stephanie Dalley, the late Roger Moorey, Oswyn Murray, Robin Osborne, Nicholas Purcell, and Susan Sherratt. Sadly, Roger Moorey and Andrew Sherratt, whose counsel was instrumental in turning ideas for a scholarly gathering into a fully-fledged symposium, are no longer with us to see the proceedings through the press. It is to their memory that this book is dedicated.

Finally, we would like to thank the anonymous reviewers of the publishers, Equinox, for their suggestions in the completion of this book, and to Valerie Hall and Heidi Robbins who saw it through the press.

References

Almagro Gorbea, M. (1991) El mundo orientalizante en la Península Ibérica. In *Atti del II Congresso Internazionale di Studi Fenici e Punici, Roma, 1987*, vol. 2. Roma, Consiglio Nazionle delle Ricerche, pp. 573–600.

Ampolo, C. (2000) Il mondo omerico e la cultura orientalizzante mediterranea. *Principi etruschi tra Mediterraneo ed Europa*, edited by A. Dore, M. Marchesi and L. Minarini. Venezia: Marsilio Editori, pp. 27–35.

Aubet, M. E. (1971) *Estudios sobre el Periodo Orientalizante*. Studia Archeologica 10. Santiago de Compostela: Universidad de Santiago de Compostela.

Aubet, M. E. (1984) La aristocracia tartésica durante el periodo orientalizante. *Opus* 3(2):445–68.

Aubet, M. E. (1996) *The Phoenicians and the West. Politics, Colonies and Trade*. Cambridge: Cambridge University Press.

Barnett, R. D. (1948) Early Greek and oriental ivories. *Journal of Hellenic Studies* 68:1–25.

Bietti Sestieri, A. M. (1997) Italy in Europe in the Early Iron Age. *Proceedings of the Prehistoric Society* 63:371–402.

Bisi, A. M. (1965) *Il grifone: storia di un motivo iconografico nell'antico oriente mediterraneo*. Roma: Centro di Studi Semitici, Istituto di Studi sul Vicino Oriente, Università di Roma.

Boardman, J. (1999) Greek colonization: the Eastern contribution. In *La colonisation grecque en Méditerranée occidentale. Actes de la rencontre scientifique en hommage à Georges Vallet organisée par le Centre Jean Bérard, l'École française de Rome, l'Istituto universitario orientale et l'Università degli studi di Napoli 'Federico II', Rome-Naples, 15-18 novembre 1995*. Rome: École française de Rome, pp. 39–49.

Botto, M. (1993) I bronzi di produzione orientale del tumulo F di Satricum. *Annali dell'Istituto Orientale di Napoli* 15:9–22.

Brown, W. L. (1960) *The Etruscan Lion*. Oxford: Clarendon Press.

Brunn, H. (1868) *Die Kunst bei Homer und ihr Verhältniss zu den Anfängen der griechischen Kunstgeschichte*. München.

Brunn, H. (1893) *Griechische Kunstgeschichte*. München: Veerlagsanstalt für Kunst und Wissenschaft.

Buranelli, F. (2000) The Vatican's Museo Gregoriano Etrusco from the nineteenth century and beyond. In *The Etruscans*, edited by M. Torelli. London: Thames and Hudson, pp. 511–13.

Burckhardt, J. (1998) *The Greeks and Greek civilization*. Translated by Sheila Stern, edited by Oswyn Murray. London and New York: HarperCollins.

Burkert, W. (1992) *The Orientalizing Revolution. Near Eastern Influence on Greek Culture in the early Archaic Age*. Harvard: Harvard University Press.

Canciani, F. (1979) Coppe 'fenicie' in Italia. *Archäologischer Anzeiger* 1:1–6.

Clermont-Ganneau, C. (1880) *L'imagerie phénicienne et la mythologie iconologique chez les grecs. 1re partie—La coupe phénicenne de Palestrina*. Paris, Ernest Leroux. [Previously published as La coupe phénicienne de Palestrina et l'une des sources de l'art et de la mythologie Helléniques, *Journal Asiatique* (février-mars) 1878: 232–70 and (avril–mai–juin) 1878: 444–544.]

Collignon, M. (1886) *A Manual of Greek Archaeology*. London: Cassell and Company.

Conze, A. (1870) *Zur Geschichte der Anfänge griechischer Kunst*. Vienna.

Coulson, W. D. E. (1983a) The Dark Age: the architecture. In *Excavations at Nichoria in Southwest Greece III: Dark Age and Byzantine Occupation*, edited by W. A. McDonald, W. D. E. Coulson and J. Rosser. Minneapolis: University of Minnesota Press, pp. 9–60.

Coulson, W. D. E. (1983b) The Dark Age: the pottery. In *Excavations at Nichoria in Southwest Greece III: Dark Age and Byzantine Occupation*, edited by W. A. McDonald, W. D. E. Coulson and J. Rosser. Minneapolis: University of Minnesota Press, pp. 61–259.

Cristofani, M. and M. Martelli (1994) Lo stile del potere e i beni di prestigio. In *Storia di Europa II, Preistoria e antichità*, edited by J. Guilaine and S. Settis. Torino: Einaudi, pp. 1147–66.

Cristofani Martelli, M. (1973) Documenti di arte orientalizzante da Chiusi. *Studi Etruschi* 41:97–120.

d'Agostino, B. (1975) Ideologia e rituale funerario in Campania nei secoli VIII e VII a.C. In *Contribution à l'étude de la société et de la colonisation eubeénnes*, by E. Lepore. Cahiers du Centre Jean Bérard 2. Naples: Centre Jean Bérard, pp. 107–110.

d'Agostino, B. (1977a) Tombe 'principesche' dell'orientalizzante antico da Pontecagnano. *Monumenti Antichi* serie miscellanea II–1, 49:1–110.

d'Agostino, B. (1977b) Grecs et 'indigènes' sur la côte tyrrhénienne au VIIe siècle: la transmission des idéologies entre élite sociales. *Annales. Economies-sociétés-civilisations*:3–18.

Della Seta, A. (1922) *Italia antica: dalla caverna preistorica al palazzo imperiale*. Bergamo: Istituto italiano d'arte grafiche.

de Longpérier, A. (1855) Notice sure les monuments antiques de l'Asie nouvellement entrés au musée du Louvre. *Journal Asiatique* 5me série, 5 (octobre–novembre):408–23.

de Longpérier, A. (1868–74) *Choix de Monuments antiques pour servir a l'Histoire de l'Art en Orient et en Occident (Musée Napoleon III)*. Paris: L. Guérin.

Delpino, F. and G. Bartoloni (2000) Il principe: stile di vita e manifestazione del potere. In *Principi etruschi. Tra Mediterraneo ed Europa*, edited by A. Dore, M. Marchesi and L. Minarini. Venezia: Marsilio Editori, pp. 221–9.

Delpino, F. and P. Flourentzos (2000) Tra oriente ed Etruria: i modelli e la formazione della cultura orientalizzante. In *Principi etruschi. Tra Mediterraneo ed Europa*, edited by A. Dore, M. Marchesi and L. Minarini. Venezia: Marsilio Editori, pp. 92–101.

Demargne, P. (1964) *Aegean Art: the Origins of Greek Art*. London: Thames and Hudson.

Dore, A., M. Marchesi and L. Minarini (eds.) (2000) *Principi etruschi. Tra Mediterraneo ed Europa*. Venezia: Marsilio Editori.

Ducati, P. (1927) *Storia dell'arte etrusca*. Firenze: Rinascimento del Libro.

Finley, M. (1962) *The World of Odysseus*. Harmondsworth: Penguin.

Foxhall, L. (1998) Cargoes of the heart's desire: the character of trade in the Archaic Mediterranean world. In *Archaic Greece: New Approaches and New Evidence*, edited by N. Fisher and H. van Wees. London: Duckworth, pp. 295–310.

Franz, A. (1998–99) Thymiateria with drooping petal-capitals: distribution and function of an Early Iron Age class of objects. *Talanta* 30–31:73–114.

Furtwängler, A. (1879) Die Bronzefunde aus Olympia und deren kunstgeschichtliche Bedeutung. *Abhandlunger der Königlichen Akademie der Wissenschaften zu Berlin*, 3–106.

Gardner, P. (1905) *A Grammar of Greek Art*. London: Macmillan.

Garnand, B. K.(2002) From infant sacrifice to the ABC's: ancient Phoenicians and modern identities. *Stanford Journal of Archaeology* 1:1–82 http: //archaeology.stanford.edu/journal/newdraft/garnand/index.html

Giardino, C. (1995) *Il mediterraneo occidentale fra XIV ed VIII secolo a.C.: cerchie minerarie e metallurgiche—The West Mediterranean between the 14th and 8th centuries BC: mining and metallurgical spheres*. BAR International Series 612. Oxford: Tempus Reparatum.

Goldman, B. (1960) The development of the lion-griffin. *American Journal of Archaeology* 64:319–28.

González de Canales, F., L. Serrano, and J. Llompart (2004) *El emporio fenicio de Huelva, ca. 900–770 a.C.* Madrid: Bibliotheca Nueva.

Gran-Aymerich, J. and É. du Puytison-Lagarce (1995) Recerches sur la période orientalisante en Étrurie et dans le midi Ibérique. *Comptes Rendus de l'Académie des Inscriptions et Belles-Lettres* (avril-juin):569–602.

Grau-Zimmermann, B. (1978) Phönikische Metallkannen in den orientalisierenden Horizonten des Mittelmeerraumes. *Madrider Mitteilungen* 19:161–218.

Grifi, L. (1841) *Monumenti di Cere Antica spiegati colle osservanze del culto di Mitra*. Roma: A. Monaldi.

Guerrero V. M. (1991) El palacio-santuario de Cancho Roano (Badajoz) y la commercializacion de ánforas fenicias indigenas. *Rivisita di Studi Fenici* 19(1):49–82.

Güterbock, H. G. (1957) Narration in Anatolian, Syrian, and Assyrian Art. *American Journal of Archaeology* 61:62–71.

Hägg, R. (ed) (1983) *The Greek Renaissance of the 8th century BC: tradition and innovation. Proceedings of the Second International Symposium at the Swedish Institute in Athens, 1–5 June 1981*. Acta Instituti Atheniensis Regni Sueciae 4, XXX. Stockholm: Paul Åström.

Harris, W. V. (ed) (2005) *Rethinking the Mediterranean*. Oxford: Oxford University Press.

Harrison, J. E. (1885) *Introductory Studies in Greek Art*. London: T. Fisher Unwin.

Harrison, J. E. (1912) *Themis: A Study in the Social Origins of Greek Religion*. Cambridge: Cambridge University Press.

Harrison, R. J. (1988) *Spain at the Dawn of History: Iberians, Phoenicians and Greeks*. London: Thames and Hudson.

Helbig, W. (1876) Cenni sopra l'arte fenicia. Lettera di W. Helbig al sig. Senatore G. Spano. *Annali dell'Istituto di Corrispondenza Archeologica* 48:197–257.

Helbig, W. (1887) *Das homerische Epos aus den Denkmälern erläutert: archäologische Untersuchungen*. 2nd edition. Leipzig: B.G. Teubner.

Hopkins, C. (1965) Two Phoenician bowls from Etruscan tombs. *Studi in onore di Luisa Banti*. Rome: L'Erma di Bretschneider, pp. 191–203.

Horden, P. and N. Purcell (2000) *The Corrupting Sea*. Oxford: Blackwell.

Karageorghis, V. (2002) Homeric Cyprus. In *Omero tremila anni dopo*, edited by F. Montanari. Roma: Edizioni di storia e letteratura, pp. 227–37.

Karageorghis, V. (2003) Heroic burials in Cyprus and other Mediterranean regions. In ΠΛΟΕΣ *Sea Routes: Interconnections in the Mediterranean 16th–6th century* BC. *Proceedings of the International Symposium held at Rethymnon, Crete in September 29th–October 2nd 2002*, edited by N. C. Stampolidis and V. Karageorghis. Athens: the University of Crete and the A.G. Leventis Foundation, pp. 339–51.

Karo, G. (1920) Orient und Hellas in archaischer Zeit. *Mitteilungen des Deutschen archäologischen Instituts, Athenische Abteilung* 44:106–56.

Knapp, A. B. (1990) Ethnicity, entrepreneurship, and exchange: Mediterranean inter-island relations in the Late Bronze Age. *Annual of the British School at Athens* 85:114–53.

Kopcke, G. (1992) What role for Phoenicians? In *Greece between East and West: 10th–8th centuries* BC. *Papers of the Meeting at the Institute of Fine Arts, New York University, March 15–16th, 1990*, edited by G. Kopcke and I. Tokumaru. Mainz: Philipp von Zabern, pp. 103–13.

Kristiansen, K. (1994) The emergence of the European world system in the Bronze Age: divergence, convergence and social evolution during the first and second millennia BC in Europe. In *Europe in the First Millennium* BC, edited by K. Kristiansen and J. Jensen. Sheffield Archaeological Monographs 6. Sheffield: J.R. Collis Publications, pp. 7–30.

Layard, A. H. (1853a) *Discoveries in the Ruins of Niniveh and Babylon with travels in Armenia, Kurdistan and the desert: being the result of a second expedition undertaken for the Trustees of the British Museum*. London: John Murray.

Layard, A. H. (1853b) *A Second Series of the Monuments of Niniveh including bas-reliefs from the palace of Sennacherib and bronzes from the ruins of Nimrud from drawings made on the spot, during a second expedition to Assyria by Austen Henry Layard*. London: John Murray.

Layard, A. H. (1858) *A Popular Account of Discoveries at Niniveh*. London: John Murray.

Lemnos, I. S. (2003) Craftsmen, traders and some wives in Early Iron Age Greece. In ΠΛΟΕΣ *Sea Routes: Interconnections in the Mediterranean 16th–6th century* BC. *Proceedings of the International Symposium held at Rethymnon, Crete in September 29th–October 2nd 2002*, edited by N. C. Stampolidis and V. Karageorghis. Athens: the University of Crete and the A.G. Leventis Foundation, pp. 187–95.

Lo Schiavo, F. (1990) La Sardegna sulle rotte dell'Occidente. In *Atti del XXIX Convegno di Studi sulla Magna Grecia, Taranto 1989*. Taranto: Istituto per la storia e l'archeologia della Magna Grecia, pp. 99–133.

Lo Schiavo, F. (1992) Un'altra fibula 'Cipriota' dalla Sardegna. In *Sardinia in the Mediterranean: a Footprint in the Sea. Studies in Sardinian Archaeology Presented to Miriam S Balmuth*, edited by R. H. Tykot and T. K. Andrews. Sheffield: Sheffield Academic Press, pp. 296–303.

Lo Schiavo, F. (1996) Storia della ricerca archeologica sulle relazioni precoloniali in Sardegna. *Parola del Passato* 290:378–86.

Lo Schiavo, F., E. MacNamara and L. Vagnetti (1985) Late Cypriot imports to Italy and their influence on local bronzework. *Papers of the British School at Rome* 53:1–71.

Lo Schiavo, F. and D. Ridgway (1987) La Sardegna e il Mediterraneo occidentale allo scorcio del II millennio. In *La Sardegna nel Mediterraneo tra il secondo e il primo Millennio, Atti del II Convegno di Studi, Cagliari 27-30 novembre 1986*. Cagliari: STEF, pp. 391–412.

Maggiani, A. (1973) Coppa fenicia da una tomba villanoviana di Vetulonia. *Studi Etruschi* 41:73–95.

Markoe, G. (1985) *Phoenician Bronze and Silver Bowls from Cyprus and the Mediterranean*. California: University of California Press.

Markoe, G. (1996) The emergence of Orientalizing in Greek art: some observations on the interchange between Greeks and Phoenicians in the eighth and seventh centuries BC. *Bulletin of the American Schools of Oriental Research* 301:47–67.

Markoe, G. (2003) Phoenician metalwork abroad: a question of export or on-site production? In ΠΛΟΕΣ *Sea Routes: Interconnections in the Mediterranean 16th–6th century* BC. *Proceedings of the*

International Symposium held at Rethymnon, Crete in September 29th–October 2nd 2002, edited by N. C. Stampolidis and V. Karageorghis. Athens: the University of Crete and the A.G. Leventis Foundation, pp. 209–16.

Marquand, A. (1888) An archaic patera from Kourion. *The American Journal of Archaeology and the History of the Fine Arts* 4(2):169–71.

Martha, J. (1889) *L'art étrusque*. Paris: Librairie de Firmin, Didot.

Mazarakis-Ainias, A. (1997) *From Rulers' Dwellings to Temples: Architecture, Religion and Society in Early Iron Age Greece*. SIMA 121. Jonsered: Paul Åstroms Forlag.

Mederos Martín, A. (1997) Cambio de rumbo: interración commercial entre el bronce final atlántico ibérico y micénio en el mediterráneo central (1425–1050 a.C.). *Trabajos de Prehistoria* 54(2):113–34.

Montelius, O. (1897) Pre-Classical chronology in Greece and Italy. *The Journal of the Anthropological Institute of Great Britain and Ireland* 26:261–71.

Morris, I. (1986) The use and abuse of Homer. *Classical Antiquity* 5:81–138.

Morris, I. (1997a) Periodization and the heroes: inventing a Dark Age. In *Inventing Ancient Culture. Historicism, periodization, and the ancient world*, edited by M. Golden and P. Toohey. London: Routledge, pp. 96–131.

Morris, I. (1997b) The Art of Citizenship. In *New Light on a Dark Age. Exploring the Culture of Geometric Greece*, edited by S. Langdon. Columbia and London: University of Missouri Press, pp. 9–43.

Morris, S. (1992) *Daidalos and the Origins of Greek Art*. Princeton: Princeton University Press.

Murray, O. (1993) *Early Greece*. London: Fontana Press.

Muscarella, O. W. (1962) The oriental origin of siren cauldron attachments. *Hesperia* 31: 317-29.

Muscarella, O. W. (1970) Near Eastern bronzes in the West: the question of origin. In *Art and Technology: a symposium on Classical Bronzes*, edited by S. Doeringer, D. G. Mitten and A. Steinberg. Cambridge, Massachusetts: the M.I.T. Press, pp. 109–28.

Myres, J. L. (1933) The Amathus bowl: a long-lost masterpiece of oriental engraving. *Journal of Hellenic Studies* 53:25–39.

Naso, A. (2000a) Aspetti del tema 'Gesellschaft und Selbstdarstellung'. In *Akten des Kolloquiums zum thema Der Orient und Etrurien. Zum Phänomen des 'Orientalisierens' in westlichen Mittelmerraum (10.-6. Jh. v. Chr.). Tübingen 12th-13th Jun 1997*, edited by F. Prayon and W. Röllig. Pisa and Roma: Istituti Editoriali Poligrafici Internazionali, pp. 227–32.

Naso, A. (2000b) Le aristocrazie etrusche in periodo orientalizzante: cultura, economia, relazioni. In *Gli Etruschi*, edited by M. Toreeli. Milano: Bompiani, pp. 111–29.

Newton, C. T. (1880) Dr Schliemann's discoveries at Mycenae. In *Essays on Art and Archaeology*. London: Macmillan, pp. 246–302.

Niemeyer, H. G. (2003) On Phoenician art and its role in trans-Mediterranean interconnections. In ΠΛΟΕΣ *Sea Routes: Interconnections in the Mediterranean 16th–6th century BC. Proceedings of the International Symposium held at Rethymnon, Crete in September 29th–October 2nd 2002*, edited by N. C. Stampolidis and V. Karageorghis. Athens: the University of Crete and the A.G. Leventis Foundation, pp. 201–208.

Niemeyer, H. G. (2004) Phoenician or Greek: is there a reasonable way out of the Al Mina debate? *Ancient West and East* 3(1):38–50.

Orsi, P. (1888) Studi illustrativi sui bronzi arcaici trovati nell'antro di Zeus Ideo. *Museo italiano di antichità classica* 2:769–904.

Osborne, R. (1993) À la grecque. A review of W. Burkert, *The Orientalizing Revolution, Near Eastern Influence on Greek Culture in the Early Archaic Period* (1992) and S. P. Morris, *Daidalos and the Origins of Greek Art* (1992). *Journal of Mediterranean Archaeology* 6(2):231–37.

Osborne, R. (1996) *Greece in the Making*. London: Routledge.

Pallottino, M. (1958) Urartu, Greece and Etruria. *East and West* 9 (1 and 2):29–52.

Pallottino, M. (1965) Orientalizing style. *Encyclopedia of World Art* 10:782–96.

Pareti, L. (1947) *La tomba Regolini-Galassi del Museo Gregoriano Etrusco e la civiltà dell'Italia centrale del sec. VII a.C.* Roma: Città del Vaticano.

Perrot, G. and C. Chipiez (1885) *Histoire de l'Art de l'Antiquité, tome 3: Phenicie, Cypre.* Paris: Hachette.

Popham, M. R. (1994) Precolonization: early Greek contact with the East. In *The Archaeology of Greek Colonisation. Essays dedicated to Sir John Boardman*, edited by G. R. Tsetskhladze and F. De Angelis. Oxford University Committee for Archaeology Monograph 40. Oxford: Oxbow Books, pp. 11–34.

Popham, M. R. (1995) An engraved Near Eastern bronze bowl from Lefkandi. *Oxford Journal of Archaeology* 14:103–107.

Popham, M. R., L. H. Sackett and P. G. Themelis (eds.) (1980) *Lefkandi I. The Iron Age. The cemeteries.* London: The British School of Archaeology at Athens.

Popham, M. R., E. Touloupa and L. H. Sackett (1987) Further excavation of the Toumba cemetery at Lefkandi, 1981. *Annual of the British School at Athens* 77:213–48.

Popham, M. R., P. G. Calligas and L. H. Sackett (1993) *Lefkandi II. The Protogeometric building at Toumba. Part 2. The excavation, architecture and finds.* Oxford: The British School of Archaeology at Athens.

Popham, M. R. and I. S. Lemos (1995) A Euboean warrior trader. *Oxford Journal of Archaeology* 14:151–57.

Popham, M. R. and I. S. Lemos (eds) (1996) *Lefkandi III. The Toumba cemetery. The excavations of 1981, 1984, 1986 and 1992–4.* Oxford: The British School at Athens.

Poulsen, F. (1912) *Der Orient und die Frühgriechische Kunst.* Leipzig: B.G. Teubner.

Prayon, F., and W. Röllig (eds.) (2000) *Akten des Kolloquiums zum thema Der Orient und Etrurien. Zum Phänomen des 'Orientalisierens' in westlichen Mittelmeerraum (10.–6. Jh.v.Chr.). Tübingen 12–13 June 1997.* Pisa and Rome: Istituti Editoriali Poligrafici Internazionali.

Purcell, N. (2003) The Boundless Sea of Unlikeness? On Defining the Mediterranean. *Mediterranean Historical Review* 18:9–29

Rathje, A. (1979) Oriental imports in Etruria in the 8th and 7th centuries BC: their origins and implications. In *Italy before the Romans. The Iron Age, Orientalising and Etruscan periods*, edited by D. Ridgway and F. R. Ridgway. London, New York, San Francisco: Academic Press, pp. 145–83.

Rathje, A. (1980) Silver relief bowls from Italy. *Analecta Romana Instituti Danici* 9:7–20.

Rathje, A. (1983) A banquet service from the Latin city of Ficana. *Analecta Romana Instituti Danici* 22:7–29.

Rathje, A. (1984) I *keimelia* orientali. *Opus* 3:341–51.

Rathje, A. (1988) Manners and customs in Central Italy in the Orientalizing period: influence from the Near East. In *East and West: Cultural Relations in the Ancient World*, edited by T. Fischer-Hansen. Acta Hyperborea 1. Copenhagen: Museum Tusculanum Press, pp. 81–90.

Rathje, A. (1990) The adoption of the Homeric banquet in Central Italy in the Orientalizing period. In *Sympotica: a symposium on the symposium*, edited by O. Murray. Oxford: Clarendon Press, pp. 279–88.

Rathje, A. (1991) Il banchetto presso i Fenici. In *Atti del II Congresso Internazionale di Studi Fenici e Punici, Roma, 1987*, vol. 3. Roma, Consiglio Nazionle delle Ricerche, pp. 1166–68.

Rathje, A. (1995) Il banchetto in Italia Centrale: quale stile di vita? In *In vino veritas*, edited by O. Murray and M. Tecusan. London: British School at Rome, pp. 167–75.

Rathje, A. (1996) Silver relief bowls from Italy. *Analecta Romana Instituti Danici* 9:7–46.

Reinach, S. (1888) *Esquisses archéologiques.* Paris: Ernest Leroux.

Renan, E. (1864) *Mission de Phénicie.* Paris: Imprimerie Impériale.

Richter, G. M. A. (1927) *Handbook of the Classical Collection.* New York: The Metropolitan Museum of Art.

Ridgeway, D. (2004) Euboeans and other among the Tyrrhenian seaboard in the 8th century BC. In *Greek Identity in the Western Mediterranean: Papers in honour of Brian Shefton*, edited by K. Loman. Leiden: Brill, pp. 15–33.

Ridgeway, W. (1901–31) *The Early Age of Greece*. Cambridge: Cambridge University Press.
Ridgeway, W. (1896) What people produced the objects called Mycenaean? *Journal of Hellenic Studies* 16:77–119.
Ridgway, D. (2003) Euboeans and others along the Tyrrhenian seaboard in the 8th century BC. In *Greek Identity in the Western Mediterranean: papers in honour of Brian Shefton*, edited by K. Lomas. Leiden and Boston: Brill, pp. 15–33.
Riegl, A. (1893) *Stifragen: Grundlegungen zu einer Geschichte der Ornamentik*. Berlin.
Riva, C. (2005) The culture of urbanization in the Mediterranean, c. 800–600 BC. In *Mediterranean Urbanization 800-600 BC*, edited by B. Cunliffe and R. Osborne. Proceedings of the British Academy 126. Oxford: British Academy, pp. 203–32.
Ruby, P. (ed.) (1999) *Les princes de la protohistoire et l'émergence de l'état. Actes de la table ronde internationale organisée par le Centre Jean Bérard et l'École française de Rome, Naples, 27–29 octobre 1994*. Naples and Rome: Centre Jean Bérard and École française de Rome.
Ruiz Delgado, M. M. (1989) Las necrópolis tartésicas: prestigio, poder y jerarguías. In *Tartessos: arqueología protohistórica del bajo Guadalquivir*, edited by M. E. Aubet Semmler. Barcelona: Sabadell, pp. 247–85.
Said, E. W. (1978) *Orientalism: Western Conceptions of the Orient*. Harmondsworth: Penguin Books.
Schliemann, H. (1878) *Mycenae: A Narrative of Researches annd Discoveries at Mycenae and Tiryns*. London: John Murray.
Shanks, M. (1995) Art and the archaeology of embodiment: some aspects of Archaic Greece. *Cambridge Archaeological Journal* 5:207–44.
Shefton, B. B. (1988) The Paradise Flower, a 'Court Style' Phoenician ornament: its history in Cyprus and the Central and Western Mediterranean. In *Cyprus and the East Mediterranean in the Iron Age: Proceedings of the Seventh British Museum Classical Colloquium*, edited by V. Tatton-Brown. London: British Museum Publications, pp. 97–117.
Smith, A. H. (1899) *Guide to the Greek and Roman Antiquities of the British Museum*. London: Trustees of the British Museum.
Stampolidis, N.C. and V. Karageorghis (eds.) (2003) *ΠΛΟΕΣ Sea Routes: Interconnections in the Mediterranean 16th–6th century BC. Proceedings of the International Symposium held at Rethymnon, Crete, Sept 29th–Oct 2nd 2002*. Athens: University of Crete and A. G. Leventis foundation.
Strøm, I. (1971) *Problems Concerning the Origin and the Early Development of the Etruscan Orientalizing Style*. Odense: Odense University Press.
Torelli, M. (1992) I fregi figurati delle regiae latine ed etrusche. Immaginario del potere arcaico. *Ostraka* 1:249–74.
Torelli, M. (2000) Le regiae etrusche e laziali tra orientalizzante e arcaismo. In *Principi etruschi tra Mediterraneo ed Europa*, edited by A. Dore, M. Marchesi and L. Minarini. Bologna: Museo Civico Archeologico, pp. 67–78.
Winter, I. J. (1976) Phoenician and North Syrian ivory carving in historical context: questions of style and distribution. *Iraq* 38: 1–22.
Winter, I. J. (1981) Is there a South Syrian style of ivory carving in the first millennium BC? *Iraq* 43:101–30.
Winter, I. J. (1988) North Syria as a bronzeworking centre in the early first millennium BC: luxury commodities at home and abroad. In *Bronzeworking Centres of Western Asia c.1000–539 BC*, edited by J. Curtis. London and New York: Keegan Paul International, pp. 193–225.
Winter, N. A. (1994) A terracotta griffin head from Poggio Civitate (Murlo). In *Murlo and the Etruscans: Art and Society in Ancient Etruria*, edited by R. Daniel and J. P. Small. Wisconsin: University of Wisconsin Press, pp. 72–75.
Zaccagnini, C. (1983) Patterns of mobility among ancient Near Eastern craftsmen. *Journal of Near Eastern Studies* 42:245–64.

2 Orientalizing: Five Historical Questions

Nicholas Purcell[1]

> That decisive epoch in which, under the influence of the Semitic East, Greek culture began its unique flowering, soon to assume cultural hegemony in the Mediterranean.[2]

Identifying the 8th and 7th centuries BC as an 'Orientalizing period' poses a number of interesting general historical challenges and difficulties. The remarks which follow concern those problems rather than the interpretation of specific patterns in the evidence. Periodization is one of the central ways in which we impose analytical order on the past.[3] It is not a simple matter of heuristic convention, since few would regard the segments into which the past is customarily divided as entirely arbitrary, selected at random only (as it might be) to offer a manageable spread of years for a particular enquiry. And selecting the features which we regard as sufficiently salient to give a general character and a label to a period is not a simple exercise in naming, but one of the most ambitious forms of historical generalization. Debating a term such as 'Orientalizing', then, is not a pedantic or nominalistic exercise. It concerns the historical construction of the age in question. My aim here is not principally to question the boundaries of the period.

The westward-pointing signposts

Three things may be taken as givens from the outset.

1. The Mediterranean in the first half of the first millennium BC experienced dramatic social, economic and cultural change. The principal characteristics of these changes make them, as a collectivity, a relatively uncontroversial object of historical and archaeological reflection.[4]
2. It is a distinctive feature of this episode that it exhibits large-scale long-distance interaction, for which archaeological evidence is far and away the most eloquent testimony. Understanding the experience of any given locality is very likely to require an analysis of contacts with numerous frequently remote regions. This is an age of high connectivity.[5] Dramatic cultural change does not entail such interaction, but in this case, as in many other periods of Mediterranean history, there is a clear relation between the two.
3. Understanding the increasingly intense connectivity of this period, and its historical consequences, moreover, is inconceivable without including in the analytical frame Anatolia, the west Asian coastlands, and Egypt, and their various relations with the Mesopotamian heartland to the east.

To that extent, it is also uncontroversial to assert that materials, representations and social forms previously attested only in the eastern Mediterranean or west Asia are attested much more widely in the western parts of the Mediterranean basin. In the discussion on which this volume is based, Jim Coulton used the attractively neutral terminology 'westward-pointing signposts' to refer to these phenomena.

This period is therefore clearly of very great historical interest. What do we want to identify as the salient features of change? To what do we want to point in our nomenclature for the epoch? Here I wish to express five reasons why I don't think it is anything which might be intended by the term 'Orientalizing'.

Artefacts and life

History before Alexander is resistant to periodization, and that difficulty should assist original and constructive generalization. The political framework which applies to history after Alexander, by contrast, has a specious authenticity which has entrenched conventional labels such as 'Hellenistic', or 'early Roman imperial'. Before Alexander, the political fragmentation of the Mediterranean makes this kind of periodization impossible. The boundary located by Greek-speakers themselves between periods before and after either the conquest of Anatolia by the Achaemenid state, or the check to the latter's ambitions in central Greece, forms a conventional period-limit. This division is overtly partisan and limited in its application. If it has remained in general use, that must be attributed to the involuted preoccupations of Greek historians, and still more to the coincidence by which this boundary also approximately coincides with the transitions in the material culture between 'archaic' and 'classical'.

Those last influential period-labels are examples of a historical cop-out, in which the task of making generalizations about a period is shirked, and the period is instead identified simply by reference to the nature of the evidence for it. (They are, indeed, more malign than that in also expressing very questionable value-judgements about the superiority of the 'classical' to what came before and after, quite apart from continuing debate about their usefulness for describing material culture itself.) Neither 'archaic' nor 'classical' makes any statement at all about the historical character of the period. The same is true, moving toward the period under discussion, for 'Geometric', and arguably for 'Dark Age', though that apparently stark proclamation of the absence of evidence has complex sub-texts.[6]

A fundamental choice, therefore, is whether to periodize primarily using the character of the evidence or rather by using its interpretation. The first is far safer, seeking only to describe, but it is indeed a cop-out, a refusal to analyse; the second is debatable, unstable, and risks being corrected, but is far more interesting and productive. This is not the place to attempt a historiographical survey of the idea of an 'Orientalizing' period. But not the least interesting thing about the idea is that it is an example of historical periodization founded on (originally) art-historical and (subsequently) archaeological classification of the evidence, which has taken on (as 'Geometric' has not) a character derived from claims about the interpretation of the period as a whole.

In their introductory remarks, Corinna Riva and Nick Vella show how what had been an essentially art-historical label underwent a singular shift in the last quarter of the 20th century so that it came to refer to a much broader gamut of historical problems.[7] In other words, it made the transition from one pole of the choice I have just outlined to the other. We might expect to welcome this. Some cases of crossover between describing the evidence and analysing the history have worked up to a point: the Lyric age, the age of Anxiety. It is naturally perfectly possible for representations or material culture to work extremely interestingly as proxies for the histories of ideas or social forms. Within the history of this period, the genesis of written Greek offers one helpful boundary-transition: and the debate as to whether it is a boundary only in the domain of available evidence, or also in the social and cultural history of the Mediterranean, is a fertile one. The explosion of equipment which can broadly be linked to the introduction of new forms of commensality is another instance. Nonetheless, it is apparent to all that it is necessary, before coining terms such as the Age of the Written or the First Mass Sympotic Period, to pose the perennial question as to whether what we can see is the most important thing, or a tracer of something less visible but more significant. The problem with 'Orientalizing' is precisely that an idea which had a certain use on the descriptive side has been transplanted to the explanatory, a domain in which it works much less well.

With 'the Orientalizing', moreover, we face a particularly disquieting example of the difficulty of assessing the importance of what we can see. The cultural transformation is much better known than any other aspect of the societies which it transformed, simply because the transformation involved the invention and dissemination of the things that are necessary for us to know anything about the period. The distribution of all the most diagnostic artefacts, painted pottery, metalwork, later three-dimensional images in stone or terracotta, and of the media through which we know anything about what these things mean, as well as writing itself and the occasions for using writing, whether economic, social, cultic or literary—all these are part of the phenomenon for which we propose to use them as evidence. This creates an introvertedness, even a circularity, which is uncomfortable by comparison with other periods of history.

So my first problem with the term is that its revival for a new purpose has posed unhelpful and confusing problems about the relationship between evidence and interpretation.

Origins are not very interesting: problems with -izing

Modelling cultural change and influence in the early Iron Age Mediterranean is bound to be difficult. In his justly influential monograph, Martin West brought a whole metaphor-chest to bear on the issue, comparing Orientalizing to: Ocean; digestion; impulses which might be sealed against; reflux movements; lines of transmission; routes and staging-posts; drawing from wells; fertilization (impregnation rather than horticulture, I suspect); strands in a web; and the flow of waters beneath the surface of a marsh.[8] From swampy hydraulics to antiperistalsis, this gives a somewhat queasy sense of change.

The art-historical term Orientalizing was 'diffusionist' in an old-fashioned way, and these liquid images rather suggest that the new historical version has retained this style of explanation. Diffusionism perhaps fits material culture better than it does the history of ideas, but is questionable at the best of times. Above all, work over the last generation on the construction of meaning in the use and movement of artefacts, what one might broadly call after the key work in the field the 'social life of things', has combined with very interesting new work on consumption to transform the debate on culture change.⁹ It is hard to see how retaining a term such as 'Orientalizing' could be justified from this perspective. Motifs originating in the east were reinterpreted and took on wholly new lives many times as they moved in social space in the Mediterranean.

That is naturally even more true of complex social formations. The tail is truly wagging the dog when we need to be reminded by the analogy of how artefacts' meanings and identities are continually reconstructed that socio-legal systems and myth-systems mutate similarly in the process of adaptation and appropriation! Put simply, a second basic problem with naming a cultural process for its hypothetical origin (let alone naming whole periods after the said process) is that the medium of exchange of culture does as much or more to explain the cultural form as the origin, near or far.

Progress in cultural history has therefore compelled us to get beyond the 'my-culture's-origins-are-better-than-yours' approach. Ultimate origins are even less interesting than proximate ones.¹⁰ If a Carian learned the latest Assyrian fashions from their versions in Sardis, sailed to Olbia with a Milesian vessel and passed the taste on to the Scythians in the *chora*, do you really want to call that 'Orientalization'? It now seems quaint to predicate a change of the place or time of the ultimate genesis of the change, rather than the milieu in which it operated. Why an Etruscan in the Tyrrhenian thought alphabetic writing a useful thing to learn is a more important question than where the person who taught the person who taught him learned it from. If it is at all justifiable to use metaphors such as lines, routes or trajectories in speaking of cultural influence, it is unlikely that these ran from east to west through the Mediterranean with any directness.¹¹ The fluidity and unpredictability of the sea make it a little like older science-fiction's notion of hyperspace, a different dimension from which widely separated parts of conventional geometry may be instantaneously reached. 'Orientalizing' on the shores of the Alboran sea started at Gades. To reach Elea, the Phokaians sailed east. In later times, Tyrrhenian pirates vexed the Aegean.

Not that explanations involving grand cultural diffusion are completely out of fashion. An interesting comparison for the traditional picture of an Orientalized Mediterranean is offered by Lynda Shaffer's work on 'southernization'.¹² This addresses a cultural transformation on the very largest scale, the influence from AD 400 to 1800 of south Asia and the Indian ocean *koine*, first transforming China, then the Arab world, and finally NW Europe. The phenomenon looks very like our 'Orientalizing', but on a gigantic scale, and over a period more than six times longer. And it suffers from precisely the weakness that by the time the end of the line is reached, the ultimate origin has lost explanatory power and indeed interest.

Proponents of 'Orientalizing' have of course realized that they need to locate the movement of material in a social framework before they can make advanced claims for the retention of eastward-looking interpretations in the face of the consumer's tendency to attribute new meaning to goods. Faced with connections which are deduced largely from the distribution of artefacts, scholars have naturally been tempted to explain the movements of artefacts through exchange. One effect of the label 'Orientalizing' has therefore been to encourage a too ready recourse to postulating commerce or trade.¹³ But this involves a very debatable view of the economy of the 8th- and 7th-century Mediterranean, and in the early 21st century risks being ideologically tendentious too.

On the non-existence of the Orient

The third problem with 'Orientalizing' is simply that it presupposes an Orient.

Now, it is a familiar enough point that European and American observers in the early 21st century have so complex a cultural relationship with various concepts of the Orient that any hermeneutic which draws on those concepts can only make darkness darker. A sneer can be found lurking in older uses of the term 'Orientalizing', like the condescension hidden in 'Chinoiserie' or 'Frenchified'. The purpose of the argument, though often less overtly, is to explain such things as the 'flowering' of Greece of which Burkert speaks in the epigraph above.

But the problem is not simply that we have a political duty to abandon a traditional one-upmanship and try to level the playing-field in a spirit of politically correct apology.[14] Reifying the Other is an ingredient in self-definition, and vigilance against casual identification with, as it might be, a Mediterranean world in opposition to similar constructions of comparable scale and complexity, is an important scholarly self discipline.[15] Even if we attempted to do without the specifics of orientalism as they have accumulated over the centuries, and therefore tried to drain it of sinister cultural poisons, a model of a Mediterranean world influenced by an entity of the size and generality that is presupposed by the Orient of 'Orientalizing' would be potentially problematic.

Nor would it be satisfactory to say that this is strictly a term used to describe the ultimate origin of certain stylistic features in material culture, and that it can therefore be reined in and prevented from acquiring broader associations which might be tinged with orientalism. That would be an impossible boundary to police: and anyway that pass has been sold for a generation, since Orientalizing was adopted as the name of a whole period, and began to refer to much wider cultural forms. If it hadn't made that leap, we should not have been able to stage a discussion in the terms of the meeting which gives rise to this volume.

Orientalism is only part of the difficulty. Even worse, nothing that archaeologists or historians can sensibly call the Orient (let alone the 'Near East') ever existed.

The Phoenician problem is a case in point. At first sight it looks as if a social group with undisputed roots on the *façade maritime* of west Asia and engaged in wide contacts from one end of the Mediterranean to the other provides a perfect vindication of the notion of 'Orientalizing': here, perhaps, is the vector of some at least of these changes, a pro-active group from the east caught in the act of purveying new ways of thinking, speaking, making and doing to the widest range of other peoples. It is not so easy. The Phoenicians are of course a construction of modern scholarship, and their cultural homogeneity is open to question. But much more importantly, they are part of the problem, not the answer to it. They are in the net. A Phoenician-writing traveller from Sardinian Nora to Gades in the second half of the 7th century is no cultural ambassador of Tyre, let alone of the Orient. And the role of even the cities of Phoenicia in mediating between interior west Asia and Cyprus or the Delta is an ingredient in the network which we are seeking to explain, not something which is detachable from it and therefore a possible explanation of it. The transmission of cultural forms within the Phoenician *koine* and the subdivisions and shifting allegiances of that *koine* are an example of the mutable, dynamic Mediterranean world of the 8th and 7th centuries, and no more prior to it logically than contemporary processes involving Etruscan- or Greek-speakers. 'Orientalizing' might have worked better when Greek culture was the main focus of interest, and when that was still thought of as essentially centred on the Aegean. But it has now to cope with a kaleidoscopic Mediterranean, in which—in accordance with what has already been said about the curious proximity of places joined by maritime connectivity— it can actually be argued that Greekness was invented at the furthest points of seaborne diaspora, *precisely because* of their distance from home.[16]

Just as 'Orientalizing' might have (largely) escaped Orientalism when it was limited to a range of elements in material culture, but can hardly do so when it seeks to explain everything from cognition to social structure, so 'the Orient', which might have served as a lazy but meaningful *point-de-repère* in an older art-history, can hardly satisfy the explanatory burden placed on it by the greatly expanded interpretation of the term. Whether Mesopotamian city-culture and its immediate zone of influence, or Hittite Anatolia and its successors, or the cities of the west Asian litoral were being invoked, 'the Orient' would be a very crude label. And the ongoing effect of the Egyptian cultural tradition would give further pause.

Instead of constituting an Orient, west Asia offers numerous and discrete gateway-zones which have relatively little in common.[17] As mediators of new ideas, participants in creative mobility, central Anatolian corridors ultimately debouching on the Maeander or Kaikos troughs, or north Syrian connections with Cilicia, or the maritime horizons of Tyre, or the links of the cities of the Philistine coastal strip, or the connections of the Delta ports, all played important parts. But so did Carthage and Samos, Syracuse and Gravisca, way-stations of cultural influence from firmly within the Mediterranean world.

Visiting the sins of the fathers: what about the -ized?

A fourth problem, moreover, is whether 'Orientalizing' carries any overtones of scale and completeness, as—for instance—'Hellenization' and 'Romanization' have sometimes been thought to. Does it suggest a period of steady but uninsistent influence, or a total transformation? Does Orientalizing, to put it another way, suggest Orientalization? If not, why not? A further culpable imprecision in 'Orientalizing' is that the term appears to exist in a kind of middle voice. It hovers between identifying active and passive participants. Do you get Orientalized? Can you Orientalize someone else? Is it usually a case of self-orientalization? Or is it really always just something that happens without anyone really noticing? The clear gradients of violence, force, appropriation and coercion in the Mediterranean of this period are belied by such a benign term.[18] For a scholarly world which is having such difficulty over Hellenization and Romanization, it is surely incautious to continue to identify a period as Orientalizing. But I do not have space to say very much about this issue, except to urge that a term that is so vague as to the intensity with which the process it describes actually applied, and to the nature of its results, can hardly be helpful. Put these two things together and we seem to have a concept which is as vulnerable to criticism as both the other -izations, except for the fact that it is much more vaguely stated.

The -izing label boldly proposes a conceptual singularity for the process of cultural change in the period which we are discussing. It needs to be established that the undoubted complexity of this period has, as a major and distinctive common denominator, a single and particular pattern of cultural influence—even before we decide whether it is useful to use the term 'Oriental' in any way to identify it. Is the emulation—in any respect, and at any level of purposiveness—of any archetypal culture or region, and especially of an 'Orient', the way we want to model that change? With the new ways of understanding material culture this has become a somewhat less serious problem, but it is perhaps only now becoming normal to recognizable how usual it was in all Mediterranean communities of this period for intellectual, political and social forms to be exogenous. And the more normal that recognition is, the stranger 'Orientalizing' seems as a label! Is the implication in the label that we are dealing with state A, transformation X and state B which followed, justifiable at all in the Mediterranean of the first half of the first millennium BC? The disappearance of the Aegean Dark Age, the discovery of how far complex societies had developed in west central Italy before the first settlements of Phoenicians and Greeks, and the re-periodization of the archaeology of Palestine are just three reasons for finding that picture difficult chronologically.

Vague about choice and compulsion, uncertain about scale and completeness, intrinsically committed to over-simplifying the culturally intricate, 'Orientalizing' raises a further issue connected with the fate of those who underwent it: it is a major cog in a deeply teleological machine. Thus Burkert explicitly made the Orientalizing the explanation of what happens next, as we see plainly in the epigraph. How desirable is it to construct a whole period as being in so strong a sense the parent of the period which is to come, and therefore responsible for so much of its character? This is the megalithic approach to modelling historical causation. We can build with finer, subtler and more manageable materials.

In its blundering way, 'Orientalizing' scarcely does justice to the plurality of the recipients. Once it was mainly the Greeks who underwent this sea-change; later the Etruscans were added. Now we need to accommodate far more recipients in all the coastlands and islands of the Mediterranean, Sardinians, Iberians, Thracians, Phoenicians, Latins, Scythians, Ligurians and so on. It defies belief that what happened in all these peri-Mediterranean contexts is best envisaged as a single irradiation from the Eastern sun.

How many miles to Babylon?

The westward-pointing signposts trace a history of aspiration to the markers of wealth and power. It was the largest, wealthiest and most awe-inspiring of early states which produced these markers. By the period which we are discussing, the Mesopotamian centre, in its reinvention under Neo-Assyrian and Neo-Babylonian kings offered a unique reference point for expressions of wealth and status. If there is a spread of interest in these markers, it is a spread in connectivity, simultaneously making accessible new symbols of achievement and the wherewithal for acquiring them. Tracing the adoption of the different signs of these aspirations may appear to mark out routes which lead back to the plains of the Nile, Tigris and Euphrates. That does not make it helpful to identify the world of the adopters, from Sidon to Syracuse, as Orientalizing. The signposts at their most lucid mark out lines of sight, framing highly diverse aspirations in a window which gave a very distant image of Hundred Gated Thebes or foolish Nineveh. For many more, the eagerly sought-after hardware or the prestigious ideas were simply the best that was enjoyed by those who were within a much narrower imaginative reach.

Two other possibilities derive from the quest for something that might be happening for which the signposts are a marker, but not a sufficient description, as suggested above.

The Sherratts have proposed that the period sees the incorporation of the Mediterranean into a world-system, as the periphery of a network that had its centre in the Fertile Crescent.[19] It would not be incompatible with this to see the phase as an instance of an intensification of the interdependence that is associated with Mediterranean connectivity, one of those periods when the rhythms and importance of Mediterranean movements increase and many new regions find integration into the interlocking networks of redistribution. This is the period in which the Mediterranean as we see it in the Greek and Roman periods was invented. It has recently been suggested that the 'early antique' Mediterranean was the eastern basin: in which case what we have traditionally called 'Orientalizing' might as well be seen as the incorporation of more of the seaworld into an ever more extensive net which would eventually integrate the whole Mediterranean as we know it.[20] That would be to make the process a sort of intensification, while allowing for the eastward-pointing signposts. I do not insist on this: it is simply to show that there are wholly different forms of description for what has seemed to so many to be a process of radiating influences.

So what *do* we want to identify as the salient features of the complex of changes which affected the Mediterranean in the first half of the first millennium BC? Modelling interaction without the *deus ex machina* of cultural propulsion from the East will be a primary goal, examining the types of relationships which are traced by the patterns on which theories of 'Orientalizing' have been based. But there is certainly no need to turn our backs on west Asia.

The future task is modelling social, economic and cultural contact without the dead weight of monolithic constructs such as the Orient—or the Mediterranean of older scholarship, a determined and deterministic region conceived as a world in itself. Moses Finley wrote of the Hellenistic world that there were 'two basically distinct "Greek" societies in existence ... there was therefore no Hellenistic economy; from the outset there were two, an ancient sector and an Oriental sector'.[21] This may or may not be true: but if it is, then it becomes a task of the highest interest and importance to examine what happened where those two distinct worlds abutted. In the second quarter of the first millennium as much as in the Hellenistic period, the nature of the interface between Asia and the Mediterranean is too little understood. If we are to respond to the challenge of what Robert Chartier has called *histoire à très large échelle*, and insert the world which we understand into a context, rather than continuing to sit in a darkened room occasionally illuminated by the flashes of a firework display in the garden, we shall drop the term Orientalizing and the baggage which goes with it.[22]

Endnotes

1. I am very grateful to Corinna Riva and Nick Vella for their invitation to participate in what proved a boisterous and very thought-provoking debate.
2. Burkert 1992:6.
3. The collection Golden and Toohey 1997 remains almost alone in presenting reflections on this important theme in ancient history in recent years: see especially, for the context of the present discussion, Morris 1997.
4. All the participants at the discussion agreed that common denominators of historical change across the Mediterranean in this period could and should be sought. It was far less clear that 'Orientalizing' was a useful term for any of these denominators, and I came away from the discussion believing in it less than I had previously.
5. For connectivity as a theme in Mediterranean history, Horden and Purcell 2000:123–72.
6. Morris 1997: esp. 98–9.
7. See introduction.

8. These all derive from a mere five pages of West 1997:626–30.
9. Appadurai 1986; Kopytoff 1986. For consumption, Miller 1998 and 1995, applied to the Mediterranean in this period by Dietler 1999. For use of these approaches by historians, see, e.g., Jardine 1996; Wills 1993.
10. A distinction interestingly developed by Osborne, this volume.
11. Nor is the Mediterranean itself seen by all as a privileged corridor of diffusion: Harris 2005:24–5.
12. Shaffer 1994, developed Shaffer 2001, and at greater length as Shaffer 2002.
13. This is in later models of periodization through global interaction, as Bentley 1996.
14. Thus Wengrow, this volume.
15. Against Mediterranean exceptionalism, Purcell 2004:13–17.
16. An idea which Irad Malkin memorably developed in his Nellie Wallace Lectures in Oxford in 2005. But the Mediterranean of this period has really been incompatible with this view from at least Morel 1984.
17. See recently van de Mieroop 2005.
18. Morris, this volume, is content to make a close link between Orientalizing and colonialism.
19. The classic Sherratt and Sherratt 1993 may be cited as an example.
20. Van de Mieroop 2005:118. For the Mediterranean thus conceived, see Purcell 2004; Horden and Purcell 2005.
21. Finley 1985:183
22. Chartier 2001. The debate in that volume of the *Annales*, Aymard 2001; Subrahmanyam 2001; Wong 2001, and its continuations in other places (especially Guillot, Lombard and Ptak 1998) deserve to be better known. See also Purcell 2004: Peregrine Horden and I return to these questions of modelling the place of Mediterranean history in its wider context in our forthcoming book *Liquid Continents*.

References

Appadurai, A. (1986) Introduction: commodities and the politics of value. In *The Social Life of Things: Commodities in Cultural Perspective*, edited by A. Appadurai. Cambridge: Cambridge University Press, pp. 3–63.

Aymard, M. (2001) De la Méditerranée à l'Asie: une comparaison nécessaire (commentaire). *Annales, histoire, sciences sociales* 56(1):43–50.

Bentley, J. H. (1996) Cross-cultural interaction and periodization in World History. *American Historical Review* 101(3): 749–70.

Burkert, W. (1992) *The Orientalizing Revolution: Near Eastern Influence on Greek Culture in the Early Archaic Age*. Cambridge, MA: Harvard University Press.

Chartier, R. (2001) La conscience de la globalité. *Annales* 56(1):119–23.

Dabringhaus, S. and R. Ptak (eds.) (1997) *China and her Neighbours: Borders, Visions of the Other, Foreign Policy 10th to 19th Century*. Wiesbaden: Harrassowitz.

Dietler, M. (1999) Consumption, cultural frontiers and identity: anthropological approaches to colonial encounters. In *Confini e frontiera nella grecità d'Occidente. Atti XXXVII Convegno Magna Grecia*. Taranto: Istituto per la storia e l'archeologia della Magna Grecia, pp. 475–501.

Finley, M. I. (1985) *The Ancient Economy*. 2nd edition. London: Hogarth.

Golden, M. and P. Toohey (eds.) (1997) *Inventing Ancient Culture: Historicism Periodization and the Ancient World*. London: Routledge.

Guillot, C., D. Lombard and R. Ptak (eds.) (1998) *From the Mediterranean to the China Sea*. Wiesbaden: Harrassowitz.

Harris, W. V. (2005) The Mediterranean and ancient history. In *Rethinking the Mediterranean*, edited by W. V. Harris. Oxford: Oxford University Press, pp. 1–42.

Horden, P. and N. Purcell (2000) *The Corrupting Sea: A Study in Mediterranean History*. Oxford: Blackwell.

Horden, P. and N. Purcell (2005) Four years of corruption. In *Rethinking the Mediterranean*, edited by W. V. Harris. Oxford: Oxford University Press, pp. 348–75.

Jardine, L. (1996) *Worldly Goods: A New History of the Renaissance*. London: Papermac.

Kopytoff, I. (1986) The cultural biography of things: commoditization as process. In *The Social Life of Things: Commodities in Cultural Perspective*, edited by A. Appadurai. Cambridge: Cambridge University Press, pp. 64–91.

Miller, D. (ed.) (1995) *Acknowledging Consumption: A Review of New Studies*. London: Routledge.

Miller, D. (1998) *Material Cultures: Why Some Things Matter*. Chicago: UCL Press.

Morel, J.-P. (1984) Greek colonization in Italy and the West. Problems of evidence and interpretation. In *Crossroads of the Mediterranean*, edited by T. Hackens, N. D. Holloway and R. R. Holloway. Providence, RI: Brown University, Center for Old World Archaeology and Art; Louvain-la-Neuve, Belgique: Institut supérieur d'archéologie et d'histoire de l'art, Collège Erasme, pp. 123–61.

Morris, I. (1997) Periodization and the heroes: inventing a Greek Dark Age. In *Inventing Ancient Culture: Historicism, Periodization and the Ancient World*, edited by M. Golden and P. Toohey. London: Routledge, pp. 96–131.

Purcell, N. (2004) The boundless sea of unlikeness? On defining the Mediterranean. *Mediterranean Historical Review* 18(2) (December 2003):9–29.

Shaffer, L. (1994) Southernization. *Journal of World History* 5:1–21.

Shaffer, L. (2001) Southernization. In M. Adas (ed.), *Agricultural and Pastoral Societies in Ancient and Classical History*. Philadelphia: Temple University Press, pp. 308–24.

Shaffer, L. (2002) *Southernization*. Washington DC: American Historical Association.

Sherratt, A. and S. Sherratt (1993) The growth of the Mediterranean economy in the early first millennium BC. *World Archaeology* 24:361–78.

Subrahmanyam, S. (2001) Du Tage au Gange au XVIe siècle: une conjoncture millénariste à l'échelle eurasiatique. *Annales* 56(1):51–84.

van de Mieroop, M. (2005) The eastern Mediterranean in early antiquity. In *Rethinking the Mediterranean*, edited by W. V. Harris. Oxford: Oxford University Press, pp. 117–40.

West, M. (1997) *The East Face of Helicon: West Asiatic Elements in Early Poetry and Myth*. Oxford: Clarendon Press.

Wills, J. E. J. (1993) European consumption and Asian production in the seventeenth and eighteenth centuries. In *Consumption and the World of Goods*, edited by J. Brewer and R. Porter. London: Routledge, pp. 133–47.

Wong, R. Bin (2001) Entre monde et nation: les régions braudéliennes en Asie. *Annales* 56(1):5–41.

3 Approaching Ancient Orientalization *via* Modern Europe[1]

David Wengrow

Introduction: Orientalism and Orientalizing

The term 'orientalizing' has a confused history in the study of the ancient Mediterranean. It was introduced by art historians with reference to the appearance of objects, imagery and techniques of Near Eastern or Egyptian derivation on the Greek mainland from the 8th to the 6th centuries BC, prior to the formation of classical culture (e.g. Poulsen 1912). These included figural images of real and fantastic animals, new skills in casting metal and clay figurines, and unprecedented forms of monumental stone sculpture and architecture (Boardman 1964). Prior to the impact of Edward Said's (1978) *Orientalism* within the humanities, their influence upon Greek development was typically described in terms of a Hegelian opposition between the 'spirits' of East and West, contrasting the active, self-conscious transformation of received knowledge by the Greeks with the 'banal', 'repetitive', 'stereotyped' products of the native Orient (e.g. Boardman 1973:19–107, *passim*; and cf. Morris 1989:41).[2]

More recently the concept of 'orientalizing' has been extended from the history of artefactual styles to a wider series of social and intellectual transformations in ancient Greece, including the inception of the aristocratic symposion, the introduction of the alphabet, and the encoding of a divine pantheon and body of myth (e.g. Burkert 1992; Murray 1993 [1978]:81–101). This coincided with the proposed restriction of orientalizing influences to a discrete chronological period (c. 750–650 BC), a view that has since been subject to a sustained critique by Sarah Morris (1992). She marshals a wide range of evidence for eastern influences in the Aegean extending continuously from the late second millennium BC (Late Bronze Age) into the first millennium BC (Iron Age). To prehistorians who have traced the westward spread of Near Eastern innovations back into Neolithic times (or, indeed, to archaeologists who have long since recognized the existence of a Bronze Age world system; e.g. Rowlands *et al.* 1987) this comes as no great surprise. Morris's case, however, is directed principally at scholars of classical antiquity.

With these factors in mind, the relationship between the concept of 'orientalization' and the discourse defined by Said as 'orientalism' seems best understood as one of opposition. The former seems to refer to processes of concrete cultural interaction, while the latter describes the fashioning of a self-image predicated upon distance from an exotic 'Other'. What is less easily agreed upon is whether and (if so) how often there have been transitions from orientalization to orientalism (or vice versa) in Europe. To pose the question in this way is itself an orientalist conceit, introducing binary oppositions and false notions of cultural authenticity into what has always been a shifting constellation of identities spanning east and west (cf. van Dommelen 1998). Orientalization and orientalism, today as in antiquity, may necessarily coexist: consider the highly successful use of traditional orientalist stereotypes in marketing Indian, Chinese and Middle Eastern food to western consumers. Nevertheless, the question has been posed and answered by a number of scholars.

In defining the scope of orientalism, Said himself (1978:55–73) cites Homer and Aeschylus as precursors to Flaubert and Nerval, implying a continuity of approach from Graeco-Roman to modern times. More recently, Morris has argued explicitly that modern European attitudes to the Orient were prefigured in the Athenian response to the Persian Wars during the 5th century BC, which led Greeks to shun and stigmatize their own eastern heritage (Morris 1992: xxii, cf. 1989:40–1). Comparably, in the conclusion to his *Early Greece*, Oswyn Murray (1993 [1978]:301) writes:

> The Persian Wars opened a new epoch. But they also closed an old one. Greek culture had been created from the fruitful interchange between east and west; that debt was now forgotten. An iron curtain had descended: east against west, despotism against liberty—the dichotomies created in the Persian Wars echo through world history …

Elsewhere, however, Morris has accepted Martin Bernal's (1987) argument that Europe's exclusive identification with ancient Greece is itself a fabrication of the last two centuries (Morris 1989:40–1). Stranger still, in responding to her critique, Bernal himself appears to consider his lack of attention to the classical roots of modern European chauvinism to be a failure, as though the historical identification of modern Europe with ancient Greece was real rather than constructed (Bernal 1989:22; 2001: 296–8). Nor does he consider whether, in using archaeology to re-establish the positive view held by the Greeks of their cultural debt to Egypt (for which, see now Bowman 2002), he is himself resurrecting an ancient prejudice, borne to us on Renaissance wings, which stigmatized the Near East but valorized many aspects of Egypt (Momigliano 1975:2–3). The recriminations of the Persian Wars may be 'echoing down the corridors of time'. But it is no longer clear who exactly is supposed to be listening.

In considering east-west relations from the perspective of historiography, I wish to keep both feet firmly rooted in the ground of cultural memory, and avoid stepping over onto the path of archaeological reconstruction. Nor do I wish to rehearse well-founded arguments regarding the relationship between anti-Semitism, the development of Indo-European studies, and the exclusion of the Phoenician contribution to history (Bernal 1987; Burkert 1992:1–8). Rather, I wish to focus upon how the ancient Orient has become implicated in the formation of the modern, western political subject. I do so, not in the hope of shedding any direct light on east-west relations in antiquity, but in an attempt to foreground currents of thought and emotion that may flow beneath the surface of a modern evaluation of those relations.

Forgetting sacred kingship

It is fascinating that Sigmund Freud, founder of modern psychoanalysis and author of *Civilization and its Discontents* (1930), chose largely Egyptian antiquities to line the shelves and cabinets of his office, which was also his consulting room (see Ucko 2001). By the early 20th century ancient Egypt had come to symbolize many of the discontents and contradictions of Judeo-Christian, democratic, capitalist society. In this it was rivalled only by the 'primitives' of early ethnographic accounts who also fascinated Freud and, partly because of the evolutionary framework within which they were studied, feature heavily in his own theory of the development of the human psyche (e.g. Freud 1919).

Among these discontents are the repressed desire to abdicate responsibility for life to a higher authority, which satisfies both spiritual and psychological needs; the desire for material rather than merely spiritual continuity after death; and the closely related desire to institute the social life of the living in some form of direct commerce with the dead (cf. Baudrillard 1993). Fustel de Coulanges (1864) speculated long ago as to how the repression of hereditary authority, and the cauterization of its ancestral rites and institutions of dynastic rule, had provided the historical cornerstone of republican morality and rule of law. These institutions had made authority coterminous with particular forms of social relationship which through their restricted media and modes of transmission (the blood-line, the ancestral estate, etc.) were rendered the inalienable possession of a small elite. Their disappearance opened the floodgates which had stifled the flow of power between 'ordinary people' and the political elite, and the Plebeians entered the 'Ancient City' of the Patricians.

Fustel de Coulanges was seeking to evoke the social conflicts at the heart of the ancient *poleis* of Greece and Rome, which his native France had sought to resolve in an entirely new way in 1789 through the violent destruction of the *Ancien Régime*, to which he turned his scholarly attention in later life (see Momigliano 1980:x–xi). The resemblance between that regime and the forms of government more recently described as 'archaic' or 'primitive' by anthropologists is traditionally underplayed in textbooks and popular dramatizations, but has been brought to light in studies such as Marc Bloch's (1924) *Les Rois Thaumaturges* and Ernst Kantorowicz's (1957) *The King's Two Bodies*. The anthropologist Marshall Sahlins (1985:77) has similarly suggested that 'the conception of divine kings we find in Hawaii or Fiji also happens to preside over the subterranean history of our own democracies'.

The extent to which the memory of sacerdotal kingship has been eradicated from Europe's consciousness of its own social development, or replaced by a cosy nostalgia fostered through the pageant of modern monarchy, is apparent in the opening passage to Henri Frankfort's *Kingship and the Gods*:

> The ancient Near East considered kingship the basis of civilization. Only savages could live without a king. Security, peace, and justice could not prevail without a ruler to champion them ... But if we refer to kingship as a political institution, we assume a point of view which would have been incomprehensible to the ancients (Frankfort 1948:3).

It was to the contemporary societies of Africa, rather than to Europe's own dynastic past, that Frankfort looked for guidance in understanding the functioning of ancient Egyptian and Mesopotamian forms of kingship. As Pierre Clastres (1987:15, 205) reminds us, though, the earliest Europeans to reach Brazil considered the Tupinamba Indians savages precisely because they were 'people without god, law, and king'. When Frankfort (1948:x) asserted that 'the achievements of the Greeks and the teachings of the Old and New Testaments' are the basis of modern Europe's alienation from the ancient Near East he was therefore presenting a partial view. As Louis Dumont (1980) observed in his study of the Indian caste system, the Revolution had also played its part in making *Homo hierarchicus* incomprehensible to *Homo aequalis*.

The attitude of those early European explorers is now largely unrecognizable to us. The notion that genuine political participation begins where kingship and divinely sanctioned rule end has become a central feature of modern western thought, inscribed in the charters of its three great political revolutions: American, French and Russian. Despite their differences it is a common feature of these charters that any government worthy of the name must, as Giambattista Vico had already perceived, 'be conformable to the nature of the governed' rather than to that of the ruler, the cosmos, or the gods (see Wilson 1972:11). The humanism of Vico's (1725) *Scienza Nuova* differed profoundly from that of the 18th-century Enlightenment in viewing the passage of social time as a cyclical process rather than a linear progression. The historical experience which, above all others, separated these two points of view—one essentially medieval and the other modern—was the French Revolution, and the rupture caused by this experience has been vividly evoked by Paul Connerton (and see also Walzer 1974):

> The trial and execution of Louis XVI was not the murder of a ruler but the revocation of a ruling principle: the principle according to which the dynastic realm was the only imaginable political system. It had indeed been possible to envisage regicide within the terms of that system ... But whatever fate might befall individual kings, the principle of dynastic succession remained intact ... This form of regicide left the dynastic system unchallenged: the benchmarks of time were still the phases of dynastic rule. The death of the king registered a break in that public time: between one king and another time stood still.

And he goes on:

> The revolutionaries needed to find some ritual process through which the aura of inviolability surrounding kingship could be explicitly repudiated ... For thousands of years the kings of France had received at their coronation holy oil as well as the crown upon their heads, after the manner of the apostles' successors. The effect was to transform the enemies of royalty into apparently sacrilegious persons. This was the effect that the public regicide of Louis sought to undo ... The anointed head was decapitated and the rite of coronation ceremonially revoked. Not simply the natural body of the king but also and above all his political body was killed. (Connerton 1989:8–9)

Revolutionary thought requires both a sense of the naturalness of its own aims, and of the unnaturalness of what it seeks to overthrow. The experience of the French Revolution, and the chronic social instability and periodic relapses into old forms of authority which followed, raised urgent new questions (cf. Dumont 1980:13–17; Giddens 1986:11–24). How does a society function without rulers? What is the place and responsibility of the individual within the collective? Are forms of knowledge and organization based on secular principles adequate to replace the precepts of a hierocratic order? New ideas of social development were required to make the new vision of the present and future understandable as part of a natural evolution from the past.

A central theme of this essay is that as a requirement of modernity the institution of kingship—especially in its sacerdotal forms—therefore had to be pushed to the margins of historical consciousness and rendered anomalous, exotic, and moribund (cf. Ozouf 1988). This resulted, on the one hand, in the creation of a new European past rooted exclusively in an idealized image of classical antiquity, which encompassed both republican ideals and imperial ambitions (Bernal 1987; Hingley 2000). On the other it led to the construction of new and remote spaces of the imagination such as 'the Orient' (Said 1978) and 'primitive society' (Kuper 1988), incompatible with and subordinate to Europe's emerging self-image as a progressive society, onto which the collective memory of sacred kingship could be grafted.

'Liberating' Egypt and exorcizing the *Ancien Régime*

> The Museé Napoleon was born of three parents, republicanism, anti-clericalism and successful aggressive war.
> ... The Revolution had set up an idol which itself demanded the offerings that were made to it. (Gould 1965:13, 40)

In order to pin these ideas a little more closely to historical events, I would now like to consider the Napoleonic occupation of Egypt, an episode defined by Said (1978:42) as the founding event of modern orientalism, setting in motion processes between East and West that 'still dominate our contemporary cultural and political perspectives'. I have already outlined some of the social and ideological forces at play when Britain's growing hold on Mughal India and the eastern trade prompted Napoleon Bonaparte to invade Egypt in 1798. With the embers of revolution still smouldering on the streets of Paris, the chief servant of the Directory confronted the Ottoman Empire in the name of liberty and in the process encountered the ancient kings of the Nile valley, a confrontation later visualized by artists such as Orange and Cogniet (see Larsen 1994:34, fig.1; Andreu *et al*. 1997:19, fig.4). Faced with this spectacle, the general of the First Republic could not resist entombing himself briefly within the Great Pyramid. The irony was short-lived, however. It was not to a Pharaonic legacy that Napoleon appealed in his victorious address to the people of Alexandria, but to an idealized Islamic past of flourishing cities and trade, free from the yoke of Mameluke tyranny. And it was with his domestic subjects, rather than the people of Egypt, in mind that Napoleon's *savants* were set to the task of documenting and appropriating the ancient monuments (see Bret 1999).

The publication of the monumental *Description de l'Égypte* (1809–28) was an event commemorated by the striking of a bronze medallion designed by J. J. Barre (Figure 3.1; and see Curl 1994:132–3, fig.81). It shows a masculine personification of Roman Gaul unveiling ancient Egypt in the form of a suppliant woman. She holds a sistrum evoking the goddess Hathor (and hence female sexuality) whose temple at Dendera is faithfully depicted in the background, and fondles the muzzle of the crocodile upon which she reclines. While undoubtedly concerned at some level with discovery or appropriation (Larsen 1994: 36), the impression given by this allegorical image is also of the pacifying and feminising of an alien power, metonymically represented by the pyramids which are visible behind the figure of Gaul.

Figure 3.1   Bronze medallion commemorating the publication of *Description de l'Égypte*, 1826. After Curl 1994:133, fig.81.

The 'domestication' of ancient Egypt also found expression in contemporary European fashions for interior design, instigated during the late 18th century by Giovanni Battista Piranesi's spectacular Egyptianizing fireplaces (Curl 1994:87–97). In France and Italy these fashions originated under the patronage of the *Ancien Régime* but were incorporated into bourgeois tastes during the early 19th century through the production of cabinets, clocks and more minor household articles such as teapots, which had been produced in Egyptianizing styles by Josiah Wedgwood for the mercantile middle classes of England as early as the 1770s (ibid.112–147).

The democratizing of fine art and sculpture had commenced in France during the pre-Revolutionary period, when objects from the noble houses had first been placed on public display. In 1783 the Palais du Louvre, containing the royal collections, was opened as a public institution, the Museum Central des Arts. It subsequently became a venue for the display of an extraordinary quantity of art objects confiscated by Bonaparte's forces following their successful campaigns in Belgium (1794) and Italy (1796–99) and was renamed the Musée Napoleon in 1803 (Gould 1965). In a letter to Napoleon the Commissioner of Art André Thouin expressed his view that 'the French spoliation of Italy was the reward of military virtue over decadence and that it was strictly comparable with what the Greeks are supposed to have done to the Egyptians and the Romans in their turn to the Greeks' (ibid.65).

Against this highly politicized background the display of Egyptian antiquities in the Musée Napoleon took on a particular social significance. A section of the museum devoted specifically to ancient Egypt was first opened by Champollion in 1826 under the restored monarchy of Charles X, occupying the former chambers of the French queens (see Andreu *et al.* 1997; Humbert 1997). The extraordinary preservation of elite burials in the *salle funéraire* meant that any citizen could stand face-to-face with royalty and measure their own being against the exposed figure of a divine king, while at the same time measuring the human size of the latter against that of his boastful monuments (Figure 3.2). What was on display here was not merely the fantastic 'otherness' of Oriental civilization (cf. Mitchell 1991) but also the very embodiment of dynastic rule, displaced onto the inscrutable remains of an ancient culture and located safely behind the threshold of modernity. The guillotine had given way to the intrusive public gaze as a means of unveiling and laying to rest the ghost of monarchy (see, in this context, 19th-century tableaux showing visitors to the Egyptian galleries; e.g. Andreu *et al.* 1997:22–3, figs.5–6). In this sense the museum anticipated in concrete form the grand themes of Michelet's (1879–80) *Histoire de la Révolution française*:

> Another thing which this History will clearly establish and holds true in every connection, is that the people were usually more important than the leaders. The deeper I have excavated, the more surely I have satisfied myself that the best was underneath, in the obscure depths … To find the people again and put it back in its proper role, I have been obliged to reduce to their proportions the ambitious marionettes whose strings it manipulated and in whom hitherto we have looked for and thought to see the secret play of history. (Michelet, cited in Wilson 1972:24)

The Renaissance background

Returning for a moment to the medallion commemorating the *Description* (Figure 3.1) we also find an allusion to the image of the goddess Isis-Athena at Sais, described by Plutarch

Figure 3.2   *La Musée Charles-X en 1863*. Engraving by A. Régis. After Andreu *et al.* 1997:23, fig.6.

during the 1st century AD in his *De Iside et Osiride*. During the Renaissance, and on the basis of Plutarch's account, 'the concept of the veiled figure of the goddess whom it is death to uncover became a frequent metaphor of revealed wisdom' (Whitehouse 1995: 20). At the heart of this Renaissance concept was a particular, pre-Revolutionary notion of the relationship between knowledge, art and power, in opposition to which the motif of 'unveiling Egypt' seems best understood. This earlier notion may be briefly explored by considering Gianlorenzo Bernini's 'Fountain of the Four Rivers', commissioned by Pope Innocent X as a foundation setting for the Egyptian obelisk he erected in the Piazza Navona in 1652, two years after its scheduled date of completion in the Holy Year 1650 (Curl 1994:74).

Simon Schama (1995:293) places Bernini's monument in its political context, noting that 'in the age of sacred hydraulics, the way in which a papal dynasty effectively colonised a Roman piazza was by creating a new fountain'. Innocent X had previously had the hieroglyphs on his obelisk studied by Athanasius Kircher, 'an unreconstructed neo-Platonist obsessed with hieroglyphs as an allegorical and esoteric crypt' (ibid.300; cf. Iversen 1961:89). Bernini's sculpted setting for the obelisk expresses an appropriately holistic and mystical cosmology, framing it within four personified male figures of river-deities symbolizing the Nile, Danube, Ganges, and Río de la Plata. The head of 'Nile' alone is shown veiled, suggesting its unknown source and reflecting the contemporary perception of Egypt as locus of hidden knowledge. The top of the obelisk is crowned by a dove holding an olive branch and symbolizing both the Pamphili dynasty of Innocent X and the Holy Ghost (Schama 1995:298).

Other dynasts, including Pope Alexander VI, claimed a more direct Egyptian ancestry by commissioning scholars to trace their family line back, via the classical sources, to the mythical figure of Osiris (Iversen 1971:183). This practice reached the western fringes of Renaissance culture where it was translated, none-too-subtly, into an early form of national agenda (Kendrick 1950:65–72). Hector Boece's *Scotorum Historia*, published in 1527, revived a belief that his native Scotland had been named after Scota, daughter of the Pharaoh of the Oppression and wife of a Greek prince. (He also claimed that King Arthur had died on the shores of the Humber, having promised Britain to the royal house of the Picts.) The English rebuttal came in the *Scriptorium illustrium majoris Britanniae* compiled by John Bale, Bishop of Ossory, and containing—in a second, expanded edition published in 1557—a remarkable genealogy (Figure 3.3).

In his bold act of revelation, then, the figure of Gaul challenges not only the mystique of Egypt as a source of origin but also the very cultural basis of an old elite which, in republican eyes, had founded its authority upon an esoteric and unenlightened worldview. His gesture forms a symbolic counterpart to the physical transplantation of fine paintings and sculpture from the Italian heart of the Renaissance to the halls of the Musée Napoleon, shattering the 'art nexus' (Gell 1998) which since the beginning of the Christian era had bound such objects and their associated meanings exclusively to the Church and the nobility (cf. Gould 1965:13).

Another aspect of this transformation was the deconstruction of Egypt's special status as a source of high culture and wisdom (Ucko and Champion 2003), which had been cultivated by European elites since the 15th century, and its incorporation into what Whitehouse (1995:16)

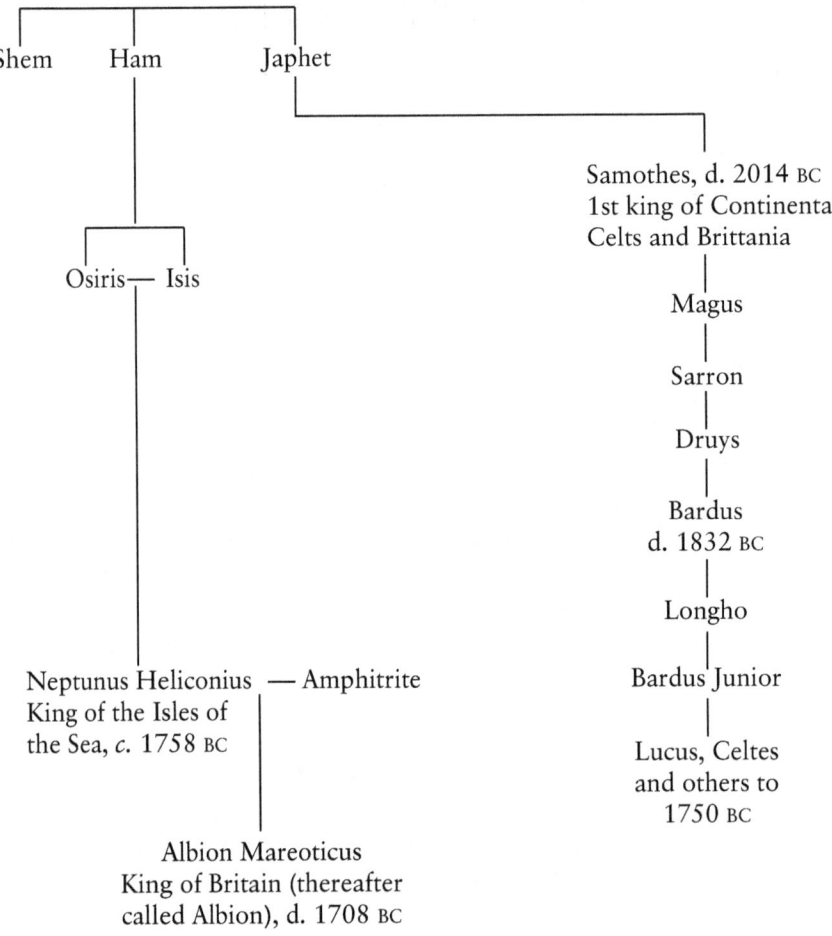

Figure 3.3   The origin of Britain according to John Bale, Bishop of Ossory (d.1563). After Kendrick 1950:68.

has termed a 'generalised oriental sphere' extending from China to the Mediterranean (cf. Said 1978:42). The novelty of this view is highlighted by a consideration of the marked difference in Renaissance attitudes towards Egypt and the Near East. As Lundquist (1995:67) points out there had 'never been a "Babyloniamania" in western art, literature, architecture, or design to rival Egypt's hold on pre-modern Europe'. This was due in large measure to the invisibility of Assyrian and Babylonian monuments prior to the beginning of large-scale tell excavations during the mid-19th century, as well as the local re-use of mud-brick over the centuries (ibid.67; and see Larsen 1996). It also reflected negative perceptions of the Near East conveyed to Renaissance scholars by their classical and biblical sources, the former crystallized in the Athenian response to the Great Persian War and the latter portraying Babylon as a site of urban corruption, idolatry and hubris (cf. McIntosh 1999). This biblical image was evoked in numerous depictions of Nimrod overseeing construction of the Tower of Babel, the most famous being the 1563 version by Pieter Brueghel the Elder (Klengel-Brandt 1982:11, pl.ii).[3]

It is perhaps in this remote space of the Renaissance imagination that we find the germ of those attitudes characterized by Said as 'Orientalist', and only later extended to Egypt (cf. Lundquist 1995:77). Such a view cannot be accepted uncritically, however. During the 16th century, negative images of the ancient Near East also resonated with contemporary rivalries between the ruling houses of Europe and the vast Ottoman Empire. The value attached to symbols of antiquity in this rivalry has been articulated through a study of the circulation of art objects between the Hapsburg and Ottoman elites (Jardine and Brotton 2000). The movement of artists, tapestries, medallions, horses, and other luxuries between courtly centres of Europe and the Orient reveals, not a distant perception of the exotic eastern 'Other', but a shared set of values within which dynastic rulers jostled for prestige: 'East and West fixed each other with an equal, reciprocal gaze [which] was intensified and revised in the subsequent contests for power and legitimation that defined the escalation in inter-imperial confrontation in the course of the sixteenth century' (ibid.63). The common desire of Charles V and Süleyman the Magnificent to inhabit the image of Alexander the Great through the commissioning of art objects is particularly striking in highlighting the contests of power through which Europe took stock of its present cultural inventory (Figure 3.4).

In the ideological aftermath of the French Revolution the parameters within which material remains of earlier hierarchies, including those of the ancient East, were reconstituted and understood in Europe and America were profoundly altered (cf. Hughes 1995). No longer simply pawns in an ongoing game of dynastic one-upmanship, they now began to take up their new and often more paradoxical places in a self-consciously Occidental discourse of universal progress.[4] The transition is anticipated in a statement that concludes the entry for 'Egypt' in Diderot's *Dictionnaire Raisonné des Sciences, des Arts et des Métiers*, which appeared in 1751: 'It was once a country to be admired; nowadays it is one to be studied' (cited in Gillispie 1987:4; cf. Laurens 1999).

From Tribe to Empire: reconciling the ancient Orient with progress

When Georges Davy, a member of Emile Durkheim's inner intellectual circle, and the renowned Egyptologist Alexandre Moret decided to write a book together in the 1920s, they could have had little sense of its future impact—albeit largely indirect—on the development of archaeological thought. The result, which they called 'From Tribe to Empire' adding the

Figure 3.4   Detail from Pieter Coecke van Aelst, *Procession of Sultan Süleyman II through the Atmedan*, woodcut from *Ces Moeurs et fachons de faire de Turcz*, 1533. After Jardine and Brotton 2000:151, illus.62 (note obelisk, top left).

subtitle 'social organization among Primitives and in the Ancient Near East' (Moret and Davy 1926), is an unintended monument to the conceptual gulf which, during the course of the 19th century, had come to separate the sociological study of human development from the older narrative history of kings, migrations and military clashes. It was not without diffidence that the authors brought the monumental remains of ancient Egypt and Mesopotamia into a direct confrontation with the intellectual values of liberal, bourgeois republicanism:

> Why does this book, which is a history book and takes Egypt and the Ancient East for its subject, open with an introduction which is sociological and the scope of which extends far beyond Egypt and seems to embrace primitive institutions in general? ... Is it ... in the expectation of providing History with that absolute beginning which History itself fails to offer us? ... however deep might be the interest of such an attempt, our contribution ... has more modest aims. It merely proposes to introduce the reader to an appreciation of the problems which the earliest history of Egypt and the Orient inevitably raises, being yet not committed to solve them. (Moret and Davy 1926:2)

What then were these profound evolutionary problems posed by the ancient East? They may be condensed into a single institution: kingship.

Based upon ethnographic accounts of native Australians, Africans and Americans, and heavily influenced by the work of Frazer, Maine, McLennan, Tylor, Morgan, Robertson Smith, and Boas (see Kuper 1988), the scholars of the *Année Sociologique* had accepted a new point of origin for the development of human political institutions: the totemic clan. The clan was 'communistic' and 'democratic' but contained no true individuals. Its unity and egalitarianism derived rather from the common participation of all members in the religious essence of a unifying symbol, the totem. Consequently the early evolution of political institutions was merged with that of mythology and spiritual beliefs. The process by which hierarchy had emerged from undifferentiated unity had also involved issues of territorial rights, rules of property and inheritance, ritualised economic competition (the *potlach*) and gender ('the masculinization of kinship and authority'). At its core however was the theme of individualisation, the absorption and embodiment of totemic force within a single person—the chief—whose power resided in his claim: 'Le clan, c'est moi' (Moret and Davy 1926: 85).

It is not hard with hindsight to see whence this scheme derived, and where it was leading. Individual authority, in its essential form, is nothing other than the transfigured spirit of the collective. Durkheim had been right: despotism, 'at least when it is not a pathological or degeneration phenomenon, is nothing but a transformed communism' (ibid.111). It follows that in its pathological form despotism is tantamount to usurpation; a failure on the part of the ruler to perceive that his authority rests ultimately upon the will of his subjects. It will be clear by now that the primitive clan *was*, in fact, a charter of origin for republican society: the 'beginning' which conventional history had failed to offer. Behind the triumphal conclusion to Davy's contribution in *From Tribe to Empire*, we can still hear distant echoes of the Bastille falling:

> This conclusion is just; for nothing comes out of nothing—Pharaoh's absolute kingship no more than any common-place natural product; and that is one of the first maxims we have laid down in these pages. Sovereignty has a 'matter,' and it cannot be created by a mere fiat of the sovereign's will. Such a will is, then, in this sense only a secondary cause. But history, *down to its latest self-revelation*, stands as a witness to warn us that a secondary cause is not necessarily an ineffectual cause, and that according as it assume this figure or that, it can modify surprisingly the 'form' of the 'matter' in which it works. (Moret and Davy 1926:112 [my emphasis])

The translator of *From Tribe to Empire*, and so of this oddly rendered passage, was V. Gordon Childe and the rest as they say is 'what happened in history' (see Childe 1936; 1942; and also Rowlands 1994; Sherratt 1997:64, 'The writing of prehistory is still a dialogue with the ghost of Childe'). More deeply entrenched in Marx than his French contemporaries, Childe perceived technology rather than collective consciousness to be the 'matter' of which both despotic and free societies are made. But while technological capacity in itself is mere 'capital', so for Childe it was the 'qualities of energy, independence, and inventiveness which distinguish the western world from Egypt, India or China' that transformed it into the instrument of liberty and progress (Childe 1925:xiii–xv).

Contemporary archaeology and the idea of the Orient

As Bruce Trigger (1979) perceived, the problem of kingship remained a root cause of Egypt's isolation from the social sciences during the late 20th century (see also Lustig 1997). Once a cornerstone of social evolutionary thought, in the tradition set down by Frazer (1890) and Hocart (1927), kingship was marginalized from the neo-evolutionary theory of the 1960s–80s which chose instead to ponder the transitions from 'tribe' to 'chiefdom' and from 'chiefdom' to 'archaic state'. Forms of status as diverse as 'warrior chief' and 'ritual leader' were subsumed within a single category, and a common criticism of the 'chiefdom' has since been that it spans too broad a range of social variation (e.g. Yoffee 1993; Kristiansen 1998).

At around the same time the anthropology of divine kingship took a semiological turn, inspired by Dumézil's analyses of Indo-European mythology and the structural anthropology of Lévi-Strauss (both grounded in comparative linguistics), and exemplified in de Heusch's (1972) study of Bantu myth and Sahlins's (1985) work on Oceania. There is no inherent reason why the study of ancient Egypt or Mesopotamia should have been excluded from this theoretical enterprise, and many of its central concerns were anticipated in the work of Henri Frankfort (1948) which, as Trigger notes, attempted to discern the consistent patterns of mythical thought and symbolic practice underlying the different forms of kingship in these two regions (Trigger 1979:32; cf. Wengrow 1999:603).

A notable attempt to break out of this self-imposed disciplinary isolation, which has already provoked ample secondary discussion (e.g. Rowlands 1989:33–4; Larsen 1994:29–33), is the debate involving K. C. Chang, G. Willey, K. Lamberg-Karlovsky and others published in the 1985 edition of *Symbols*, the journal of the Peabody Museum. These scholars broadly agreed that the Western attainment of technological progress, rational bureaucracy, and secular political thought are rooted in the constitutional fabric of the ancient Mesopotamian city-state. They argued that its genesis during the fourth millennium BC represented a unique departure from a universal pattern of experience found in the other early civilizations of the Old and New Worlds such as those of China, the Maya, and Egypt. There political and economic life remained embedded within distinct cosmological systems which encouraged conformity to a pre-determined order encompassing both the human and non-human domains, and centred upon the mediation between kingship and divinity. By contrast, Mesopotamian civilization developed a cultural ethic based upon the conquering of nature by technological means, which was transmitted to modern Europe via ancient Greece and Rome, and upon which the values of individual freedom and rule of law are founded (Lamberg-Karlovsky 1985).

Quite apart from their obliteration of 'Occidental despotism' from the historical record and their unusual interpretation of Mesopotamian kingship and cosmology, these accounts do not appear to consider whether concepts such as 'freedom' and 'progress' might themselves be 'strategies of legitimation of a social order vis-à-vis the natural order' (Kus 1982:53; cf. Pfaffenberger 1988). This was elegantly expressed in a Marxian vein by the anthropologist Franz Steiner in his 1944 essay 'On the process of civilization':

> We have dropped the idea of measuring our powers with nature, as this is simply an allegory with the help of which predatory social elites transfigure the beliefs appropriate to their own technology. There is no such thing as the powers of nature on the one hand, those of 'the human being' on the other, an ensuing struggle, a growth of human powers, and finally a defeat of nature. That is simply the trite myth of capitalism. (Steiner, reproduced in Adler and Fardon 1999:125)

The primary dissenter in the *Symbols* debate was a Professor of Latin who asserted that 'the origin of the democratic concept of society did not reach Greece from contact with the Near East or Mesopotamia, where equity and justice were a gift of the ruler, not the right of the ruled, but stemmed from an Indo-European concept of social organization' (Hammond, cited in Larsen 1994:33). The retention of this point of view among some classicists and ancient historians creates a problem for archaeologists seeking to respond constructively to Said's (1978) critique of 'Orientalism'. Such responses often take the form of a call for the deconstruction of historical narratives which value the study of the ancient East only in so far as it contributed to 'the rise of the West', a view symbolized on the relief which adorns the entrance to the Oriental Institute in Chicago (Larsen 1989; 1994; and see also Kohl 1989; Bahrani 1998). Zeinab Bahrani, for instance, regrets that 'Countless texts from the

Western historical tradition describe how civilisation was passed from the Near East through Greece and Rome to the modern West and this is hardly a point of contention any longer' (1998:163). But if so then why has Martin Bernal's (1987) *Black Athena*, a book which claims that Graeco-Roman civilization had strong Near Eastern and Egyptian roots, generated such heated and lengthy controversy (e.g. Lefkowitz and Rogers 1996; Bernal 2001)? There is an irony here. While archaeologists working in the core areas of 'the Orient' are increasingly distancing themselves from Eurocentric notions of progress in order to consider other pasts, many of those working in the Mediterranean region are still fighting a battle to prove how important oriental influences were in the formation of classical civilization.

Conclusion

> That dead man is Old France, and that bier, the coffin of the Old Monarchy. Therein let us bury, and for ever, the dreams in which we once fondly trusted—paternal royalty, the government of grace, the clemency of monarchy, and the charity of the priest; filial confidence, implicit belief in the gods here below. (Michelet [1879–1880] 1967:55)

The contradictions and paradoxes implicit in the Napoleonic encounter with ancient Egypt remain with us, in the uneasy coexistence of Egyptology with a strong public desire to retain a source of mystery, sensuous experience and self-knowledge (cf. Roth 1998). They are also manifest in the ambiguous place which Egyptology itself continues to occupy between the humanities and the social sciences. The name given to the study of Egypt (like Assyri-*ology* and anthrop-*ology*) distinguishes it from that of Graeco-Roman civilization (see Bowman 2002) and incorporates it into a field of knowledge conceived as the scientific study of the 'other', but often practised as the humanistic search for 'self'.

In discussing the relationship between republican values and the study of the ancient Orient I have also attempted to highlight the extent to which modern, western identity as a whole is anchored in the images and material remains of remote times and places. In Hollywood films, novels and fringe literature on the origins of extinct civilizations, western societies are still confronting fears about their own origins which manifest themselves as possessive demons, vampires or other supernatural beings occupying the spaces between bourgeois consciousness and the ancient (and sometimes modern) East. A common structural element within many of these narratives, from Bram Stoker's *Dracula* to William Blatty's *The Exorcist*, is the invasion of the western body by pathological forces from a hierocratic, dynastic past. Georges Dumézil (at least in Sahlins's 1985:73 reading of him) might have argued for a deep Indo-European origin to the popularity of these stories, but undoubtedly they also express basic insecurities about the condition of modernity, and the integrity of 'the West'.

Acknowledgments

I am grateful to Alan Bowman, Eleanor Robson and Andrew Sherratt for providing valuable references, and to Corinna Riva and Nick Vella for the opportunity to participate in their symposium.

Endnotes

1. This paper is adapted from an earlier publication by the author, with the title: 'Forgetting the *Ancien Régime*: republican values and the study of the ancient Orient', published in D. Jeffreys (ed.), *Views of Ancient Egypt since Napoleon Bonaparte: Imperialism, Colonialism and Modern Appropriations* (London: UCL Press, 2003), pp. 179–93. I am most grateful to UCL Press, an imprint of Cavendish Publishing Limited, and to Peter Ucko, the series editor of 'Encounters With Ancient Egypt', for permission to reproduce much of that piece here.
2. In this sense, the Orient has often served as the false conscience of global capital and 'coca-colonization', as well as of western political experience. It is particularly ironic that the desire of modern Greeks to 'occidentalize' by consuming mass-produced Americanalia is perceived by some Americans and northern Europeans as a betrayal of 'traditional' Greek values (Herzfeld 1995).
3. The Renaissance portrayal of the building of the Tower of Babel, showing construction workers cowering before the magisterial figure of the king and pleading for respite, is a fascinating inversion of how ancient Mesopotamian rulers actually portrayed themselves (something unknown of course to Renaissance artists). In commemorative art and inscriptions the rulers of ancient Babylonia and Assyria are represented as the chief physical participants in the process of constructing monumental buildings, which constituted a basic act of royal mediation between humanity and divine will (see, e.g., Suter 2000). The gods are nowhere to be seen in the bright blue skies above Brueghel's tower.
4. Gillispie (1987:4) suggests that the Marquis de Condorcet was 'the first leader of opinion to use the term "Occident", the West, in its modern sense, connoting the combination of cultural family with civilized norm'.

References

Adler, J. and R. Fardon (eds.) (1999) *Orientpolitik, Value, and Civilisation. Franz Baermann Steiner, Selected Writings*. Vol. 2. New York and Oxford: Berghahn.

Andreu, G., M.-H. Rutschowscaya and C. Ziegler (eds.) (1997) *L'Égypte ancienne au Louvre*. Paris: Hachette.

Bahrani, Z. (1998) Conjuring Mesopotamia: imaginative geography and a world past. In *Archaeology under Fire: Nationalism, Politics and Heritage in the Eastern Mediterranean and the Middle East*, edited by L. Meskell. London: Routledge, pp. 159–74.

Baudrillard, J. (1993) *Symbolic Exchange and Death*. London: Sage.

Bernal, M. (1987) *Black Athena: the Afroasiatic Roots of Classical Civilization*. London: Free Association.

Bernal, M. (1989) Black Athena and the APA. *Arethusa* 22:17–38.

Bernal, M. (2001) *Black Athena Writes Back: Martin Bernal Responds to his Critics*. Durham, NC: Duke University Press.

Bloch, M. (1924) *Les Rois Thaumaturges: Étude sur le Caractère Surnaturel Attribué à la Puissance Royale Particulièrement en France et en Angleterre*. Strasbourg and London: Oxford University Press.

Boardman, J. (1964) *The Greeks Overseas*. Harmondsworth: Penguin.

Boardman, J. (1973) *Greek Art*. London: Book Club Associates, Thames and Hudson.

Bowman, A. (2002) Recolonising Egypt. In *Classics in Progress. Essays in Ancient Greece and Rome*, edited by T. P. Wiseman. Oxford: British Academy, pp. 193–244.

Bret, P. (ed.) (1999) *L'éxpedition d'Égypte: une entreprise des lumières, 1798–1801*. Paris: Technique et Documentation.

Burkert, W. (1992) *The Orientalizing Revolution: Near Eastern Influence on Greek Culture in the Early Archaic Age*, translated by M. E. Pinder and W. Burkert. Cambridge, MA and London: Harvard University Press.

Childe, V. G. (1925) *The Dawn of European Civilisation*. London: Routledge and Kegan Paul.

Childe, V. G. (1936) *Man Makes Himself*. London: Watts and Co.

Childe, V. G. (1942) *What Happened in History*. Harmondsworth: Penguin Press.

Clastres, P. (1987) *Society Against the State: Essays in Political Anthropology*. New York: Zone Books.
Connerton, P. (1989) *How Societies Remember*. Cambridge: Cambridge University Press.
Curl, J. S. (1994) *Egyptomania. The Egyptian Revival: A Recurring Theme in the History of Taste*. Manchester, New York: Manchester University Press.
de Heusch, L. (1972) *The Drunken King or the Origins of the State*. London: Routledge.
Dumézil, G. (1968–73) *Mythe et Épopée*. Paris: Gallimard.
Dumont, L. (1980) *Homo Hierarchicus: the Caste System and its Implications*. Chicago and London: University of Chicago Press.
Frankfort, H. (1948) *Kingship and the Gods: A Study of Ancient Near Eastern Religion as the Integration of Society and Nature*. Chicago: University of Chicago Press.
Frazer, J. G. (1911) [1890] *The Golden Bough: A Study in Magic and Religion*. London: Macmillan.
Freud, S. (1919) *Totem and Taboo: Resemblances between the Psychic Lives of Savages and Neurotics*. London: Routledge and Sons.
Freud, S. (1930) *Civilization and its Discontents*. London: Hogarth Press.
Fustel de Coulanges, N. D. (1980) [1864] *The Ancient City: A Study on the Religion, Laws, and Institutions of Greece and Rome*. Baltimore: Johns Hopkins University Press.
Gell, A. (1998) *Art and Agency: An Anthropological Theory*. Oxford: Clarendon Press.
Giddens, A. (1986) *Durkheim on Politics and the State*. Cambridge: Polity.
Gillispie, C. C. (1987) Historical introduction. In *Monuments of Egypt. The Napoleonic Expedition. The Complete Archaeological Plates from La Description de l'Égypte*, edited by C. C. Gillispie and M. Dewachter. Princeton, NJ: Princeton Architectural Press, pp. 1–29.
Gould, C. (1965) *Trophy of Conquest: The Musée Napoléon and the creation of the Louvre*. London: Faber and Faber.
Herzfeld, M. (1995) Hellenism and Occidentalism: the permutations of performance in Greek bourgeois identity. In *Occidentalism: Images of the West*, edited by J. G. Carrier. Oxford: Clarendon Press, pp. 218–33.
Hingley, R. (2000) *Roman Officers and English Gentlemen: The Imperial Origins of Roman Archaeology*. London and New York: Routledge.
Hocart, A. (1927) *Kingship*. London: Oxford University Press.
Hughes, P. (1995) Ruins of time: estranging history and ethnology in the Enlightenment and after. In *Time: Histories and Ethnologies*, edited by D. O. Hughes and T. R. Trautman. Michigan: University of Michigan Press, pp. 269–90.
Humbert, J-M. (1997) *L'Égypte à Paris*. Paris: Action Artistique de la Ville de Paris.
Iversen, E. (1961) *The Myth of Egypt and its Hieroglyphs in European Tradition*. Copenhagen: Gad.
Iversen, E. (1971) The hieroglyphic tradition. In *The Legacy of Egypt*, edited by J. R. Harris. Oxford: Clarendon Press, pp. 170–96.
Jardine, L. and J. Brotton (2000) *Global Interests: Renaissance Art between East and West*. London: Reaktion Books.
Kantorowicz, E. H. (1957) *The King's Two Bodies: A Study in Mediaeval Political Theology*. Princeton: Princeton University Press.
Kendrick, T. D. (1950) *British Antiquity*. London: Metheun and Co.
Klengel-Brandt, E. (1982) *Der Turm von Babylon: Legende und Geschichte eines Bauwerkes*. Berlin: Koehler and Amelang.
Kohl, P. (1989) The material culture of the modern era in the ancient Orient: suggestions for future work. In *Domination and Resistance*, edited by D. Miller, M. J. Rowlands and C. Y. Tilley. London: Unwin Hyman, pp. 240–5.
Kristiansen, K. (1998) Chiefdoms, states and systems of social evolution. In *Social Transformation in Archaeology: Global and Local Perspectives*, edited by K. Kristiansen and M. Rowlands. London and New York: Routledge, pp. 243–67.
Kristiansen, K. and M. Rowlands (eds.) (1998) *Social Transformations in Archaeology: Global and Local Perspectives*. London and New York: Routledge.

Kuper, A. (1988) *The Invention of Primitive Society: Transformations of an Illusion.* London: Routledge.

Kus, S. (1982) Matters material and ideal. In *Symbolic and Structural Archaeology*, edited by I. Hodder. Cambridge: Cambridge University Press, pp. 47–62.

Lamberg-Karlovsky, C. C. (1985) The Near Eastern 'breakout' and the Mesopotamian social contract. *Symbols* (Spring Issue). Cambridge, MA: Peabody Museum.

Larsen, M. T. (1989) Orientalism and Near Eastern Archaeology. In *Domination and Resistance*, edited by D.Miller, M. J. Rowlands and C. Y. Tilley. London: Unwin Hyman, pp. 229–39.

Larsen, M. T. (1994) The appropriation of the Near Eastern past: contrasts and contradictions. In *The East and the Meaning of History: International Conference (23–27 November 1992)*. Università degli studi di Roma 'La Sapienza'. Dipartimento di studi orientali; 13. Rome: Università di Roma 'La Sapienza', pp. 29–51.

Larsen, M. T. (1996) *The Conquest of Assyria: Excavations in an Antique Land, 1840–1860*. London: Routledge.

Laurens, H. (1999) Les lumières et l'Égypte. In *L'éxpedition d'Égypte: une entreprise des Lumières, 1789–1801*, edited by P. Bret. Paris: Technique et Documentation, pp. 1–6.

Lefkowitz, M. R. and G. M. Rogers (1996) *Black Athena Revisited.* London: Chapel Hill.

Lundquist, J. M. (1995) Babylon in European thought. In *Civilizations of the Ancient Near East vol. 1*, edited by J. M. Sasson. New York: Charles Scribner's Sons, pp. 67–80.

Lustig, J. (ed.) (1997) *Anthropology and Egyptology: A Developing Dialogue.* Sheffield: Sheffield Academic Press.

McIntosh, R. J. (1999) Western perceptions of urbanism and invisible African towns. In *Beyond Chiefdoms: Pathways to Complexity in Africa*, edited by S. K. McIntosh. Cambridge: Cambridge University Press, pp. 56–65.

Meskell, L. (1998) *Archaeology under Fire: Nationalism, Politics and Heritage in the Eastern Mediterranean and the Middle East.* London: Routledge.

Michelet, J. (1967) [1879–80] *History of the French Revolution*, translated by G. Wright. Chicago and London: University of Chicago Press.

Miller, D., M. J. Rowlands, and C. Y. Tilley (eds.) (1989) *Domination and Resistance.* One World Archaeology series, 3. London: Unwin Hyman.

Mitchell, T. (1991) *Colonising Egypt.* Cambridge: Cambridge University Press.

Momigliano, A. (1980) Foreword. In *The Ancient City: A Study on the Religion, Laws, and Institutions of Greece and Rome*, by N. D. Fustel de Coulanges. Baltimore: Johns Hopkins University Press, pp. ix–xv.

Momigliano, A. (1975) *Alien Wisdom: The Limits of Hellenization.* Cambridge: Cambridge University Press.

Moret, A. and Davy, G. (1926) *From Tribe to Empire: Social Organization among Primitives and in the Ancient Near East.* 'History of Civilisation' series. London: Kegan Paul.

Morris, S. (1989) Daidalos and Kadmos: Classicism and 'Orientalism'. *Arethusa*:39–54.

Morris, S. (1992) *Daidalos and the Origins of Greek Art.* Princeton: Princeton University Press.

Murray, O. (1993) [1978] *Early Greece.* 2nd edition. Cambridge, MA: Harvard University Press.

Ozouf, M. (1988) *Festivals and the French Revolution.* Cambridge, MA and London: Harvard University Press.

Pfaffenberger, B. (1988) Fetishized objects and humanized nature: towards a social anthropology of technology. *Man* (N.S.) 23:236–52.

Poulsen, F. (1912) *Der Orient und die Frühgriechische Kunst.* Leipzig: B.G. Teubner.

Roth, A. M. (1998) Ancient Egypt in America: claiming the riches. In *Archaeology under Fire*, edited by L. Meskell, pp. 17–229.

Rowlands, M. (1989) A question of complexity. In *Domination and Resistance*, edited by D.Miller, M. J. Rowlands and C. Y. Tilley. London: Unwin Hyman, pp. 29–40.

Rowlands, M. (1994) Childe and the archaeology of freedom. In *The Archaeology of V. Gordon Childe: Contemporary Perspectives*, edited by D. Harris. London: UCL Press, pp. 35–50.

Rowlands, M. J., K. Kristiansen and M. T. Larsen (eds.) (1987) *Centre and Periphery in the Ancient World*. Cambridge: Cambridge University Press.
Sahlins, M. (1985) *Islands of History*. Chicago: University of Chicago Press.
Said, E. (1978) *Orientalism*. New York: Vintage.
Sasson, J. M. (1995) *Civlizations of the Ancient Near East*, Volume 1. New York: Charles Scribner's Sons.
Schama, S. (1995) *Landscape and Memory*. London: Fontana Press.
Sherratt, A. (1997) *Economy and Society in Prehistoric Europe: Changing Perspectives*. Edinburgh: Edinburgh University Press.
Suter, C. (2000) *Gudea's Temple Building: the Representation of an Early Mesopotamian Ruler in Text and Image*. Groningen: Styx.
Trigger, B. G. (1979) Egypt and the comparative study of early civilizations. In *Egypt and the Social Sciences: Five Studies*, edited by K. Weeks. Cairo: American University in Cairo Press, pp. 23–56.
Ucko, P. J. (2001) Unprovenanced material culture and Freud's collection of antiquities. *Journal of Material Culture* 6(3):269–322.
Ucko, P. J. and T. Champion (eds.) (2003) *The Wisdom of Egypt: Changing Visions through the Ages*. London: UCL Press.
van Dommelen, P. (1998) *On Colonial Grounds: A Comparative Study of Colonialism and Rural Settlement in First Millennium BC West Central Sardinia*. Leiden: Faculty of Archaeology, University of Leiden.
Vico, G. B. (1968) [1725] *The New Science of Giambattista Vico* (transl. of the 3rd ed. of 'La Scienza Nuova' (1744) by Thomas Goddard Bergin and Max Harold Fisch). Ithaca: Cornell University Press.
Walzer, M. (1974) *Regicide and Revolution: Speeches at the Trial of Louis XVI*. London: Cambridge University Press.
Wengrow, D. (1999) The intellectual adventure of Henri Frankfort: a missing chapter in the history of archaeological thought. *American Journal of Archaeology* 103:597–613.
Whitehouse, H. (1995) Egypt in European thought. In *Civilizations of the Ancient Near East*, edited by J. M. Sasson. New York: Charles Scribner's Sons, pp. 15–32.
Wilson, E. (1972) *To the Finland Station: A Study in the Writing and Acting of History*. London: Fontana/Collins.
Yoffee, N. (1993) Too many chiefs? (or, safe texts for the '90s). In *Archaeological Theory: Who Sets the Agenda?*, edited by N. Yoffee and A. Sherratt. Cambridge: Cambridge University Press, pp. 60–78.

4 Orientalization and Prehistoric Cyprus: The Social Life of Oriental Goods

A. Bernard Knapp

Introduction

'Orientalization' is a concept most frequently encountered in discussions of the Iron Age Mediterranean world (e.g. Burkert 1992; Cuozzo 1994; Morris 1992). Its impact, real or imagined, typically is thought to affect an area stretching from the Aegean to Italy and even to Levantine Spain. The current debate over the viability of this concept—whether it is useful in interpreting the dynamics of inter-Mediterranean social contact and cultural change, or whether it is simply a 'factoid' of contemporary historiography—is one that has been less pertinent in discourses on Mediterranean prehistory, and at the same time less apparent on Cyprus and in the eastern Mediterranean (cf. Peltenburg 1991, on both counts), perhaps because of their proximity to or involvement in what is deemed to be the 'ancient Orient'.

Given this situation, and at the same time attempting to contribute to the debate that forms the central theme of this volume, I approach issues related to Orientalization from a different vantage point. To set the background, and to extend the discussion along a related but perhaps unexpected trajectory, I consider the relationship between Orientalization and *Orientalism* (Said 1978), especially in light of concerns about the relevance of modern historiographic constructs for interpreting the past.

To come to grips with Orientalization in the *prehistoric* eastern Mediterranean, I follow to some extent the methodology that characterizes Iron Age approaches to this issue. That is, I consider the meanings of the import of Egyptian and Near Eastern objects, and their associated symbolism and royal ideology, into Late Bronze Age Cyprus. I do so explicitly from the perspective of considering the social life of these objects, as well as notions of distance and access to the 'exotic', as possible sources of social power for and amongst Cypriot elites (see also Knapp 1998).

The extensive and comprehensively published archaeological record of Late Bronze Age Cyprus includes the following objects and iconographic components, directly relevant to such an approach:

1. several gold, metal, faience and glyptic items decorated with animal motifs, sphinxes, bull-, lion- or griffin-headed beings;
2. female and kilted male figures shown dominating lions or griffins;
3. hieroglyphic signs and other images;
4. several carved ivory objects portraying struggles between lions and bulls, hunting scenes, warriors combating griffins, sphinxes and vegetation motifs.

All these items, many with a very complex biography and iconography, suggest a sophisticated manipulation of the Near Eastern ideology of kingship and royal power (e.g. Caubet 1986; Feldman 1998, 2002a, 2002b; Keswani 1989). This adoption of Near Eastern objects and icons of power may have served initially to centralize and legitimize the political economy at Enkomi (Webb 2005), but subsequently it functioned to disperse the wealth derived from copper production and interregional trade more widely throughout the island.

In what follows, I discuss first the relationship between Orientalization and *Orientalism*, and then present an overview of the relevant archaeological evidence. To situate the study in its cultural context, I provide a brief discussion of the geopolitical configuration of Late Bronze Age Cyprus. I then consider the social lives, and the likely role of 'Oriental' luxury goods within Cypriot (elite) society, discussing both the objects and their iconography. I continue with consideration of how the distance between 'Oriental' states and Cyprus, as well as the very notion of (ancient) Orientalism, may have helped to establish, stabilize and legitimize social power amongst Cypriot elites. I conclude with a more nuanced discussion of how distance, the accumulated histories of luxury objects, and power all were entangled in the ways that the Oriental 'other' impacted on Late Cypriot society. Finally, I assess the value of the Orientalization concept for a better understanding of the dynamics of eastern Mediterranean prehistory.

Orientalization and *Orientalism* in Cyprus

Edward Said's (1978) *Orientalism* refers to a negative, postcolonial concept associated with the (early) modern era and should not be confused with Orientalization in the Bronze or Iron Ages. The relevance of *Orientalism* to this study stems in part from the fact that 'Orientalizing' evidence has at times been overlooked or ignored in discussions of culture contact, acculturation and the direction or influence of cultural change in the eastern Mediterranean (Bernal 1987, 2001; Bass 1997; cf. Webb 2005). It is therefore important to attempt to isolate an *ancient* view of Orientalism and its otherness. If Said's *Orientalism* is, in one sense, an 'archive of information' commonly held by 19th and 20th century colonial powers in the west and geared specifically to ensure domination over the Orient (Said 1978:32–42), then an ancient view of Orientalism, I suggest, was distinctively different in its social and ideological significance and impact.

One of the few studies that even mentions Cyprus in the context of (modern) attitudes to *Orientalism*—in particular that of Bernal's *Black Athena* (1987, 1991)—is Walz's (1997) review of the Cypriot role in Near Eastern-Aegean contacts during the Bronze Age. Steadfastly Cypro-centric throughout his study, Walz seeks to demonstrate how Cyprus, notwithstanding its unsubstantiated image as a crossroads between 'Orient and Occident' (Karageorghis 1982, 1986), is in fact often ignored or assigned a passive role in studies of Near Eastern trade with the Aegean or Cyprus. Bernal, for his part, does not deny that Cyprus played a crucial role in Bronze Age eastern Mediterranean trade. Rather he argues that such a role has perpetuated 'Aryanist and isolationist' attitudes amongst archaeologists by acting as a 'filter between East and West, allowing them to be in contact *without actually touching*' (Bernal 1991:494, original emphasis, cited by Walz 1997:4). If, as it seems, Bernal de-emphasizes the Cypriot role because of its ideological implications (Walz 1997:4), Walz tends to overstate that same role without recognizing that he is not alone in portraying the politico-economic status and social position of Cyprus in the study of eastern Mediterranean interaction spheres.

For Mediterranean polities of the Late Bronze Age, contact with the distant and exotic Orient—ideological, economic, individual—was a desirable commodity, one that served to enhance the social status of Mediterranean elites and to perpetuate their exclusionary political position alongside other Mediterranean and Levantine elites. In other words, if modern *Orientalism* served to establish and legitimize colonial regimes in the Middle East, Africa and Asia, ancient Orientalism enabled 'western' (i.e. Mediterranean) elites, through their knowledge of and contact with—but *not* power over—ancient Near Eastern realms, to establish, stabilize and expand their own authority at home. Orientalization, therefore, should not be seen so exclusively as representing the passive impact of ancient Near Eastern culture, material culture, art and ideology on the Aegean and eastern Mediterranean. Rather it may be seen as an active strategy adopted by Mediterranean—especially Aegean and Cypriot—elites of the Late Bronze Age to amplify their own socio-political and economic status.

Because 'The Orient ... had been since antiquity a place of romance, exotic beings, haunting memories and landscapes, remarkable experiences' (Said 1978:1), it is entirely appropriate in considering the relationship between distance, knowledge and social power to engage with *Orientalism* in re-considering the value and relevance of Orientalization. Indeed, Herodotos was equally enchanted by the magic, the allure and the antiquities of ancient Egypt (Morris 1992, 1996:169). Or, as the Sherratts (1998:330) put it more generally: 'there is also the interpretation of *ex Oriente lux*. The ancient Greeks themselves were not unaware of their indebtedness to lands further east for the origin of many of the crucial arts of civilisation.'

Another issue that must be borne in mind is the way that modern scholars (including myself) always assume some level of mutual exclusivity between the (secondary) states of the eastern Mediterranean and the (primary) states of western Asia, when in fact the social and cultural identities within either of those areas were multiple, variable and complex. We need to bear in mind, and seek to delineate better, the constant tension between connectedness and otherness that must have motivated interactions between these culture arenas, to consider how that tension may have motivated and been mediated by spheres of interaction—ideological, iconographic and individual—that permeated the entire region (Marian Feldman, personal communication, 2002).

Orientalization and prehistoric Cyprus: an archaeological overview

Throughout the Aegean and eastern Mediterranean during the second millennium BC, archaeological and iconographic evidence for an artistic and ideological *koine* continues to mount (Feldman 1998, 2002a; Keswani 1989; Knapp 1998; Peltenburg 1991; Sherratt 1994; Webb 2005). In each case, the evidence for this phenomenon must be assessed cautiously and contextually if we are to gain any insight into the commercial, ideological, artistic and social dynamics that characterized the region, and helped to legitimize and perpetuate its elites. It is argued here that the experience and knowledge gained by Mediterranean traders and political elites is a direct result of their contacts with the distant polities of ancient western Asia, and of the objects they exchanged and displayed. Both factors were key sources of social power, invisible commodities and tangible goods that motivated trade, modified cultural attitudes, made reputations, stimulated acculturation and continuously transformed social practices.

For a 'secondary' state such as Cyprus (Keswani 1996; Peltenburg 1996; Webb 2005), contacts with the ancient Orient were motivated at least partly by the wish of local elites to enhance their social and political position. For the 'primary' states of western Asia, these same contacts would have been stimulated equally by economic and political concerns. I should suggest, and will try to defend the proposition that co-optation of certain aspects of Near Eastern iconography, images, objects, artists or ideas into localized contexts on Cyprus represents social as well as individual exchange. The coding of elite motifs used in Cypriot, Aegean and Levantine jewellery, metalwork, frescoes, ivories, and faience or pottery vessels is seldom discussed with reference to the ideational aspects of long-distance trade, or even to the possible exchange of craftspeople as producers of art—works and renowned objects that capitalized on the significance of distance and the other.

I have discussed elsewhere (Knapp 1998) how recent finds of 'Minoan'-style wall-paintings at Tell ed Dab'a in the Egyptian delta and at Tel Kabri in Israel should be seen not as indicators of travelling Minoan artists and craftspeople, nor as the result of inter-marriage between the different states. Rather they should be regarded as indicative of the role that distance and the exotic played in Bronze Age Mediterranean maritime travel and trade. On Cyprus, the social, economic and ideological transformations that characterize the Late Bronze Age have already been linked in part to a major growth in interaction with the older civilizations of the Near East. Keswani (1989), for example, maintains that towards the end of the 13th century BC, Cypriot elites sought to distinguish themselves by using various prestige goods imported from Egypt and the Near East, or by imitating prototypes from those areas.

In what follows, after setting the context with a brief overview of the geopolitical configuration on Late Bronze Age Cyprus, I present various material items, luxury objects that represented social and individual exchanges between the Orient and the Occident. Can closer consideration of the social lives of such objects inform and elaborate on an ancient view of Orientalism and in turn help us to develop a more nuanced and multivalent concept of Orientalization?

Cyprus and the Near East: the Late Bronze Age

Late Bronze Age geopolitical configurations

In order to discuss the Orientalizing phenomenon with respect to Late Bronze Age Cyprus, it is necessary first to outline the geopolitical configuration on the island, insofar as it is known or surmised. During the course of the Bronze Age, Cypriot society was transformed from an isolated, village-based culture into an international, urban-centred, possibly state-level polity. Interpretations of these developments differ radically. Frankel *et al.* (1996; Frankel 2000), for example, maintain that migrating or invading Anatolian colonists made a major impact on Cypriot Bronze Age culture whereas others (e.g. Knapp 1990, 2001; Manning 1993) hold that local responses to social pressures and economic demand provided the stimulus for change. When it comes to the Late Bronze Age, the development of social complexity is seen as stemming from processes of urbanization, state formation, and/or 'heterarchical' society (e.g. Keswani 1996; Knapp 1986; Negbi 1986; Peltenburg 1996).

One factor seems indisputable: during the 17th–16th centuries BC, a single pre-eminent polity emerged at the site of Enkomi on the east coast of Cyprus (Knapp 1988; Muhly 1989; Peltenburg 1996). The earliest Late Bronze Age levels excavated at other sites—e.g. Hala Sultan Tekke *Vyzakia*, Kalavasos *Ayios Dhimitrios*, Alassa *Palaeotaverna*—have been limited in exposure, and it is thus quite difficult to demonstrate one way or another their political or economic relationship to Enkomi. Whether or not the authority of Enkomi's elites extended to the entire island therefore remains uncertain, but several factors indicate that whoever controlled the polity centred at Enkomi also exercised control over the intensified mining, production and export of Cypriot copper. Peltenburg (1996) suggests that this hegemony may be seen archaeologically in a series of fortifications that safeguarded the transport of copper from the Troodos mining regions to Enkomi. Once the raw copper was further refined and prepared for export in industrial sectors at the site, elites at Enkomi not only would have controlled the overseas distribution of copper, they also would have had direct access to overseas markets and their managers, and in particular to the luxury goods that began to trickle into the island at this time. In turn, these direct interactions with the exotic polities, factions, communities and individuals in the Near East would have enhanced the aura of power sought by Cypriot elites.

By the 14th–13th centuries BC, this situation had changed. If Enkomi once held pre-eminent status amongst the regional polities on Cyprus, its dominance finally gave way to a series of local polities administered by local elites. These elites had gained control of copper production and distribution on a local or regional level, mobilized agricultural goods and surpluses to support industrial, artistic and other specialists, and commanded other material and symbolic resources (Webb 2005). Goren *et al.* (2003) recently have argued that either Alassa *Palaeotaverna* or Kalavasos *Ayios Dhimitrios* now became the pre-eminent polity of *Alashiya* (the Bronze Age name for Cyprus). Although their argument is compelling, we need a comprehensive reassessment of all the relevant documentary and archaeological evidence before we can begin to elaborate on the foundation they have provided. Wherever the political centre may have been situated, all these regional polities operated within a well organized, hierarchical system of primary and secondary centres, mining communities and agricultural support villages, other production sites (pottery, olive oil, etc.), and transhipment points that facilitated social, economic and ideological exchanges on the island (Keswani 1993, 1996; Knapp 1997, 2003; Webb and Frankel 1994).

Although the details of this geopolitical configuration might be debated (e.g. Baurain 1984; Merrillees 1986, 1992; Steel 2003; Wachsmann 1986) and certainly will be refined as more evidence accumulates, its general features are accepted by most specialists involved in the study of Late Bronze Age Cyprus. Less certain are the organizational strategies that facilitated the production, distribution and consumption of resources amongst the island's regional polities, and the identity and status of those who dictated these policies. The elites involved must have established new mechanisms and ideological sanctions geared to motivate trade, legitimize their own authority, ensure compliance amongst the various factions involved in the mining, smelting and transport of copper, and overall to integrate society more generally. In what follows, I consider how the import of Egyptian and Near Eastern objects and symbols of value, authority and royal ideology impacted on these new organizational strategies.

Luxury goods, distance and social power

Amongst the major transformations that characterized the Cypriot Late Bronze Age was a notable increase in interactions with the state-level polities of both the Near East and the Aegean. Keswani maintains that by the 13th century BC (and in some cases much earlier), Cypriot elites distinguished themselves and legitimized their roles through the display of imported ivory, gold and faience objects, as well as ceremonial *rhyta* acquired from or imitating those of their Near Eastern and Aegean counterparts. She argues that the 'cosmic symbolism' of several gold, metal, stone and glyptic items from Enkomi, decorated with animal motifs, sphinxes, hieroglyphic signs and other images, along with the intricate iconography of several carved ivory objects, suggest 'a closer identification with, or a more sophisticated manipulation of, the Near Eastern ideology of kingship and political legitimacy' (Keswani 1989:69–70). Changes in the iconography and design of various Cypriot products, based on luxury objects imported to Cyprus, traditionally have been associated with the presence of Near Eastern or Aegean craftspeople, or of various invaders and migrating groups, like the Sea Peoples, Lycians or Hittites. Keswani (1989:70) rightly asserts, however, that more fundamental politico-ideological transformations were at work, characterized by Near Eastern or Aegean representations of power and authority raised to cosmic dimensions.

From a very different perspective but one that equally links luxury goods with social power, Feldman (1998, 2002a) reconsiders the 'International Style' of a small number of prestige goods from Ugarit on the Syrian coast. Made of ivory, alabaster, gold and faience, these items share hybrid motifs and compositional devices, and served as symbolic resources that promoted and enhanced the identity and status of royal elites throughout western Asia and the eastern Mediterranean, including the Aegean and Cyprus. Feldman has taken a long-standing but ill-defined concept ('International Style') of a commonly shared repertoire of motifs found on luxury goods throughout this region (e.g. Crowley 1989; Kantor 1947; Poursat 1977; Smith 1965; Vercoutter 1956) and redefined it. By looking at the shared formal attributes of a wide range of luxury objects, she construes the International Style anew as 'a more narrowly bounded visual expression of specific cultural circumstances that coexisted with other artistic modes' (Feldman 2002a:7). Some of the gold, ivory and alabaster items analysed at length by Feldman share certain designs and motifs with those presented by Keswani. Equally important for the present study, Feldman isolates two primary thematic categories: (1) combative subjects in states of extreme motion (animal attack and hunting scenes) and (2) more orderly renderings of herbivores and vegetation (heraldic scenes with animals flanking stylized vegetation). The combative themes are represented by lions, griffins, sphinxes and bulls, whilst the heraldic themes are illustrated by goats, bulls, leonine creatures and palmettes, rosettes or other flowers. Feldman (2002a:17–23) suggests that the combative themes reflect martial prowess whilst the heraldic scenes represent fertility and prosperity under divine auspices. Both themes resonate deeply with an iconography based on the ancient Near Eastern concept of kingship, in both its military and protective aspects.

The social life of 'Oriental' luxury goods on Cyprus

I can add little to the richly detailed empirical, art historical and theoretical aspects of these studies by Keswani and Feldman. Nor, indeed, is it necessary to recapitulate to any extent their more than ample stylistic, spatial and chronological presentations of a wide range of luxury goods found throughout the eastern Mediterranean. Instead, I propose to consider the 'social life' of these and other objects, who sought them and why they did so. In particular, I argue that elites on Late Bronze Age Cyprus purposely adopted and reinterpreted Levantine and Egyptian royal and ideological symbols to enhance their own power and prestige, both on Cyprus and within wider Mediterranean social and political interaction spheres.

In this line of argument, I draw upon Appadurai's (1986) notions on the social life of things (or commodities), and Kopytoff's (1986) landmark study on the cultural biography of things.

I emphasize, however, the social life of objects as opposed to their cultural biography, because the latter concept was formulated primarily to consider unique items as they move through different contexts and usages, if not individual hands, and thus acquire a *specific* biography. The social history of things, in contrast, is concerned with larger scale dynamics and longer term changes (in demand, meaning, etc.) in various classes or types of objects, changes that transcend the individual biographies of particular items in those classes or types. As Appadurai (1986:34) explained it: 'Thus a particular relic may have a specific biography, but whole types of relic, and the class of things called "relic" itself, may have a larger historical ebb and flow, in the course of which its meaning may shift significantly.' Nonetheless, the social history of things cannot be fully separated from the cultural biography of specific objects because the former—over long periods of time and at diverse social levels—constrains the form, meaning and structure of the latter with respect to their specific, shorter term, more intimate trajectories (Appadurai 1986:36). I return to these concepts at various points throughout this study.

To assess the situation on Cyprus more closely, I employ only a *representative sample* of the material that portrays Near Eastern contacts, without excluding evidence from the Aegean. To limit the chronological scope of this study within manageable proportions, I include only material dating from the Late Cypriot (LC) IIA–LC IIIA (Protohistoric Bronze Age 2) era, about 1450–1190 BC (for earlier Cypro-Levantine/Egyptian contacts, see most recently Manning 2001:80–84; Marcus 2002; Webb 2000).

Keswani (1989:70) suggests that Near Eastern symbols of royal power become much more prevalent from LC IIC onwards (i.e. around 1300–1200 BC), when organizational changes, metalworking activity and specialized craft production are seen to proliferate at Enkomi. Although some of these developments only become prominent at Cypriot sites in LC IIC or LC IIIA levels, they must have had antecedents extending back at least to the beginning of the LC II period, about 1450 BC (Knapp 1988). In fact, excavations at sites such as Alassa *Palaeotaverna*, Kalavasos *Ayios Dhimitrios*, Maroni *Vournes*, and Hala Sultan Tekke *Vyzakia* now reveal some of these earlier stages (summarized with references in Knapp 1994: 282–90).

From several tombs at Enkomi comes an array of objects crafted in or emulating goods from Egypt (for full references on the following items, see Keswani 1989:62–68, 71–74). British Tomb 93, for example, contained:

1. an ornate necklace identified as an Egyptian *ousekh* collar
2. a scarab bearing the name of Tiy, wife of Amenophis III
3. a silver finger ring engraved with the name of Amenophis IV, and
4. several stamped gold bands with sphinxes, lions, goats, rosettes and palmettes, all motifs associated with Near Eastern royal insignia.

Several LC IIC tombs reveal an array of Near Eastern luxury goods such as faience, glass and ivory (French Tomb 5, Swedish Tomb 11, Cypriot Tomb 10). British Tomb 66 contained the most elaborate array of faience and glazed pottery, whilst Swedish Tomb 18 yielded the richest collection of ivories, including a comb and other toilet articles. Two hematite cylinder seals carved in Syro-Mitannian style were recovered from British Tomb 93, whilst British Tomb 66 produced one faience seal carved in Mitannian style. The contents of many of these same tombs (e.g. Swedish Tombs 3 and 18, British Tomb 12) included large numbers of Mycenaean kraters, some with chariot scenes, others with depictions of bulls, goats, birds and fish. Keswani

(1989:66) observes that British Tombs 66 and 93, along with Swedish Tombs 3 and 18, are qualitatively and quantitatively distinct from the other tomb groups.

The luxury objects in these tombs—gold and silver bowls, signet rings, faience vessels, ivories—were made by specialist craftspeople from the rarest of materials. They exhibit all the criteria associated with luxury goods (Appadurai 1986: 38): complexity of acquisition and restricted access ('scarcity'); the capacity to signal complex social messages ('semiotic virtuosity'); specialized knowledge for 'appropriate' consumption ('regulation by fashion'); and close linkage to specific people or personalities. These goods were the exclusive possessions of individuals who enjoyed very high status in the community, exotic and renown items that would have been imbued with a distinctive social life and selective informational value well known to the people who used and displayed them, or who were buried with them.

Peltenburg (1986) compiled and discussed a group of small Egyptian and Egyptianizing luxury objects (in glass, faience, alabaster and carnelian) and scarabs from LC IIC–LC IIIB contexts. Most of the LC III goods, even if they are 'holdovers' from the LC IIC period (Peltenburg 1986:170), derive from settlement rather than mortuary contexts, and Keswani (1989:67) suggests that they may have been curated as social valuables, with the attendant biographical significance, rather than permanently disposed of in burials.

Dated to the very end of the Late Cypriot II period (around 1200 BC) are some exquisite bronze tripods and four-sided stands (British Tombs 58, 97 and possibly 15), revealing elaborate craftsmanship and suggesting cultic associations (Catling 1984; Papasavvas 2003). Other prominent luxury items from tombs of this period include the elaborately carved ivory pyxides (British Tombs 24, 75), mirror standards (British Tombs 16, 17, 33), and a gaming board depicting a figure wearing a feather-like headdress (British Tomb 58). These ivories portray scenes that may have served to symbolize elite dominance, both in the political sphere and in the cosmic order: struggles between lions and bulls, hunting scenes, warriors combating griffins, a man leading a sphinx (Keswani 1989:68; Lagarce and Lagarce 1986:137). The style as well as the iconography of the ivories distinguish them from other mortuary goods and, in Keswani's opinion, reveal the politico-ideological manipulation by Cypriot elites of Near Eastern symbols of kingship and royal power.

Four elite tombs at Kalavasos *Ayios Dhimitrios*, just west of a monumental (ceremonial?) structure termed Building X (South 2000:349–53), should also be noted here. Tomb 11 served as the final resting place of three women and four infants; it contained a striking number of luxury goods, including gold, ivory, glass and sets of material—a cup, two bull rhyta, two glass vessels, two ivory palettes in the form of ducks, and other pottery vessels—that had been placed in two kraters (Goring 1989:102). To the south of Building X, the partially looted Tomb 13 contained intact gold jewellery, faience and alabaster vessels, several ivory objects, and a few vessels imported from the Levant. South (2000:354–5) also mentions the recovery of numerous Mycenaean vessels from this tomb, the most striking of which is another chariot krater depicting a building crowned by (Aegean-inspired) horns of consecration, with a female figure portrayed inside the building (Steel 1994). Tomb 14 included a range of luxury goods, including Mycenaean and Red Lustrous pottery, a gold diadem and many small fragments of gold foil, finger rings and beads, three complete bronze daggers and many small fragments of bronze, some very fragmentary ivory pieces and two ivory disks, and some square glass plaques along with faience 'gaming' pieces (South 2000:353–4). Finally, in Tomb 12 (subsidiary chamber to Tomb 13), which contained the skeletons of a five- or six-year-old child and four infants, the excavators uncovered a 6 cm high silver figurine of Hittite design, depicting a male figure (a 'protective god') standing or riding on a deer (South 1997:163 and plate XV:1).

Throughout her presentation of International Style luxury items from Ugarit, Feldman refers to several ivories and faience pieces from Cyprus that share the themes and compositions of this iconographic *koine*. A polychrome faience vessel from Kition *Bamboula*, for example, displays hunting scenes with lions and gazelles (?) on the shoulder as well as goats flanking some voluted palmettes on the body (Yon and Caubet 1985: figs. 33, 35). The famous LC IIC conical rhyton of Levanto-Egyptian style, from Kition *Chrysopolitissa*, is also noteworthy in this context. Decorated with hunting scenes, bulls, a goat, stylized flowers and two hunters with short kilts and tassled headdresses, the combination of Egyptian, Orientalizing and Aegean motifs singles out this vessel as a prime example of the International Style (Karageorghis 1974:116–26, plate XCIV). The LC IIIA ivory gaming board from British Tomb 58 at Enkomi (mentioned above) portrays various horned and hoofed animals, in flying gallop, fleeing before a chariot holding an archer, as well as a large bull with lowered horns facing the chariot (Murray *et al.* 1900:12–14, plate I). Feldman (1998:133) associates the bull as well as a vignette of a man spearing a rearing lion to the left of the hunting scene on this splendid ivory piece with similar details on a gold bowl and gold plate from Ugarit (Schaeffer 1949:5, plates II–V, VIII). The Enkomi ivory thus is linked not only to these prestigious golden vessels from Ugarit—all three certainly part of an internationalizing iconographic trend—but also to the wider eastern Mediterranean sphere of luxury goods. Finally, and again taking up the hunting theme, an ivory mirror handle from British Tomb 17 at Enkomi depicts a man in hand-to-hand combat with a winged griffin (Murray *et al.* 1900:11, plate II, no. 872A).

This list could be extended at length, with respect to both artefacts and iconography (see, for example, Åström 1984, 1994, 2000; Cline 1994; Jacobsson 1994; Merrillees 2000; Peltenburg 1986, 1991). My intention here, however, has been to demonstrate by means of some selected examples the existence on Cyprus of luxury objects closely linked to items in similar styles found in contemporary Egypt, the Levant and the Aegean. Feldman (1998:111–78) offers more detailed analyses of several of these objects.

The cultural biographies (Gosden and Marshall 1999) and social lives of all these objects will have been complex, often singular, and frequently changing in meaning as they passed from their site of production to their ultimate point of deposition (primarily mortuary). The meanings of each of these luxury goods, and their links to the people who crafted, exchanged and consumed them, were entangled in evolving relationships and were transformed as time passed, and as the goods or people moved about, accumulating life histories (Thomas 1991). These objects became invested with meaning through, and as part of, the social interactions in which they were involved, as for example the scarab carved with the name of Amenophis III's wife Tiy, or the silver finger ring engraved with Amenophis IV's name, both found in British Tomb 93. The complex biography and meanings of these two objects, as well as those of any others noted in this study, cannot be understood by viewing them only at their (primarily) mortuary point of final consumption (Kopytoff 1986). Rather it must be realized that they accumulated different histories and divergent meanings as their existence and ownership changed, in these examples from the original adornment (or marriage celebration, in the case of the Tiy/Amenhotep III scarab) of their named owners to their final signification as objects from afar, paraphernalia of power for the Cypriot elites with whom they were buried. The intrinsic significance of these objects for the people who owned, exchanged or displayed them, as well as an archaeological understanding of them, must derive from the people and events and travels with which they were intimately linked throughout their histories. The fame of such objects, and the renown of the people who owned them, are mutual, inasmuch as the objects attain value by being linked to (powerful) individuals, whilst an individual's status is enhanced by owning, exchanging or displaying a well-known—and often well-travelled—object. In other words, luxury objects such as these can best be understood not just by looking at their terminal cultural context in elite burials, but also by taking into account their original context of production and use, all the circumstances and contingencies through which they travelled, and their ultimate (archaeological) context (Gosden and Marshall 1999:174).

It is not possible, nor does it serve the purpose of this study, to treat all of these individual items in detail; each one, or at least each iconographic or material class or group, deserves a study on its own. In what follows, therefore, I consider how the movement of such luxury objects—between the ancient Orient and Cyprus—is enmeshed with the concept of distance, and how the accumulated histories of these goods as well as their travels may have impacted on the organisation of Late Cypriot society. I argue, to reiterate, that they served to solidify further the social power that accrued to those Cypriot elites who had exclusive access to exotica that flowed into the island from ancient western Asia and Egypt.

Discussion: distance, power and Orientalization

Objects, information and experiences obtained from a distance are often imbued with latent power, and have the potential to increase the prestige and status of those who acquire them (Helms 1988:261–3, and *passim*). Thus long-distance travel and/or trading ventures designed to acquire raw materials or manufactured goods also may result in the acquisition of exotic information or luxury objects that could enhance the traveller's social position at home (Broodbank 1993:331). Appadurai (1986:41) suggests that certain 'economic objects' (commodities), entangled in the socio-political circumstances surrounding their exchange, represent complex social forms of knowledge. The tension between distance and knowledge, therefore, affects not just the flow of goods but their value, and objects realize value through their social potential as well as their life histories.

To take a well known example, one that offers clear insights into the predominantly prehistoric situation on Late Bronze Age Cyprus, I discuss here briefly the celebrated *kula* ring of island Melanesia. Appadurai (1986:18–22) uses the same ethnographic example to portray what he terms 'tournaments of value', periodic events that involve issues of status, rank or fame for individual actors as well as the disposition of socially valued tokens. My purpose in discussing the Melanesian situation is not simply to include what seems to have become in the archaeological literature on trade and exchange a mandatory, cross-cultural, case study. Rather I present these ethnographically based concepts because they provide a dynamic counterpoint to the types and spheres of regal interaction attested by an extensive corpus of cuneiform documents from the Late Bronze Age eastern Mediterranean, and because they may help us to perceive how the social histories of the luxury goods discussed in this study were intimately engaged with those interaction spheres.

The *kula* represents a pre-industrial, trans-local exchange system, where specific kinds of valuables (necklaces, arm-shells) circulate in opposing directions (Leach and Leach 1983;

Malinowski 1922; Munn 1990). The *kula* flourishes in the Massim group of islands just east of Papua New Guinea and is linked to other, nearby, regional exchange systems (e.g. *kune, hiri*—see Frankel and Rhoads 1994; Irwin 1983; Knapp 1989:185–8). These systems allow 'men of substance' to make or break their reputations by acquiring and exchanging prestige goods, individual objects of renown whose histories and ownership were well known to all participants in the system (Appadurai 1986:18; Gosden and Marshall 1999:170–2).

Two further concepts associated with *kula* exchange—*kitoum* and *keda*—are also relevant. *Kitoum* provides the conceptual and instrumental link between the larger 'paths' that *kula* valuables follow, and the smaller, more intimate and regular, local exchanges that together make up the social and economic world of the Massim (Appadurai 1986:18–22; Irwin 1983). Some Massim people use the term *keda* ('road, path') to describe the journey taken by *kula* valuables from island to island. But *keda* can also refer to the social or ideological links between *kula*-traders or, most abstractly, it may symbolize the paths to power and status enjoyed by those enmeshed in this exchange of valuables (Campbell 1983:203–4). The polysemic concept of *keda* thus interweaves the circulation of renowned goods, the human agents involved in their circulation, and the paths to social power that result. *Kitoum*, moreover, represents the articulation between the exchange of prestige-laden objects and more personalized modes of exchange that co-occurred with *kula*.

Helms (1993:145) has argued that luxury goods acquired from afar, or produced at home by transforming exotic raw materials, may encode images and ideals of authority. The flow of such 'kingly things' (Gluckman 1983; Appadurai 1986:22), although deliberately separated from commercial exchange spheres, serves to establish and maintain a certain regal exclusivity, to display social privilege, and to promote a commercial advantage. The human agents involved in *kula* manipulate the movement of valuables, link that movement to more mundane (commercial) modes of exchange, and adapt it to enhance their own social status and privileges. Most of the objects that make up this exclusive sphere of exchange are 'enclaved' (Appadurai 1986:22) and cannot even represent commodities. Often they are referred to as 'primitive valuables': like gifts, they are insensitive to supply and demand, and tend to promote self-aggrandizement. Above all, these are objects with a history, prized for their exotic qualities and valued for the eminence of their ownership.

Obviously there is no direct correspondence between Melanesian *kitoum* and *keda*, on the one hand, and on the other the commercial or social exchanges that operated in the Late Bronze Age eastern Mediterranean. I maintain nonetheless that these ethnographic concepts provide not just a dynamic counterpoint to, but one possible way to help us interpret the organizational strategies that underpinned royal diplomacy and characterized the spheres of elite interaction attested by an extensive corpus of cuneiform documents from the Late Bronze Age (see amongst others Beckman 1996; Knapp 1996; Moran 1992). These 14th–13th century BC letters—exchanged between rulers and court officials in Egypt, Babylonia, Anatolia, various Levantine city-states, and Cyprus—reveal a sophisticated socio-political system based on a type of royal gift exchange and implemented by a royal interaction sphere that linked together a diversity of peoples, cultures, objects and ideologies (for a recent overview, see Feldman 2002a:23–4). Morris (1992:95), with reference to Aegean, Egyptian and Ugaritic documents treating *Keftiu/Kptr*, Kothar-wa-Hasis, Daidalos (*da-da-re-jo*) and Hephaistos, suggests that a Late Bronze Age eastern Mediterranean literary *koine* existed in tandem with the iconographic one; she argues that such a *koine* offers a more accurate view of the Orientalizing experience as an interactive, acculturative exchange.

Taken together, the recent ethnographic and ancient cuneiform evidence indicate that the regular exchange of luxury goods and raw materials may have been entangled in more complex realities, wherein prestige items acquired from afar were intimately linked to the accumulation of wealth and social power. Just as the acquisition and exchange of renowned objects with distinctive life histories enabled powerful individuals to enhance their status in Massim society, so too did the acquisition, display or consumption of luxury objects from the Orient, with their own social histories, serve to perpetuate an elite, if not regal exclusivity and to promote a commercial advantage for the rulers of Late Bronze Age Cyprus.

The iconography, symbolism and historical or legendary status inherent in Oriental luxury objects formed a key component of interregional exchange in the Bronze Age eastern Mediterranean. On Cyprus, the images that appeared on many of the items executed in the International Style (e.g. leonine creatures, sphinxes, griffins, chariots) were unattested before the beginning of the Late Cypriot period. These imports in some cases would have been symbolically reinterpreted or historically invested with new meaning (e.g. the scarab of Queen Tiy and Amenophis IV's silver finger ring, noted above). In other cases, they were altered or produced anew from raw materials unavailable on Cyprus (e.g. the lapis lazuli cylinder seals reworked with gold foil on Cyprus and then transhipped to a Mycenaean ruler in Boiotian Thebes—Porada 1982:68–70), almost certainly to conform to the perceived social and ideological needs of local elites. These elites sought to amplify their position and embellish their status by drawing on a repertoire of objects, images and icons that referred to an extensive and shared, status-laden eastern Mediterranean system. The symbolism and biographic aura embedded in these luxury goods reflected a foreign political ideology, one that offered Cypriot elites a 'blueprint' for power and authority, whether amongst themselves or between themselves and the merchants, managers and craftspeople whose compliance they sought (Webb 2005).

The significance attached to both the people and the objects must have had comparable meanings and values. The mechanisms through which such values and meanings of Oriental objects were transmitted to non-elites on Cyprus, or the extent to which they were shared within Cypriot society, are matters for further study. It is clear, nonetheless, that luxury items imported from distant lands, decorated with the insignia of a widely recognized iconographic or artistic *koine*, and often with a reputation that preceded them, were important social objects in their own right. They were imbued with a social history that instantly linked their new owners with other elites in the eastern Mediterranean interaction sphere. The highest social status and the aura of power associated with Oriental dynasts thus accrued to those involved in the exchange of these inordinately significant luxury objects. Such goods, consequently, were pivotal for Cypriot elites who sought to establish and legitimize their social power and politico-ideological status.

Conclusions

By the 14th century BC, Cypriot elites at sites such as Alassa *Palaeotaverna*, Kalavasos *Ayios Dhimitrios*, Maroni *Vournes* and Kition began to display the trappings of Oriental wealth and power that previously had been Enkomi's exclusive domain. Regional or local elites thus sought to adopt objects and images of Near Eastern or Aegean kingly authority, icons and exotica that linked them with the distant, mystical civilizations of the ancient Near East. Knowledge of

Oriental dynasts—of their individualizing objects and their paraphernalia of power—invested local elites with a level of social prestige and political authority that enabled them to compete with Enkomi. Many of the luxury objects and iconographica presented by Feldman, Keswani and others were linked to new social and political institutions of more diverse—and more fractured—sources of power than had existed previously. The ideology that now sanctioned these new polities was anchored in a range of highly charged luxury goods and symbols that made it possible for local agents to marshal the resources they needed to meet their own social needs and political ends. These elites thus played on the icons, objects and images of distance and the exotic—all with their own historical ebb and flow—to reaffirm their authority and status within Late Cypriot society.

Although I have limited my consideration of 'Orientalization in Antiquity' to Cyprus, some of the observations should serve as an impetus to consider more explicitly the concept of *Orientalism*, and to expand, refine and validate our notions of Orientalization. In many respects, these two concepts form the inverse of each other: whereas *Orientalism* is a 'western', or foreign concept imposed on the east, Orientalization is a concept constructed in the west that draws on objects and ideas from the east but uses them creatively to produce 'western', or more accurately hybrid meanings and conceptualizations (Peter van Dommelen, personal communication, 2003; see also his paper in this volume on the notion of 'hybridity'). *Orientalism* is a colonialist enterprise that denies eastern agency; Orientalization is a notion that literally encapsulates and demands local agency, whether eastern or western. The luxury objects representing social and individual exchanges between Orient and Occident help to inform an ancient view of Orientalism that is qualitatively different from the postcolonial concept of *Orientalism*. In all their iconographic, artistic, manufacturing and material distinctiveness, in their embedded biographies and social histories, these goods serve to illustrate the dynamics of Orientalizing exchange and to demonstrate that a more nuanced understanding of Orientalization involves an appreciation of the following issues:

1. the status-seeking aspirations of Cypriot (or Mycenaean, or Levantine) elites who absorbed the language and symbolism of Near Eastern ostentation and display;
2. the commercial and ideological aspirations of Near Eastern dynasts in expanding their spheres of influence and interaction;
3. the mutual aspirations of all participants in the international iconographic and exchange systems of the time; and, perhaps most importantly
4. the journeys taken by these luxury objects amongst the courtly societies of the Aegean, the eastern Mediterranean and the ancient Orient.

Material goods play an active role in constructing social and symbolic meaning within and between different societies and cultures. Luxury objects, especially those obtained from a distance or from individuals with highly charged social positions, enjoy a biography that can be used in social strategies of exclusion or recruitment and thus form a dynamic component of social change (Sherratt and Sherratt 1991:354). The Orientalizing symbols and iconography that characterized and defined the luxury objects exchanged in the Late Bronze Age eastern Mediterranean provided both a construction and a legitimization of individual social realities. These goods, and the social meanings imbued in their production, decoration, distribution and consumption, gave rise to an international, iconographic and stylistic *koine* throughout the Aegean and eastern Mediterranean, a cosmopolitanism widely recognized by the dynasts and elites—as well as their merchants, messengers and entourages—who controlled and invigorated social dynamics and social change throughout the region.

> In a sense, Orientalism was a library or archive of information commonly and, in some of its aspects, unanimously held. What bound the archive together was a family of ideas and a unifying set of values proven in various ways to be effective. These ideas explained the behaviour of Orientals .... (Said 1978:42).

Just so, but in positive contrast, does an ancient Orientalism—and the contemporary concept of Orientalization—help to explain the behaviour of those local elites who pursued interaction with Orientals in the Late Bronze Age eastern Mediterranean.

Acknowledgments

My thanks to Corinna Riva (University of Glasgow) and Nick Vella (University of Malta) for organizing the symposium on 'Orientalization in Antiquity' at St John's College, Oxford (7–8 September 2002), and for inviting me to take part. Thanks are also due to the British Academy for travel and other support. I am grateful to Marian Feldman (U.C. Berkeley) for very helpful discussions on the topic of 'luxury goods' over the past few years, although she is in no way responsible for the ways I have sought to understand the meanings of those goods. I also thank her and especially Peter van Dommelen (University of Glasgow) for insightful comments on both the original and current versions of this paper. Thanks also to Priscilla Keswani for comments on the original version.

References

Åström, P. (1984) Aegyptiaca at Hala Sultan Tekke. *Opuscula Atheniensia* 15:17–24.
Åström, P. (1994) More Aegyptiaca at the Late Bronze Age site of Hala Sultan Tekke. In *Hommages à Jean Leclant* 3, edited by C. Berger, G. Clerc and N. Grimal. Bibliogtheque d'Étude 106.3. Paris: Institute Français d'Archéologie Orientale, pp. 5–8.
Åström, P. (2000) Recent discoveries at Hala Sultan Tekke. In *Proceedings of the Third International Conference on Cypriot Archaeology* (Nicosia, 16–20 April 1996), edited by G. C. Ioannides and S. A. Hadjistellis. Nicosia: Society of Cypriot Studies, pp. 423–28.
Appadurai, A. (1986) Toward an anthropology of things. In *The Social Life of Things*, edited by A. Appadurai. Cambridge: Cambridge University Press, pp. 3–63.
Bass, G. F. (1997) Beneath the Wine Dark Sea: nautical archaeology and Phoenicians of the Odyssey. In *Greeks and Barbarians: Essays on the Interactions between Greeks and Non-Greeks in Antiquity and the Consequences for Eurocentrism*, edited by J. Coleman and C. Walz. Occasional Publications of the Department of Near Eastern Studies and the Program of Jewish Studies, Cornell University, Number 4. Bethesda, Maryland: CDL Press, pp. 77–101.
Baurain, C. (1984) *Chypre et la Méditerranée Orientale au Bronze Récent: Synthèse Historique*. Études Chypriotes 4. Paris: E. de Boccard.
Beckman, G. (ed.) (1996) *Hittite Diplomatic Texts*. Society for Biblical Literature, Writings from the Ancient World 7. Atlanta, Georgia: Scholars Press.
Bernal, M. (1987) *Black Athena: The Afroasiatic Roots of Classical Civilization*. Volume 1: *The Fabrication of Ancient Greece 1785–1985*. London: Free Association Books.
Bernal, M. (1991) *Black Athena: The Afroasiatic Roots of Classical Civilization*. Volume 2: *The Archaeological and Documentary Evidence*. New Brunswick, NJ: Rutgers University Press.

Bernal, M. (2001) *Black Athena Writes Back: Martin Bernal Responds to his Critics*. Durham, NC and London: Duke University Press.

Broodbank, C. (1993) Ulysses without sails: trade, distance, knowledge and power in the early Cyclades. *World Archaeology* 24:315–31.

Burkert, W. (trans. M. E. Pinder and W. Burkert) (1992) *The Orientalizing Revolution: Near Eastern Influence on Greek Culture in the Early Archaic Age*. Cambridge: Harvard University Press.

Campbell, S. F. (1983) Kula in Vakuta: the mechanics of Keda. In *The Kula: New Perspectives on Massim Exchange*, edited by J. W. Leach and E. Leach. Cambridge: Cambridge University Press, pp. 201–27.

Catling, H. W. (1984) Workshop and heirloom: prehistoric bronze stands in the east Mediterranean. *Report of the Department of Antiquities, Cyprus*:69–91.

Caubet, A. (1986) La thème du lion á Chypre au Bronze Récent: a propos de trouvailles de Kition-Bamboula. In *Acts of the International Archaeological Symposium: Cyprus between the Orient and the Occident* (Nicosia 8–14 September, 1985), edited by V. Karageorghis. Nicosia: Department of Antiquities, Cyprus, pp. 300–10.

Cline, E. H. (1994) *Sailing the Wine-Dark Sea: International Trade and the Late Bronze Age Aegean*. BAR, Int Series 591. Oxford: Archeopress.

Crowley, J. L. (1989) *The Aegean and the East: An Investigation into the Transference of Artistic Motifs between the Aegean, Egypt, and the Near East in the Bronze Age*. Studies in Mediterranean Archaeology, Pocketbook 51. Jonsered, Sweden: P. Åström's Förlag.

Cuozzo, M. (1994) Patterns of organisation and funerary customs in the cemetery of Pontecagnano (Salerno) during the Orientalizing period. *Journal of European Archaeology* 2:263–98.

Feldman, M. H. (1998) Luxury Goods from Ras Shamra-Ugarit and Their Role in the International Relations of the Eastern Mediterranean during the Late Bronze Age. Unpublished PhD thesis, Harvard University (Department of Fine Arts), Cambridge, MA.

Feldman, M. H. (2002a) Luxurious forms: redefining a Mediterranean 'International Style', 1400–1200 B.C.E. *Art Bulletin* 84:6–29.

Feldman, M. H. (2002b) The iconography of power: reading Late Bronze Age symbols. *Archaeology Odyssey* 5(3):26–34, 61–2.

Frankel, D. (2000) Migration and ethnicity in prehistoric Cyprus: technology as habitus. *European Journal of Archaeology* 3:167–87.

Frankel, D. and J. W. Rhoads (eds.) (1994) *Archaeology of a Coastal Exchange System: Sites and Ceramics of the Papuan Gulf*. Research Papers in Archaeology and Natural History 25. Canberra: Research School of Pacific and Asian Studies, Australian National University.

Frankel, D., J. M. Webb and C. Eslick (1996) Anatolia and Cyprus in the third millennium BCE. A speculative model of interaction. In *Cultural Interaction in the Ancient Near East*, edited by G. Bunnens. Abr Nahrain Supplement 5. Louvain: Peeters, pp. 37–50.

Gluckman, M. (1983) Essays on Lozi land and royal property. In *Research in Economic Anthropology 5*, edited by G. Dalton. Greenwich, Connecticut: JAI Press (first published 1943), pp. 1–94.

Goren, Y., S. Bunimovitz, I. Finkelstein and N. Na'aman (2003) The location of Alashiya: new evidence from petrographic investigation of Alashiyan tablets from el-Amarna and Ugarit. *American Journal of Archaeology* 107:233–55.

Goring, E. (1989) Death in everyday life: aspects of burial practice in the Late Bronze Age. In *Early Society in Cyprus*, edited by E. J. Peltenburg. Edinburgh: Edinburgh University Press, pp. 95–105.

Gosden, C. and Y. Marshall (1999) The cultural biography of objects. *World Archaeology* 31:169–78.

Helms, M. W. (1988) *Ulysses' Sail: An Ethnographic Odyssey of Power, Knowledge, and Geographical Distance*. Princeton: Princeton University Press.

Helms, M. W. (1993) *Craft and the Kingly Ideal: Art, Trade and Power*. Austin: University of Texas Press.

Irwin, G. (1983) Chieftainship, kula and trade in Massim prehistory. In *The Kula: New Prespectives in Massim Exchange*, edited by J. Leach and E. R. Leach. Cambridge: Cambridge University Press, pp. 29–72.

Jacobsson, I. (1994) *Aegyptiaca from Late Bronze Age Cyprus.* Studies in Mediterranean Archaeology 112. Jonsered, Sweden: P. Åström's Förlag.

Kantor, H. J. (1947) *The Aegean and the Orient in the Second Millennium B.C.* Archaeological Institute of America: Monograph 1. Bloomington, Indiana: Archaeological Institute of America.

Karageorghis, V. (1974) *Excavations at Kition* I. *The Tombs.* 2 Volumes. Nicosia: Cyprus Department of Antiquities.

Karageorghis, V. (1982) *Cyprus. From the Stone Age to the Romans.* London: Thames and Hudson.

Karageorghis, V. (ed.) (1986) *Acts of the International Archaeological Symposium: Cyprus between the Orient and the Occident* (Nicosia 8–14 September, 1985). Nicosia: Department of Antiquities.

Keswani, P. S. (1989) Dimensions of social hierarchy in Late Bronze Age Cyprus: an analysis of the mortuary data from Enkomi. *Journal of Mediterranean Archaeology* 2:49–86.

Keswani, P. S. (1993) Models of local exchange in Late Bronze Age Cyprus. *Bulletin of the American Schools of Oriental Research* 292:73–83.

Keswani, P. S. (1996) Hierarchies, heterarchies, and urbanization processes: the view from Bronze Age Cyprus. *Journal of Mediterranean Archaeology* 9:211–49.

Knapp, A. B. (1986) Production, exchange and socio-political complexity on Bronze Age Cyprus. *Oxford Journal of Archaeology* 5:35–60.

Knapp, A. B. (1988) Ideology, archaeology and polity. *Man* 23:133–63.

Knapp, A. B. (1989) Paradise gained and paradise lost: intensification, specialization, complexity and collapse. *Asian Perspectives* 28:179–214.

Knapp, A. B. (1990) Production, location and integration in Bronze Age Cyprus. *Current Anthropology* 31:147–76.

Knapp, A. B. (1994) Emergence, development and decline on Bronze Age Cyprus. In *Development and Decline in the Mediterranean Bronze Age*, edited by C. Mathers and S. Stoddart. Sheffield Archaeological Monograph 8. Sheffield: John Collis Publications, pp. 271–304.

Knapp, A. B. (1996) *Near Eastern and Aegean Texts from the Third to the First Millennia BC.* Sources for the History of Cyprus II (General Editors, P. W. Wallace and A. G. Orphanides). Altamont, New York: Greece/Cyprus Research Center.

Knapp, A. B. (1997) *The Archaeology of Late Bronze Age Cypriot Society: The Study of Settlement, Survey and Landscape.* Department of Archaeology, University of Glasgow, Occasional Paper 4. Glasgow.

Knapp, A. B. (1998) Mediterranean Bronze Age trade: distance, power and place. In *The Aegean and the Orient in the Second Millennium: Proceedings of the 50th Anniversary Symposium, Cincinnati 18–20 April 1997*, edited by E. H. Cline and D. Harris-Cline. Aegaeum 18. Liège: Université de Liège, pp. 260–80.

Knapp, A. B. (2001) Archaeology and ethnicity: a dangerous liason. *Archaeologia Cypria* 4:29–46.

Knapp, A. B. (2003) The archaeology of community on Bronze Age Cyprus: Politiko *Phorades* in context. *American Journal of Archaeology* 107:559–80.

Kopytoff, I. (1986) The cultural biography of things: commoditization as process. In *The Social Life of Things: Commodities in Cultural Perspective*, edited by A. Appadurai. Cambridge: Cambridge University Press, pp. 64–91.

Lagarce, J. and E. Lagarce (1986) Les découvertes d'Enkomi et leur place dans la culture internationale du Bronze Récent: la metallurgie. In *Enkomi et le Bronze Récent en Chypre*, edited by J.-C. Courtois, J. Lagarce and E. Lagarce. Nicosia: Leventis Foundation, pp. 60–100.

Leach, J. W. and E. R. Leach (eds.) (1983) *The Kula: New Perspectives on Massim Exchange.* Cambridge: Cambridge University Press.

Malinowski, B. (1922) *Argonauts of the Western Pacific.* London: Routledge.

Manning, S.W. (1993) Prestige, distinction and competition: the anatomy of socio economic complexity in 4th–2nd millennium B.C.E. Cyprus. *Bulletin of the American Schools of Oriental Research* 292: 35–58.

Manning, S.W. (2001) The chronology and foreign connections of the Late Cypriot I period: times they are a-changin. In *The Chronology of Base-ring Ware and Bichrome Wheel-made Ware* (Stockholm,

18–19 May 2000), edited by P. Åström. Konferenser 54. Stockholm: Kungl. Vitterhets Historie och Antikvitets Akademien, pp. 69–94.

Marcus, E. (2002) The southern Levant and maritime trade during the Middle Bronze IIA period. In *Aharon Kempinski Memorial Volume: Studies in Archaeology and Related Disciplines*, edited by E. D. Oren and S. Ahituv. Beer-Sheva 15. Beersheva: Ben-Gurion University of the Negev Press, pp. 241–63.

Merrillees, R. S. (1986) Political conditions in the eastern Mediterranean during the Late Bronze Age. *Biblical Archaeologist* 49:42–50.

Merrillees, R. S. (1992) The government of Cyprus in the Late Bronze Age. In *Acta Cypria* 3: *Acts of an International Congress on Cypriote Archaeology held in Goteborg (22–24 August 1991)*, edited by P. Åström. Studies in Mediterranean Archaeology and Literature, Pocketbook 120. Jonsered, Sweden: P. Åström's Förlag, pp. 310–29.

Merrillees, R. S. (2000) The glyptic of Late Bronze Age Cyprus: an historiographical review. In *Proceedings of the Third International Conference on Cypriot Archaeology* (Nicosia, 16–20 April 1996), edited by G. C. Ioannides and S. A. Hadjistellis. Nicosia: Society of Cypriot Studies, pp. 289–300.

Moran, W. L. (1992) *The Amarna Letters*. Baltimore: Johns Hopkins University Press.

Morris, S. P. (1992) *Daidalos and the Origins of Greek Art*. Princeton: Princeton University Press.

Morris, S. P. (1996) The legacy of Black Athena. In *Black Athena Revisited*, edited by M. R. Lefkowitz and G. M. Rogers. Chapel Hill, North Carolina: University of North Carolina Press, pp. 167–74.

Muhly, J. D. (1989) The organisation of the copper industry in Late Bronze Age Cyprus. In *Early Society in Cyprus*, edited by E. J. Peltenburg. Edinburgh: Edinburgh University Press, pp. 298–314.

Munn, N. D. (1990) Constructing regional worlds in experience: kula exchange, witchcraft and Gawan local events. *Man* 25:1–17.

Murray, A. S., A. H. Smith and H. B. Walters (1900) *Excavations in Cyprus*. London: British Museum Publications.

Negbi, O. (1986) The climax of urban development in Bronze Age Cyprus. *Report of the Department of Antiquities, Cyprus*:97–121.

Papasavvas, G. (2003) Cypriot casting technology I: the stands. *Report of the Department of Antiquities, Cyprus*: 23–51.

Peltenburg, E. J. (1986) Ramesside Egypt and Cyprus. In *Acts of the International Archaeological Symposium: Cyprus between the Orient and the Occident* (Nicosia 8–14 September, 1985), edited by V. Karageorghis. Nicosia: Department of Antiquities, pp.149–79.

Peltenburg, E. J. (1991) Greeting gifts and luxury faience: a context for Orientalizing trends in Late Mycenaean Greece. In *Bronze Age Trade in the Mediterranean*, edited by N. H. Gale. Studies in Mediterranean Archaeology 90. Göteborg, Sweden: P. Åström's Förlag, pp. 162–79.

Peltenburg, E. J. (1996) From isolation to state formation in Cyprus, c.3500–1500 B.C. In *The Development of the Cypriot Economy: From the Prehistoric Period to the Present Day*, edited by V. Karageorghis and D. Michaelides. Nicosia: Bank of Cyprus, University of Cyprus, pp. 17–44.

Porada, E. (1982) The cylinder seals found at Thebes in Boeotia. *Archiv fur Orientforschung* 28:1–70.

Poursat, J.-C. (1977) *Les ivoires myceniens*. Athens, Paris: École Française d'Athènes.

Said, E. W. (1978) *Orientalism*. New York: Pantheon.

Schaeffer, C. F. A. (1949) *Ugaritica* II. *Mission de Ras Shamra* 5. Bibliothèque Archéologique et Historique 47. Paris: Geuthner.

Sherratt, A. G. and E. S. Sherratt (1991) From luxuries to commodities: the nature of Mediterranean Bronze Age trading systems. In *Bronze Age Trade in the Mediterranean*, edited by N. H. Gale. Studies in Mediterranean Archaeology 90. Göteborg, Sweden: P. Åström's Förlag, pp. 351–86.

Sherratt, A. G. and E. S. Sherratt (1998) Small worlds: interaction and identity in the ancient Mediterranean. In *The Aegean and the Orient in the Second Millennium: Proceedings of the 50th Anniversary Symposium, Cincinnati 18–20 April 1997*, edited by E. H. Cline and D. Harris-Cline. Aegaeum 18. Liège: Université de Liège, pp. 329–43.

Sherratt, S. (1994) Comments on Ora Negbi, The 'Libyan Landscape' from Thera: a review of Aegean

enterprises overseas in the Late Minoan IA period (JMA 7.1). *Journal of Mediterranean Archaeology* 7:237–40.
Smith, W. S. (1965) *Interconnections in the Ancient Near East: A Study of the Relationships between the Arts of Egypt, the Aegean, and Western Asia*. New Haven: Yale University Press.
South, A. K. (1997) Kalavasos-Ayios Dhimitrios 1992–1996. *Report of the Department of Antiquities, Cyprus*, pp. 151–75.
South, A. K. (2000) Late Bronze Age burials at Kalavasos *Ayios Dhimitrios*. In *Acts of the Third International Congress of Cypriot Studies*, edited by G. C. Ioannides and S. A. Hadjistellis. Nicosia: Society of Cypriot Studies, pp. 345–64.
Steel, L. (1994) Representations of a shrine on a Mycenaean chariot krater from Kalavasos-*Ayios Dhimitrios*, Cyprus. *Annual of the British School at Athens* 89:201–11.
Steel, L. (2003) *Cyprus before History: From the Earliest Settlers to the End of the Bronze Age*. London: Duckworth.
Thomas, N. (1991) *Entangled Objects: Exchange, Material Culture, and Colonialism in the Pacific*. Cambridge, MA: Harvard University Press.
Vercoutter, J. (1956) *L'Égypte et le monde Égéen Préhéllenique*. Bibliothèque des Études 22. Cairo: Institut Français d'archéologie orientale.
Wachsmann, S. (1986) Is Cyprus ancient Alashiya? New evidence from an Egyptian tablet. *Biblical Archaeologist* 49:37–40.
Walz, C. A. (1997) Black Athena and the role of Cyprus in Near Eastern/ Mycenaean contact. In *Greeks and Barbarians: Essays on the Interactions between Greeks and Non-Greeks in Antiquity and the Consequences for Eurocentrism*, edited by J. Coleman and C. Walz. Occasional Publications of the Department of Near Eastern Studies and the Program of Jewish Studies, Cornell University, Number 4. Bethesda, Maryland: CDL Press, pp. 1–27.
Webb, J. M. (2005) Ideology, iconography and identity: the role of foreign goods and images in the establishment of social hierarchy in Late Bronze Age Cyprus. In *Archaeological Perspectives on the Transmission and Transformation of Culture in the Eastern Mediterranean*, edited by J. Clarke. Levant Supplementary Series 2. Oxford: Council for British Research in the Levant and Oxbow Books, pp. 176–82.
Webb, J. M. and D. Frankel (1994) Making an impression: storage and surplus finance in Late Bronze Age Cyprus. *Journal of Mediterranean Archaeology* 7:5–26.
Yon, M. and A. Caubet (1985) *Le Sondage L-N13. Bronze Récent et Géométrique*. Volume 1. Kition Bamboula III. Paris: Recherche sur les Civilisations.

5 The View from East Greece: Miletus, Samos and Ephesus

Sarah P. Morris

'Orientalizing': state of the question?

Our symposium focussed on a set of relationships—material, cultural, and historical—between Greece and its Eastern neighbours, which modern scholarship terms an 'Orientalizing' phase of early Greek experience. Our objective was not only a fresh look at the topic through new finds and innovative models, but also a critical look at the very concept: is it a valid heuristic term, or a dated construct of early modern historiography?

Historical Perspective

Beyond the histories of scholarship which have proliferated in recent studies of early Greece (Burkert 2003:12), we need to track more significant changes in attitude. Borrowing from the history of gender studies, I would characterize three 'waves' of Orientalizing scholarship in archaeology, at first preoccupied with identifying and classifying foreign imports in the Greek material record, and assessing their impact on Greek forms (Morris 2003:2). Here we risk the same dangers as in early work on women in antiquity, focussing first on 'finding them', then adding this new evidence to our view of classical Greek culture—the old 'add women and stir' response, which soon shifted to consider how to change the entire picture of antiquity. In the 'Orientalizing' field, polarized choices once faced the archaeologist: an object must necessarily be *either* Near Eastern *or* Greek and the differences should be clear and explicable. These have now ceded to a much more complex vision of interaction and production, imagining immigrant artists, intermarriage and other social processes to explain the migration of material culture and its producers.

The 'second wave' shifted its view from the *objects* to the *contexts* and individuals that produced and consumed them: why are these objects here? who or what brought them to or from Greece? how were they viewed and valued? Here we have borrowed widely from cultural anthropology and its models of gift exchange in primitive societies, and elite interaction in non-western societies. Among the most popular and influential models have proved Mary Helms's study of distance and power in New World chiefdoms (Helms 1993), and Nicholas Thomas's study of early modern European exchange with the Pacific (Thomas 1991). But we are lacking in ancient Greece the rich texts of encounter that these modern ethnohistories enjoy. Moreover, Greek merchants, mercenaries and artisans from small city-states were awed by the 'world cultures' (Egypt, Assyria) whose opportunities attracted them in the archaic period: this made them more modest players, unlike expansionist European empires encountering new worlds. Prior to Greek colonization, and in fact not until the fateful encounter with Persians on the battlefield, few Greeks approached the Near East with the sense of superiority that European explorers and missionaries brought to the Americas, and the Pacific. Thus ancient 'Orientalizing' witnessed the development in reverse of modern encounters, perhaps the very opposite of those romantic European travellers who felt 'civilized' by 'savages'. Given these reservations, it is difficult to adopt the full implications of 'entangled objects' framed by Nicholas Thomas in the Pacific, as much as modern scholars have sought to.

But at least we have outgrown the lame use of 'trade' as a self-explanatory force, to capture instead patterns of consumption, the effect on emerging elites and the 'materialization' of ideology in imported objects (DeMarrais et al. 1996). This contextual approach has led to an inevitable third wave, with much serious self-criticism about Eurocentric assumptions, and the drive to forge post-colonial methodologies for understanding both material and relationships. It is at this stage that our symposium took place and that we asked ourselves whether we should abandon 'Orientalization' entirely, and if so, replace it with what? My answer will conclude this exploration.

Methodologies

In approaching an answer to our question, I will set forth a few principles basic to my own research on Greek interaction with the Near East:

1. The trail of exotica we track as archaeologists is merely the visible but minor record of larger cargo, invisible 'soft things' such as commodities (wine, oil), raw materials (metals), manufactured goods (textiles) that drove international traffic (Knapp 1991). The most significant cargo may have been human: mobile populations (Purcell 1990; Weiler 1996; Kaplan 1998), from migrants to mercenaries to slaves, produced the most meaningful and lasting 'Orientalizing' effects, but remain visible primarily in texts.

A letter from an Assyrian official to Tiglath-Pileser III (744–727) places the first 'Ionians' on the Levantine coast just after the middle of the 8th century (Parker 2000; cf. Lanfranchi 2000:15–16):

> The Ionians came (and) attacked the cities of Samsimuruna,
> Harisu, and [xxx]. A cavalryman came to the city of Dana[bu]
> (to report this). I gathered up the available men and went
> (after them). (They) did not get anything. When they saw my troops, they got into their boats
> and [disappeared] into the middle of the sea.

Lanfranchi has suggested that by the time of Sargon II, this kind of 'Ionian' aggression by sea was related to or even coordinated with simultaneous Phrygian aggression by land in Cilicia (2000:16–21). Initially, however, Greeks must have operated for their own profit, attacking cities not yet incorporated into greater Assyria, for the sake of booty, typical of the unheroic profit motive of Greeks in the Near East at the time (Winter 1995). This Assyrian document also illustrates a phase before such marauders were actively recruited by Near Eastern dynasts for local service (e.g. Herodotus 2.152), largely in the 6th century. Personal enrichment through mercenary service is familiar from Alcaeus (frag. 16): his brother, Antimenidas, returned to Lesbos from a Babylonian campaign (against Askhelon, or Jerusalem? Quinn

1961) with a sword fitted with a gold and ivory hilt. In a new inscription, an Egyptian basalt statue said to be found in a cave near Priene was dedicated by one 'Pedon', who served under Psammetichos and was rewarded with *aristeia*, a gold bracelet and a city (*polis*), *aretes eneka* (Şahin 1987; Masson and Yoyotte 1988; Ampolo and Bresciani 1988). Both gold object and command of a city were traditional forms of royal recompense to officers in Egypt. Such documents complement the activity of Ionian and Carian mercenaries in Egypt, who left their signatures on royal statues at Abu Simbel (Boardman 1999:115–16). We should also calculate the participation of the fairer sex: women like Rhodopis (a Thracian slave) were brought to Egypt by Greeks (a slave trader of Samos) and became wealthy as courtesans (Herodotus 1.134). One might pair prostitution with mercenary service to recognize women as well as men in Greek enterprise overseas (Weiler 1996 even argues that prostitution was an Orientalizing institution borrowed from the East by Greece). Serving foreign masters in war or love, or otherwise performing as 'attached specialists' to foreign courts, brought exotic rewards, surely a significant source of major traffic in Orientalia. Meanwhile, Greek tyrants enjoyed close *xenia* relations with foreign dynasts (Psammetichus and the Kypselids, Polykrates and Amasis), funded through gifts, secured through marriage and other alliances, perhaps nurtured by military support. Thus while I will concentrate on exotic objects from three locales in Ionia, my aim is to test them for the larger picture implied in these literary sources, and the lasting legacy of the Near East.

2. My second argument has these relationships begin in the Bronze Age. For example, mercenaries were long a chief export from southwest Asia Minor. By the archaic period, 'Kar'

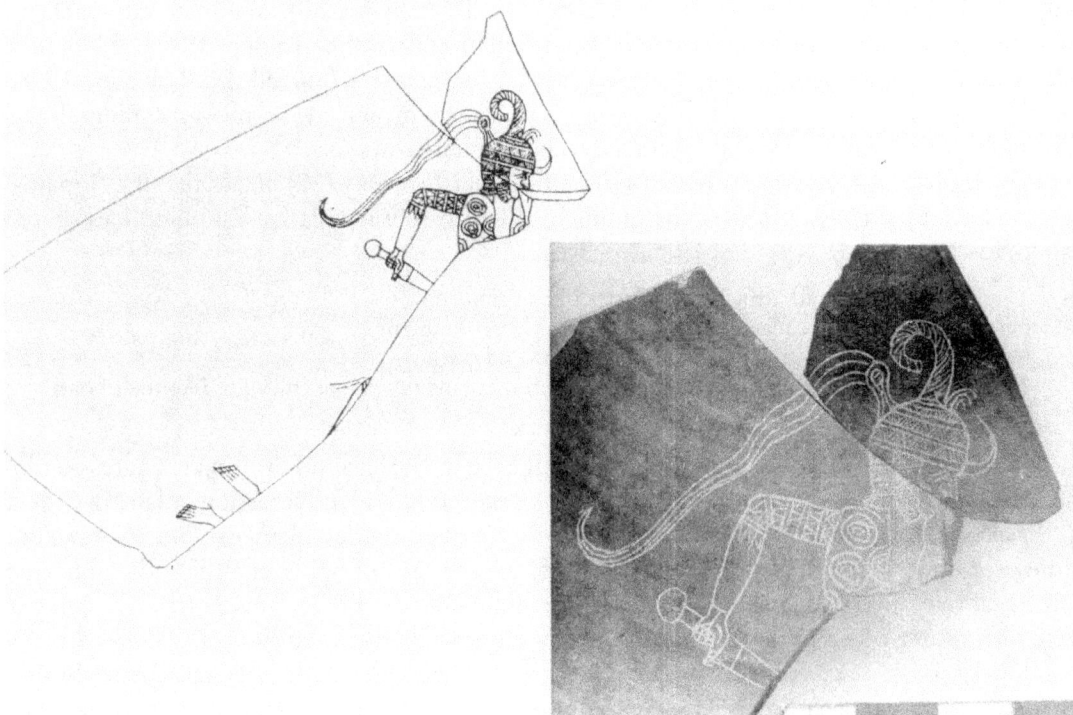

Figure 5.1   Hittite bowl from Hattusas with graffito of Aegean (?) warrior. Photo by author after Kurt Bittel, *Revue Archéologique* 1976, 11, fig. 3.

(Carian) is a synonym for hired soldiers (Archilochus frag. 216: Kaplan 1998), and Carian weapons were famous (Snodgrass 1964), but even in the Bronze Age, Aegean-style weapons were familiar in Central Anatolia (Figure 5.1). In another example of historical continuity, the strong Aegean identity of Bronze Age Miletus survives in its autonomous status under Persia and in its relative scarcity of Anatolian imports (compared to Ephesus, for example). 'Ionian' raids on cities of the Levantine coast, of the kind chronicled in the Assyrian letter cited above, closely resembled those of the 'Ahhiyawa' in western Anatolia in the Bronze Age, who alternated between alliance and attack in their relations with cities subject to the Hatti. As in the first millennium, Aegean opportunists operated in the shadow of larger empires, from which they profited as frequently as they suffered. Recent consensus views Greek-Near Eastern relations across millennia (Karageorghis and Stampolidis 1998) more often than in the past. This expanded perspective, initiated in my own view of long-term relations in the Mediterranean (Morris 1992), loosens 'Orientalizing' from the early archaic *polis*, as this symposium has done, to consider its diachronic powers in antiquity.

3. If mobile individuals are more crucial players than immobile objects, even more significant is the intellectual heritage of this exchange, which transcends archaeology. Monumental architecture, sculpture and orthogonal city-planning show a visible debt to Near Eastern models, but how do we get from graffiti left by soldiers on Egyptian statues to the adoption of those sculptural forms at home? More lasting institutions to consider are coinage and writing, both borrowed from the Levant (on coinage, see Kroll 2001; Schaps 2001, 2004; Thompson 2003), and deeper intellectual exchange through contact with Assyrian and Babylonian mathematics and astronomy (Halperin 2003). This is harder to trace on the ground, but the most critical part, as Nicholas Purcell emphasized at the symposium. While we focus on archaeological and historical records, surely our ultimate goal is to capture the lasting legacy of East-West exchange (e.g. Dalley and Reyes 1998).

Case Studies in Ionia

Against this background, it is particularly appropriate to focus on coastal Asia Minor and its islands, as the earliest Aegean zone of contact with non-Greeks since the Bronze Age. The epic tradition remembers this region for the earliest encounters with barbarians: the Carians of Miletus, allies of Troy, are the earliest *barbarophonoi* in Greek testimonia (*Iliad* 2.867–9). Moreover, the area enjoyed close relations with Egypt and the Levant, even Mesopotamia, perhaps since the Bronze Age, including through mercenary services (Haider 1990; Niemeier 2001). Finally, as the westernmost region incorporated into the Persian empire, via the defeat of Lydia and loss of its territories to Cyrus in 546 BC, Ionia was the first Greek region whose elite rulers (tyrants) developed close client relations with Persia. Revolution when those relations failed set in motion the conflict with Persia that shaped 'Orientalism' as a Greek discourse. Thus it was in Ionia that Athens first witnessed the art of intimacy with Persia, and how to reject it under changed political conditions. In this way, Ionia provided the *paideusis* of Greece for relations with the Near East, by its failure to make that relationship work over time. If we have shifted our gaze in literature recently eastward from Aeschylus in Athens to Phrynichus and Timotheus in Miletus (Hutzfeldt 1999), we should make equivalent adjustments in our archaeological agendas.

I will examine this relationship within the 'golden triangle' of Ionia: three powerful Greek cities (Samos, Miletus, Ephesus), whose material and historical record allows us to re-examine these phases and modes of interaction. Archaic habitation levels from these three cities are scarce (for Miletus: Kalabaktepe, see now Senff 2000; for Ephesus, Kerschner *et al.* 2000). Thus we cannot compare closely Eastern evidence from these Greek cities with the residential areas of Al Mina, Tel Sukas, Ras el-Bassit, and other Levantine sites to complement the picture in Ionia (Haider 1996). Nor are archaic cemeteries of East Greece as well explored as those at Athens, Lefkandi, or Knossos. So we must concentrate on East Greek sanctuaries, without a good sense of how 'Oriental' the average local household was, and how much Near Eastern contact there was in daily life and death.

1) Ephesus: *Potnia Aswiya*

As I have argued recently (Morris 2001a, 2001b), Ephesus exemplifies the kind of city with a rich Anatolian past, prior to new Orientalizing contacts. Newly visible is the city's prehistory, centred on the conspicuous citadel of the third and second millennia, later the site of a medieval castle and modern Selçuk. This was the core of second-millennium *Apasas* in Hittite texts, a city whose alliance Hattusas (the Hittite capital) sought against renegade neighbours (Uhhaziti, etc.), and whose remains include plenty of Mycenaean pottery. Thus it occupied a status between the Hittite cities of the heartland and the 'Ahhiyawa' we associate with 'Achaean' Greek-speakers, on the islands and/or mainland of Greece. In legend, Greeks remembered the cult of Artemis as a foundation by the Amazons, perhaps a memory of its early, un-Greek history, if not a misunderstanding of images of the Hittites themselves.

Some elements of this heritage have survived, I have argued, in the cult and image of Artemis of Ephesus, a Greek goddess grafted onto an Anatolian deity by the first Greek settlers. They occupied a new site on adjacent hills for their city, but continued to worship Artemis at the foot of the prehistoric citadel. Her statue, much copied in Roman antiquity, has been described as 'many-breasted' ever since the Church Fathers condemned her appearance, and her image survives as a nurturing figure of Nature in the Renaissance, and a modern 'fertility' or 'mother' goddess. Long thought a late antique extravaganza, it is now more likely that even the early statue was decorated with these 'bulbs'. They are not shaped or coloured like breasts in copies, and in fact are worn by native Carian gods like Zeus as martial (?) attributes, not as breasts. Small-scale versions of these shapes in amber have been recovered in early archaic levels of the sanctuary, and are likely predecessors of her later multiple appendages. Research in Hittite texts convinces me that they incorporate a Greek transformation of an old Anatolian cult attribute, the *kursas* or animal-skin bag that resembles in function a cornucopia (Morris 2001a, 2001b). In art and word such a *kursas* became the *aegis* of Athena, also 'shaggy' in word but scaly in appearance, while in Ionia it survived to decorate the Greek replacement for an early Anatolian city goddess of *Apasas*.

Thus creative engagement with non-Greek traditions, and vivid results, was already in progress in this part of the world before the period traditionally marked as 'Orientalizing'. In order to understand East Greek interaction with local barbarians later (Carians and Lydians, eventually Phoenicians and Persians), I believe it is necessary to appreciate these earlier contacts and exchanges with which Greek speakers in the Bronze Age must have been familiar.

Ephesus enjoyed its closest relations with Lydia, as the 'natural port of Sardis' (Georges 1994: Herodotus 6.54, 100) with whom it shared a goddess of local nomenclature (if 'Artimu' is indeed Anatolian). Unlike Miletus (attacked by Ardys), or Smyrna (besieged by Alyattes), Ephesus resisted Lydia but was then incorporated into its cultural milieu, and shared cults at Sardis. More than its neighbours at Miletus and Samos, where Anatolian artefacts are outnumbered by imports from the eastern Mediterranean, Ephesus retained close connections with Lydia and developed what Hanfmann (1975:13) termed a 'mixo-Lydian' character in its material culture. It was Gyges of Lydia who first approached the Assyrians for help against the Cimmerians, and Croesus whose ambitions against Persia cost not only him but the Greeks of Ionia their independence. And it was the Lydians who employed Greek artists like Theodorus of Samos and Glaukos of Chios. A close relationship with Phrygia can also be observed in bronze fibulae and belts from the Artemision, half of which are 'Phrygian' in style, but include many Greek imitations (Klebinder 2002). Phrygian textiles may have accompanied these votives, and Artemis of Ephesus wears a Phrygian belt (Bammer 1991–92:38–43; cf. Boardman 1999:90–91). These recall early relations between Phrygia and Asian Greeks (Midas married a Greek princess from Kyme: Aristotle frag. 616), and the role of Phrygia in first engaging the Greeks with Assyria (as Lanfranchi 2000:17–21 argues). In concentrating on the primary text-producing cultures in the Orientalizing experience—Greeks and Assyrians—we have neglected their vital intermediaries—Caria, Lydia, Phrygia—with whom both had early and constant contact. This may be the most crucial lesson of examining these three Ionian cities.

Let us consider those small finds that I condemned as trivial, in my preface on methodology. A number of new Phoenician imports, along with potential Semitic practices involving animal bones, have been attributed to Phoenician presence at Ephesus (Bammer 1985, 1991–92). In all three Greek cities under scrutiny, we must engage with an important article by Imma Kilian-Dirlmeier (1985), of closer relevance to Samos. Among imports at Ephesus, can we single out one set as evidence of migrants? Phoenicians may have survived in Ionia, if Thales of Miletus was indeed of Phoenician descent (Herodotus 1.170). But Phoenician imports must be interpreted in the context of other objects from Cyprus, Egypt, and North Syria, and local industries. Ephesus presents us our first set of 'entangled objects' in all their complications: were foreigners visiting Ephesus and dedicating native trinkets to Artemis? Or, did Greek entrepreneurs bring votives to the goddess from distant ports of call? Greater entanglement attends the earliest coinage of western Asia, whose first examples stem from the Artemision at Ephesus: was this a co-innovation of Lydians, Greeks, and Phoenicians (Kroll 2001)?

The colossal temple initiated in the 6th century at Ephesus included columns contributed by Croesus, shows Lydian mason's marks, and exhibits an archaic sculptural style much indebted to Lydia. The architects responsible for the temple, Chersiphron ('Handy-Man?') and 'Metagenes' (perhaps a second-generation migrant?), originally from Crete, probably borrowed lifting techniques from Egypt, but relied on Theodorus, fresh from the temple project on Samos, for the temple foundations. In imagining the monumental scale and hypostyle effect of these structures, we inevitably turn to Egypt to explain as well as visualize the tremendous leap in scale from Greek predecessor structures. Thus the small finds we carefully catalogue, although often more eloquent, are eclipsed in the original Orientalizing experience by the impact of these temples, which dramatically transformed the sacred landscape of all three cities.

2) Samos: Sanctuary and Sages

On Samos, the lone-standing column of its unfinished archaic temple, designed to be the largest in the Greek world, is a reminder of its disrupted fate: once powerful under the tyranny of Polykrates, it fell victim to internal *stasis* and the failure of its external relations (Shipley 1987). Theodorus and Rhoikos, local sculptors and engineers, were responsible for the first (and perhaps second) phase of this temple, and were later recruited to cope with similar groundwater problems at Ephesus. Theodorus also made a bronze statue based on Egyptian techniques (Diodorus I. 98.5–9), for which the giant Isches kouros found 20 years ago remains the most vivid proof of direct inspiration by Egypt (Kyrieleis 1996); many assume Theodorus visited Egypt. Thus the sanctuary epitomizes a city with close relations with Egypt, and local fruits of foreign contact.

The sanctuary of Hera has produced the largest corpus of Oriental imports in Greece. They include exotic fauna, such as hippo teeth, the skull of a Nile crocodile and the horn of an African antelope, trophies of a trip to Egypt (Boessneck and von den Driesch 1981). While such animal products are often foreign tribute, as in the Theban tombs of Bronze Age Egypt, these are more likely dedications by Greeks, not gifts from abroad. More substantial is the remarkable range of imported ivories and bronzes dedicated to Hera at Samos, making it the richest source for these finds not only in Greece but in the Near East: two-thirds of the non-ceramic finds from Samos are from Egypt, Cyprus and Syria. Kilian-Dirlmeier (1985) and Kyrieleis (1979) argue for the presence of foreigners as dedicants of these objects, so wide a spectrum do they represent, and so intimately do the dedicants seem to understand the practice of non-Greek religion.

Certainly some of the votives are dedicated purposively, by worshippers who understand their foreign cult significance. Thus the Babylonian bronze figures leading dogs represent the healing powers of the goddess Gula of Isin, appropriate to other concerns at this sanctuary (Burkert 1992:75–79). Egyptian scarabs from the Heraion at Samos, like those dedicated to the same goddess at Perachora, show amuletic signs relevant to Egyptian magic (Skon-Jedele 1994:1402–54). Bronze mirrors inscribed to Mut but dedicated to Hera, again at both sanctuaries, as well as bronze censers and a situla, imply further familiarity with non-Greek religion, or at least with non-Greek deities and their Greek equivalents (cf. Herodotus 2.50). These kinds of votives argue for a mixed community, one 'bilingual' in its religious sensibilities, if not in language itself, and surely speak for female as well as male worshippers.

These objects remind us how foreign kings honoured Greek gods: the most famous was Croesus of Lydia, who showered Pythian Apollo with gold (Herodotus 1.50–51, 92), but also gifted the Laconians with gold for their statue (1.69). Necho of Egypt dedicated his battle outfits to Apollo at Didyma (2.159), and Amasis gave images of himself and of Athena at Lindos, Cyrene, and of Hera to Samos (2.182). Such diplomatic pieties may have even have prevailed in the Bronze Age: Midas of Phrygia was remembered by Herodotus as the first foreigner to honor a Greek god (at Delphi: 1.14), but the Hittites did so much earlier. King Mursilis II, stricken by aphasia, was bidden to bring the 'gods of Lazpa [Lesbos] and Ahhiya[wa]: [Aegean Greeks]' to cure him (Morris 2001a:428). I have argued that such piety towards Greek gods by foreign rulers, at least in the Iron Age, allowed them to establish permanent relations of prestige not possible through political channels, given unstable regimes (tyrants) or rotating officials in democratic cities (Morris 1997:65–6). But small figurines, the objects that survive in sanctuaries, surely represent a more modest population, or objects looted from Assyrian palaces (Curtis 1994) rather than gifted by rulers, and rarely reflect these higher relations. Do they demonstrate gifts made by foreigners?

Let us consider closely one of the most crucial objects of all, the bronze horse frontlet decorated with figures of naked women and beasts, a 'Mistress of Animals' (Figure 5.2).

Made in a North Syrian workshop, it was inscribed by a 9th-century ruler of Damascus (Haza'el), as booty from his capture of Umqi. But it was found in a 6th-century deposit at Samos, no sign of a gift by a foreign ruler. Moreover, other frontlets and a horse-blinker from Samos match two blinkers from a similar bridle at the sanctuary of Apollo at Eretria, one inscribed with the identical message, and companions from Miletus. The inscriptions tempt us to see direct relations between rulers and Greek sanctuaries, of the kind we know existed in history. But can we point to them in such objects? Many of them display a significant gap in time between their manufacture in the Near East and their deposition in a Greek sanctuary, as if they had circulated widely, and none are whole outfits, unlike parallels buried with horses and chariots in 'royal' graves in Cyprus (Donder 1980).

As I will reiterate below, I remain reluctant to see these as elite gifts to Greeks, or any equivalent to the kind of diplomatic exchange common in the Near East (Morris 1997: 63–7). I would instead treat these Syrian horse-trappings like the bronze bowl with Luwian

Figure 5.2 North Syrian horse frontlet, bronze, from Samos. DAI Samos 88/1022. Height 27.3 cm and maximum width 17.3 cm.

inscription from Gurgum (Maraş) buried with an early Greek woman at Tragana in central Greece (Muhly 1999:525). They are all likely to be booty from North Syrian cities, looted in a Greek raid or Assyrian campaign, shared back home with families and deities. Many stem from harness ornaments, like the bronze bells found at Samos and Sparta (Villing 2002). We should imagine women as well as men participating in these redistributions, if courtesans like Rhodopis (whose freedom was eventually purchased by a Greek, but she remained in Egypt to practise her trade) gifted Greek gods at Delphi with signs of wealth—iron spits—earned abroad (Herodotus 2.135).

Relations between the tyrant of Samos, Polycrates, and the Egyptian king Amasis are well known since Herodotus (3.40–43). The story of the ring designed by Theodorus may reflect an exchange of wealthy gifts sealing their *xenia*, a friendship whose betrayal by Amasis lies at the heart of this story. More intriguing is the way the tyrant recruited and supported talent for his city: the engineer Eupalinos from Megara (Herodotus 3.60), the poet Anakreon of Teos (Strabo 14.268), the physician Democedes (Herodotus 3.125)—and is said to have assembled a library as well. This is good Near Eastern behaviour in a ruler (compare the cultural policies of Nabonidus of Babylon), an aspect of Mesopotamian influence more comprehensive than isolated imports or immigrants, and one widely useful to tyrants throughout Greece.

Last but not least, let us consider the intellectual heritage of archaic Samos. If not visible in the foreign lessons applied to a native temple, the Heraion, did Egyptian or Babylonian geometry inform the design of Samos's greatest monument, the aqueduct of Eupalinos (Kienast 1995)? Megara and Samos alone do not account for the ambition of this project. We should compare innovations such as new techniques of measurement to the adoption of new standards of weight, coinage, and the alphabet, signs of adjustment to leading economies. In recent views of these transformations, 'royal' measures often became Greek (see Burkert 1996 on the *basileion pechus*), and Babylonian standards were discarded for Euboic ones (Kroll 2001). The prehistory of money has recently been recast as 'an Asiatic notion' (Schaps 2001), not because the first ancient coins are Lydian (Karwiese 1995), but for their developmental antecedents in the Near East (Thompson 2003). Unlike the alphabet, there are no precise predecessors in the Levant, nor does the area adopt coinage as rapidly as Greece: thus it is all the more critical to recognize its non-Greek conceptual roots. What role did the need to pay Greek mercenaries and prostitutes (in non-Greek contexts) play as a stimulus for the invention of coinage?

Pythagoras of Samos was a pivotal figure, an exemplar of those 'sages' whom Greeks associated with Ionia. In exile, he is said to have travelled to Egypt (Iamblichus): others asserted that he served in the Assyrian army (historically impossible), was captured by Cambyses and brought to Babylon, or studied with an Assyrian sage (Dalley and Reyes 1998:97). These anecdotes indicate at least that his learning was thought to come from the Near East, a probable source of his mathematics and geometry. Techniques of triangulation applied to urban and rural land measurement in early Greece the theorem we call Pythagorean, derived from Babylonian mathematics, perhaps via Egypt (Boyd and Jameson 1981:334–5). Learning allegedly acquired by Greeks from the Near East is complicated by the *topos* that attributes innovation to foreign factors, to be distinguished from evidence for genuine influence (Lloyd 1982; Lefkowitz 1997). But in the sum of skills commanded by figures like Pythagoras, and their relations to dynasts (it is not clear whether Pythagoras fled the tyranny of Polykrates when he went to Sicily, or benefitted from it), these figures with multiple skills played a Near Eastern role in Ionia.

3) Miletus: *proschema* of Ionia

In ending with Miletus, we close the triangle of three sites that formed the 'principal foyer' or gateway to Asia, with a leading city remembered by Herodotus (5.28) as the 'ornament' of Asia (Gorman 2001). Like Ephesus, Miletus has a significant Aegean prehistory, figuring in Hittite texts as Millawanda, home to renegade rulers and inconstant alliances with the central Anatolian powers. In archaeology, recent years have enriched its Aegean connections with evidence for a vivid Minoan occupation, and a Mycenaean one. More than any other city in western Asia Minor, many of which retained a strong Anatolian flavour in the second millennium, Miletus was as Aegean in its material culture (e.g. Minoan/izing pottery) as many cities in the Cyclades or the Dodecanese (Greaves 2002:45–73).

However, Homer remembers a Miletus of Carians, speaking a barbarian tongue (*barbarophonoi*) and characterized by warriors like Nastes ('native dweller?') dressed in gold, 'like a girl' (*Iliad* 2.872). The ambivalent ancestry of the city, both Greek (like Nastes's brother, Amphimachos) and Anatolian, is vivid in this passage that anticipates, with its negative view of luxurious male costume as effeminate, the anti-Ionian view we know from later Greek sources (Kurke 1992). Indeed, one could argue that Ionian epic generates the first anti-barbarian message against its nearest neighbours (by demonizing Trojans and Phrygians), as Irene Winter has argued is visible in Homer's portrayal of Phoenicians (Winter 1995). What we have lost by way of East Greek perspectives on Anatolians, in the works of Asios of Samos, Magnus of Smyrna, Kallinos of Ephesus, and Herodotus's uncle, Panyassis, can only be surmised. However, we can no longer invoke the grand dismissal of Nineveh by Phocylides as local Orientalism: this famous fragment has recently been re-attributed to a Hellenistic Jew of 1st century AD Alexandria (Korenjak and Rollinger 2001). But as suggested earlier, native Anatolians like the Carians are rarely envisioned within the landscape of Miletus. We can only imagine what the ancestry of Thales, 'half-Carian, half-Phoenician, and all Greek' (Vermeule 1983:142), or of Histaieus son of Tymnes, who fought for the Persians (Herodotus 7.98), spells for local multi-culturalism. It was Carians like Chares of Teichioussa who dedicated some of the most famous 'Branchidae' statues on the Sacred Way to Didyma (Greaves 2002:117–20). Certainly the Carians, unlike the Greeks, moved closer to the Persians after the fall of Miletus, when they were awarded upland territories (Herodotus 6.20). At the battle of Salamis they manned 70 ships 'in Greek style', in the Persian fleet, including one captained by Artemisia, but like the Lycians wielded daggers and *drepana* (curved Persian swords? Herodotus 7.92–3).

Miletus was once the most powerful colonizing city of Greece, founding settlements in northern Greece and the Black Sea, and played a leading role in the settlement at Naukratis granted to the Greeks by the Egyptian pharaoh (Herodotus 2.179). It may also have been the primary exporter of 'Carian' and Ionian mercenaries to Egypt, and indeed have enjoyed that relationship in the second millennium. We have already considered a direct testament to such service, allegedly from Priene: 'Pedon' ('leaper', or opportunist?) was rewarded with gifts (*aristeia*) for his service to Psammetichos, a gold bracelet and a city (?), '*eneka aretes*'. Another Egyptian pharaoh, Necho, dedicated his military outfits to Apollo at the Milesian extra-urban sanctuary of Didyma (Herodotus 2.159), in thanks for victory. Are these relationships reflected in the archaeological record at sanctuaries?

New field research by German archaeologists at Miletus has mapped out in full the sacred landscape of the area. Its leading city sanctuary of Athena crowned the acropolis, with others to Artemis (on Kalabaktepe) and Apollo Delphinios, an extra-urban shrine to Aphrodite (Zeytintepe), and international oracular shrine of Apollo at Didyma (Branchidae), linked to the city by the Sacred Way (Niemeier 1999; Greaves 2002:82–130). Although several are rich in Orientalia—see the Egyptian finds from the Aphrodite sanctuary (Hölbl 1999)—there are no Lydian or Phrygian votives: a reflection of political relations? Newly published finds from the Athena sanctuary, excavated decades ago (see Held 2000 for objects described in this paragraph), illustrate a set of Oriental imports which mirror those of Samos closely. At least eight griffin-cauldrons (7th–6th century BC) have been identified from these excavations, making it the third leading site of such Orientalizing objects (after Olympia and Samos). The Persian destruction also buried Egyptian bronzes comparable to those found in the Heraion at Samos, and Near Eastern objects as old as the 9th century BC, along with bronze horse-trappings from North Syria. One right blinker (with a sphinx in relief) and two frontlets (nose-pieces) resemble those found at Eretria and Samos. A rectangular bronze panel with winged figure is likely to represent another horse-bridle decoration, as does a Cypriote bronze plaque with Near Eastern sun-moon symbols.

All these objects were buried in the debris of the destruction of Miletus by the Persians in 494 BC, along with the monumental temple of Athena (with two archaic phases: Niemeier 1999). Probably dedicated centuries after their manufacture and primary use in the Levant, they join the pieces from Samos and Eretria as parts of elaborate horse trappings, dismembered and re-distributed in those early Greek regions which participated in the 'Eastern adventure': Euboea and Ionia. A significant portion of that adventure involved, evidently, dedicating part of the booty back at home to a leading city deity: Apollo at Eretria, Hera at Samos, and Athena at Miletus. Or, were they redistributed in Central Greece through the Lelantine War in which Miletus backed Eretria against Chalkis, ally of its own rival, Samos? This was one way for Near Eastern trophies, brought back to Ionia by mercenaries, to travel further. We have not exploited fully the power of these objects to inform Greek history. Few Greek mercenaries served as cavalry, rather than as foot-soldiers fighting in close combat (Herodotus's 'bronze men': 2.152), or rode horses with such outfits in Near Eastern service. Rather, Greeks acquired horse gear, visible in action on Assyrian reliefs, and statuettes also shown being captured from cities, the same way in which they received rewards from the luxuriously fitted tents of the Persians, after the battle of Plataea (9.80–82). At least, that is how I view these objects, as indirect testimony to the Eastern adventure, most likely brought home by mercenaries fighting for or against an expansionist Assyria, Babylon, or Persia (Niemeier 2001). Indeed, those recruited by Psammetichus were already abroad in search of plunder—like those stopped by Assyria in the 8th century (Parker 2000)—and promised rewards for fighting (Herodotus 2.152). As prizes from overseas warfare, they could reflect personal gifts (*aristeia*, like Pedon's gold bracelet) or mere plunder, and force us to re-examine the magnificent sword wielded by the brother of Alcaeus. Was this a gift from a grateful Babylonian 'ally', or a lucky capture by a Greek mercenary? (Cyrus allowed his soldiers to plunder Sardis until Croesus reminded him that it was 'his own' city they were plundering: Herodotus 1.88–89). I suspect the latter, by which I am deliberately subscribing to the more scurrilous scenario of Greek opportunism rather than valour rewarded. Yet royal rewards are precisely what Pedon claimed as the source of his lavish gifts from Egypt. Thus I conclude my overview of the Orientalia from three wealthy sanctuaries with this argument for their origin: that they reflect a secondary phase of Greek enterprise in the Near East (in plunder and fighting), not primary gifts from non-Greeks (cf. Shipley 1987). I will continue to play the sceptic about relations between Greek elites and Near Eastern dynasts, as far as concerns the archaeological record. This shows us only objects out of circulation in sanctuaries, but rarely their original owners or donors, or grander royal donations of the kind reported for Amasis and Necho.

While these sanctuaries near or at cities may have seen more urban traffic, it was the oracle of Apollo at Didyma that attracted international fame and wealth. By the time of the Ionian revolt, Hecataeus of Miletus could propose melting down its riches to finance a navy against the Persians (Herodotus 5.36). The Hellenistic temple lies over its early finds and the first colossal structure. But its likely predecessor matched Samos and Ephesus in its ambitious size, which dwarfs human scale. In monumental structures like these, the Greeks emulated foreign achievements, but also made vivid their own sense of inadequacy in time as well as scale. When Hecataeus of Miletus claimed to the Egyptians his descent from a god through 16 ancestors, and they responded by showing him statues of over 345 of their own (2.143), any Greek would have felt the lack of generations in history and memory. Just as early Greek chroniclers fabricated king-lists to match those in Lydia and Egypt (Burkert 1995), patrons and builders designed enormous temples and statues to compensate for a lack of depth in time, not just size. Thus the emulation of Near Eastern scale was in part an attempt to manufacture history through monuments, a Greek drive eventually fulfilled in and after the Persian Wars (Morris 1992: Part IV).

Here I would like to move away from artefacts towards the intellectual traditions developed in western Asia in the archaic period, perhaps its most significant contribution to Greek culture and indeed the Western heritage. While early Phoenician traffic may not have produced direct effects of this kind (Patzek 1996), archaic Ionia was a more likely breeding ground for lasting cultural influence. A pioneer in early Greek poetry since Homer, Ionia (especially Miletus) became a hotbed of new intellectual disciplines in the early archaic period, from cosmology to geography to the earliest scientific thought. While Pythagoras of Samos may have had possible Oriental inspirations, it is at Miletus that those relations bore the most abundant fruit. Inadequately collected as 'Pre-Socratic philosophy', the largely fragmentary texts of early Ionian thinkers remain our richest source of Near Eastern influence on Greece. Over the years, scholars have pointed out various convergences in these texts with Eastern traditions: West (1971) saw the influence of Persia in the later 6th century, perhaps a result of the revolt and exile of the Magi. Others pointed out how much early Greek geography and the first world maps (e.g. Herodotus 5.41) owed to Babylon (Horowitz 1988, 1998; Kahn 1960:83–4; Kuhrt 2002:13–19). Most recently and fruitfully, Baruch Halperin (2003) has explored links of both Greek and early Israelite cosmogonies to Assyrian and Babylonian astronomies. A significant mode of transmission, in his view, was the deliberate and selective recruitment of intellectual elites from western Asia Minor by Assyrian and Babylonian courts, to create international cultural capitals based at palatial centres. Both Babylonian and Persian policies encouraged specialists like doctors, seers and artisans to join royal ensembles (Nylander 1970; Kuhrt 2002: 12). This brings early Greek views of migrant specialists (the famous quartet of prophet, poet, builder and healer: *Od.* 17.383–5) in harmony with similar Assyrian practices. Cohorts of scribes, diviners, exorcists, physicians, and singers were recruited as spiritual advisors ('masters': *ummanu*) by Assyrian kings (Tadmor 1986).

In moving into this dimension, we remind ourselves how partial (in both senses) is the archaeological record, and how invisible remain many of the primary relationships which constituted Greek-Near Eastern contact. The two-way traffic they once sustained should dissolve our polarizing tendency, the legacy of early modern framing of these relationships. Re-introducing the manifold experiences which 'Orientalized' Greece may not solve perennial explanatory impasses, and texts still tend to guide our interpretation of material.

Historical epilogue: *Ionia capta*?

The ultimate (in several senses of the word) Oriental enlistment of Greeks was performed by Persia, when it set up Milesian aristocrats as 'client rulers', tyrants serving in essence as satraps (Georges 2000). This relationship supported further expansion of mutual interests, for example into the north Aegean to gain a foothold near valuable silver sources. Ever since Gyges supported a Milesian colony at Abydos, near his hometown of Daskyleion, the Lydians, followed by the Persians, encouraged Ionian exploration of mineral deposits (electrum on the Propontis, silver in Thrace and Macedonia) of vital value to these non-Greek expansionist states dependent on minted coinage. Recent discoveries in northern Greece (the Thermaic Gulf and the Chalkidike) document intensive East Aegean activity, long familiar from colonies in Thrace and monumental Ionic architecture (the temples at Kavala and Therme). Ionian, Lydian and Carian graffiti at sites in Thessaloniki, along with East Greek pottery and other artefacts—Clazomenian sarcophagus burials at Akanthos (Kaltsas 1998: pl.35), East Greek pottery at Torone and other Greek cities of the Chalkidike (Paspalas 2001:312–15, 322–3), Carian graffiti at Stageira—demonstrate significant interests in this area as early as the 7th century (Tiverios 1999; Tsiafakis 2000; Tzanavari and Christides 1995). One suspects that northern metal sources in the 'Chalkidike' account for this traffic across the Aegean. As late as the 4th century, a Gyges of Torone supplied Samos with grain (Shipley 1987:170, 204); his Lydian name and eastern connections suggest how long this traffic linked markets East and West.

As in other lessons, Athens pursued northern expansion after her defeat of Persia (and of pro-Persian cities in Ionia and the north Aegean), with expeditions to Eion and Amphipolis in Thrace, an enterprise already pioneered by her own tyrants: Miltiades in Thrace, the Peisistratids in the Troad. It is no accident that pro-Persian tyrants first led this drive to the north, and that their exiled descendants—Hippias—advised Xerxes on how to capture Greece.

The collapse of this relationship, through competition among Persian and Greek elites seeking royal favour and local power, led to the disaster tactfully remembered as the Ionian revolt. And by then, Athens was drawn into the conflict (Herodotus 5.97); the rest is history. Thus the fate of Miletus, rather than Athens, introduced the break with the East that shaped modern Orientalism. The fall of Miletus, like the capture (and comeback) of Athens, was remembered by poets both Ionian (Timotheus: Hutzfeldt 1999) and Athenians (Phrynichus) whom it pained as a reminder of their own (*oikeia*) misfortunes (Herodotus 6.21). But by then Athens had captured the art of performance from Ionia (West 1999). And the failure of Miletus to cope with Persians as patrons, then enemies, enhanced the victory of Athens (as I read Herodotus: Morris 1992:272–88; cf. Balcer 1991). Thus the final chapter of archaic Ionian history sows the seeds of modern Orientalism, before Athens did.

In short, in recent years the primary discourse of Orientalism has shifted from the literature of classical Athens to the material culture of archaic Ionia, where we can observe more vividly, in archaeology, Greece's dialogue with the Near East and its demise. Here we can appreciate the crucial role of native Anatolians, subjects of both Greek and Near Eastern texts but primary agents of innovations like coinage (Lydia), writing (new dates claimed for early levels at Gordion have revived theories of the Phrygian transmission of the alphabet to Greece), and Homeric traditions (Högemann 2003). Thus a more nuanced regional view of the multiple players and effects involved in 'Orientalization' greatly diversifies and enriches our view of a fascinating, abiding and productive ancient relationship.

Conclusions: To Orientalize, Or Not?

This symposium has confronted whether 'Orientalizing' and 'Orientalization' are valid as heuristic terms for the relations between cultures in the ancient Mediterranean, or whether they are simply a modern construct. The three cities I have analysed for their particular dynamics, visible in material culture and intellectual activity, amply display the human and material grounds for interaction. But do they support or deny any use for the concept of 'Orientalizing'?

Despite calls to abandon the phrase, I believe that we should sustain some version of this term, for several reasons:

1. First of all, if we include in 'Orientalizing' a deliberate attitude towards the East, there was clearly an appetite for the display and imitation of exotic luxury goods, if one imagines a sanctuary like that of Hera at Samos in the 7th century, crowded with bronze cauldrons and their griffins, Cypriot stone statues, furniture inlaid with ivory, bronze horse trappings, and even exotic animal trophies. The imitation of these forms, in local arts, suggests this appetite extended to the sincerest form of flattery, and encouraged local *ersatz* industries. Thus a desire for objects from the Near East also inspired a local commodity industry. This frames 'Orientalizing' as an ancient reality in terms of a deliberate fashion, which is why modern scholars have resorted to the likes of 'Perserie' to describe a particular classical phase of this relationship (Miller 1997). The active verb, and transitive participle, is thus particularly useful and relevant in expressing ancient taste and imitation as a deliberate, meditated activity, however bald its associations with an early modern imperial notion of the 'Orient', which clearly indicates no more than the timing of its coinage.

2. Second, ancient Greek voices themselves acknowledge Near Eastern origins of innovations we call 'Oriental', most explicitly in their memory of the adoption of alphabetic writing. Not only does a Phoenician called 'Kadmos' (conveniently assimilated as a Greek hero by marriage) introduce this innovation to Greeks, and alphabet signs are called 'Kadmeia grammata' (Herodotus) but more striking, to write alphabetic signs is to 'Phoenicianize' (*poinikazein*), for a Cretan scribe is entitled a '*poinikastas*' (SEG XXVII, 631; Morris 1992:160). Thus in noun and verb certain regions of Greece expressed, just as we do in 'Orientalizing', the notion that 'Phoenicianizing' involved using Near Eastern traditions, in this case writing. In the archaic period the alphabet was evidently so novel in a culture that had forgotten Bronze Age writing systems, that writing was understood and described as the

most Near Eastern of institutions. But might other voices have expressed the notion that to carve monumental statues of stone was 'Egyptianizing' for early Greek sculptors, or casting certain kinds of bronze objects 'to Syrianize'?

In other striking ways, 'Phoenicians' are credited with fertilizing early Greek culture, not only in the shapes but in the very contents of early written texts. Recognizing Near Eastern sources for early Greek theogonies is a result of the modern decipherment of cuneiform Akkadian and Hittite texts. But at least one early figure, Pherekydes of Syros, perhaps the first Greek prose writer (rivaled by 'Kadmos' of Miletus!) and author of both scientific treatises and poetic cosmogonies in the 6th century, is said to have 'taken sources (*labon aphormas*) from the Phoenicians' for his theology of the god Ophion and the Ophionidai (Philo of Byblos, apud Eusebius *Praep. Ev.* I. 10, 50; Schibli 1990:81–4). Our authority for this is late, but at least more closely acquainted with genuine Phoenician mythological texts, such as those of Sanchuniathon, than we are. And it may have been no more than this report by Philo that inspired the Suda's claim that Pherekydes 'taught himself having acquired secret Phoenician books', much as I would love to believe that this indicates Pherekydes was one of the first Greeks to read cuneiform. With all due caution we must exert in not taking literally ancient claims for Near Eastern sources (Lefkowitz 1997), this could illustrate the notion that there was an ancient concept of 'Orientalizing', called 'Phoenicianizing'.

No doubt Andrew and Susan Sherratt, who argued at our symposium that 'Orientalizing' should be recast as 'Phoenicianizing', for the sake of the prominent role played by the Phoenicians as artists and explorers in the early Mediterranean, would be delighted to substitute the ancient term for the modern. And indeed as those who provided the most frequent contact for early Greeks with the Near East, short of travelling there, it would be appropriate. But it may be more honest to retain 'Orientalizing' with all of its Eurocentric trappings, as a parallel to ancient Greek use of the term 'Phoenician', which already carried a Western bias since Homer (Winter 1995). In the end, this exploration has taught me that the relationship with the Near East was also one deliberately conceptualized as such by our ancient subjects, and deserves to be treated as more than a bias of modern classification. This offers us all a valuable lesson from our symposium, and a lasting gift from its organizers.

References

Ampolo, C. and E. Bresciani (1988) Psammetico re d'Egitto e il mercenario Pedon. *Egitto e Vicino Oriente* 11:237–53.

Balcer, J. (1991) The East Greeks under Persian rule: a reassessment. In *Achaemenid History VI. Asia Minor and Egypt: Old Cultures in a New Empire*, edited by H. Sancisi-Weerdenburg and A. Kuhrt. Leiden: Brill, pp. 57–65.

Bammer, A. (1985) Spuren der Phönizier im Artemision von Ephesos. *Anatolian Studies* 35:103–108.

Bammer, A. (1991–92) Multikulturelle Aspekte der frühen Kunst im Artemision von Ephesos. *Jahreshefte des Österreichischen Archäologischen Instituts* 61:16–54.

Boardman, J. (1999) *The Greeks Overseas: Their Early Colonies and Trade*. 2nd ed. London: Thames and Hudson.

Boessneck, J. and A. von den Driesch (1981) Reste exotischer Tiere aus dem Heraion von Samos. *Athenische Mitteilungen* 96:245–8.

Boyd, T. and M. Jameson (1981) Urban and rural land division in ancient Greece. *Hesperia* 50:327–42.

Burkert, W. (1992) *The Orientalizing Revolution: Near Eastern Influence on Greek Culture in the Early Archaic Age*. Cambridge, MA: Harvard University Press.

Burkert, W. (1995) Lydia between East and West, or how to date the Trojan war: A study in Herodotus. In *The Ages of Homer: A Tribute to Emily Townsend Vermeule*, edited by J. Carter and S. Morris. Austin, TX: University of Texas Press, pp. 139–48.

Burkert, W. (1996) 'Königs-Ellen' bei Alkaios: Griechen am Rand der östlichen Monarchien. *Museum Helveticum* 53:69–72.

Burkert, W. (2003) *Die Griechen und der Orient*. Munich: C.H. Beck.

Curtis, J. (1994) Mesopotamian bronzes from Greek sites: the workshops of origin. *Iraq* 16:1–22.

Dalley, S. and A. T. Reyes (1998) Mesopotamian contact and influence in the Greek world. In *The Legacy of Mesopotamia*, edited by S. Dalley. Oxford: Oxford University Press, pp. 85–106.

DeMarrais, E., L. J. Castillo and T. Earle (1996) Ideology, materialization, and power strategies. *Current Anthropology* 37:15–31.

Donder, H. (1980) *Zaumzeug in Griechenland und Zypern*. Prähistorische Bronzefunde XVI, 3. Munich: C.H. Beck.

Ehrhardt, N. (1998) Didyma und Milet in archaischer Zeit. *Chiron* 28:11–20.

Georges, P. (1994) *Barbarian Asia and the Greek Experience. From the Archaic Period to the Age of Xenophon*. Baltimore: Johns Hopkins University Press.

Georges, P. (2000) Persian Ionia under Darius: the revolt reconsidered. *Historia* 49: 1–39.

Gorman, V. (2001) *Miletos, the Ornament of Asia. A history of the city to 400 B.C.E.* Ann Arbor: University of Michigan Press.

Greaves, A. (2002) *Miletos: A History*. London and New York: Routledge.

Guralnick, E. (2004) A group of Near Eastern bronzes from Olympia. *American Journal of Archaeology* 108:187–222.

Haider, P. (1990) Ägäer in ägyptischen Diensten (1550–1200). *Laverna* 1:18–49.

Haider, P. (1996) Griechen im Vorderen Orient und in Ägypten bis ca. 590 v. Chr. In *Wege der Genese griechischer Identität. Die Bedeutung der früharchaischen Zeit*. Berlin: Akademie Verlag, pp. 59–115.

Halperin, B. (2003) Late Israelite astronomies and the early Greeks. In *Symbiosis, Symbolism and the Power of the Past: Canaan, Ancient Israel and their Neighbours from the Late Bronze Age through Roman Palestine*, edited by W. G. Dever and S. Gitin. Proceedings of the Centennial Symposium. W. F. Albright Institute of Archaeological Research and American Schools of Oriental Research. Jerusalem, May 29–31, 2000. Winona Lake: Eisenbrauns, pp. 323–52.

Hanfmann, G. (1975) *From Croesus to Constantine: The Cities of Western Asia Minor in Greek and Roman Times*. Jerome Lectures. Ann Arbor: University of Michigan Press.

Held, W. (2000) *Das Heiligtum der Athena in Milet*. Milesische Forschungen 2. Mainz: Von Zabern.

Helms, M. (1993) *Craft and the Kingly Ideal. Art, Trade and Power*. Austin, TX: The University of Texas Press.

Högemann, P. (2003) Das ionische Griechentum und seine altanatolische Umwelt im Spiegel Homers. In *Die Griechen und der Vordere Orient. Beiträge zum Kultur- und Religionskontakt zwischen Griechenland und dem Vorderen Orient im 1. Jahrtausend v. Chr*, edited by M. Witte and S. Alkier. Orbis Biblicus et Orientalis 191. Göttingen: Vandenhoeck and Rupprecht, pp. 1–24.

Hölbl, G. (1999) Aegyptiaka vom Aphrotidetempel auf dem Zeytintepe. *Archäologischer Anzeiger* 114:345–71.

Horowitz, W. (1988) The Babylonian map of the world. *Iraq* 50:147–65.

Horowitz, W. (1998) *Mesopotamian Cosmic Geography*. Winona Lake: Eisenbrauns.

Hutzfeldt, B. (1999) *Das Bild der Perser in der griechischen Dichtung des 5. vorchristlichen Jahrhunderts*. Wiesbaden: Ludwig Reichert.

Kahn, C. (1960) *Anaximander and the Origins of Greek Cosmology*. New York: Columbia University Press.

Kaltsas, N. (1998) *Akanthos I: H Anaskaphe sto nekrotapheio kata to 1979*. Athens: Tameion Arkhaiologikon Poron kai Apallotrioseion.

Kaplan, P. (1998) Καὶ δη 'πίκουρος ὥστε Κάρ κεκλήσομαι: the mercenary in early Greece. *APA abstracts*: 17.

Karageorghis, V. and N. C. Stampolidis (eds.) (1998) *Eastern Mediterranean: Cyprus-Dodecanese-Crete 16th–6th c. B.C. Proceedings of an International Conference*. Crete: University of Crete and Leventis Foundation.

Karwiese, S. (1995) *Die Münzprägung von Ephesos. Die Anfänge: Die ältesten Prägungen und der Beginn der Münzprägung überhaupt*. Vienna: Böhlau.

Kerschner, M., M. Lawall, P. Scherber and E. Trinkl. (2000) Ephesos in archaischer und klassischer Zeit. Die Ausgrabungen in der Siedlung Smyrna. In *Die Ägäis und das Westliche Mittelmeer. Beziehungen und Wechselwirkungen 8. bis. 5. Jh. v. Chr.*, edited by F. Kritzinger. Vienna: Verlag der Österreichischen Akademie der Wissenschaften, pp. 45–54.

Kienast, H. (1995) *Die Wasserleitung des Eupalinos auf Samos*. Samos 19. Bonn: Rudolf Habelt.

Kilian-Dirlmeier, I. (1985) Fremde Weihungen in griechischen Heiligtümern vom 8. bis zum Beginn des 7. Jhdts. v. Chr. *Jahrbuch des Römisch-Germanischen Zentralmuseums Mainz* 32:215–54.

Klebinder, G. (2002) Ephesos und Phrygien. Eine Untersuchung der Beziehungen anhand der Bronzen aus dem frühen Artemision von Ephesos. In *Temenos: Festgabe für Florens Felten und Stefan Hiller*, edited by B. Asamer et al. Vienna: Phoibos Verlag, pp. 75–82.

Knapp, A. B. (1991) Spice, drugs, grain and grog: organic goods in Bronze Age East Mediterranean trade. In *Bronze Age Trade in the Mediterranean*, edited by N. Gale. Oxford: British Archaeological Reports, pp. 21–68.

Korenjak, M. and R. Rollinger (2001) Καὶ τόδε Φωκυλιδέω? 'Phokylides' und der Fall Ninives. *Philologus* 145:195–202.

Kroll, J. (2001) Observations on monetary instruments in pre-coinage Greece. In *Hacksilber to Coinage: New Insights into the Monetary History of the Near East and Greece*, edited by M. Balmuth. Numismatic Studies 24. New York: American Numismatic Society, pp. 77–91.

Kuhrt, A. (2002) *'Greeks' and 'Greece' in Mesopotamian and Persian Perspectives*. J. L. Myres Memorial Lecture, Oxford, May 2001. Oxford: Leopard's Head Press.

Kurke, L. (1992) The politics of *habrosyne* in Archaic Greece. *Classical Antiquity* 11:91–120.

Kyrieleis, H. (1979) Babylonische Bronzen aus dem Heraion von Samos. *Jahrbuch des Deutschen Archäologischen Instituts* 94:32–48.

Kyrieleis, H. (1996) *Der grosse Kuros von Samos*. Samos X. Bonn: Rudolf Habelt.

Lanfranchi, G. (2000) The ideological and political impact of the Assyrian imperial expansion on the Greek world in the 8th and 7th centuries BC. In *The Heirs of Assyria*, edited by S. M. Aro and R. M. Whiting. Helsinki: The Neo-Assyrian Text Corpus Project, pp. 7–34.

Lefkowitz, M. (1997) Some ancient advocates of Greek cultural dependency. In *Greeks and Barbarians. Essays on the Interactions between Greeks and Non-Greeks in Antiquity and the Consequences for Eurocentrism*, edited by J. Coleman and C. Walz. Bethesda, MD: CDL Press, pp. 237–53.

Lloyd, G. E. (1982) The debt of Greek philosophy and science to the Ancient Near East. *Pedilavium* [reprinted in *Methods and Problems in Greek Science*. Cambridge: Cambridge University Press. 1991].

Masson, O. and J. Yoyotte (1988) Inscription mentionnant Psammétique Ier. *Epigraphica Anatolica* 11:171–9.

Miller, M. (1997) *Athens and Persia in the Fifth Century BC. A Study in Receptivity*. Cambridge: Cambridge University Press.

Morris, S. (1992) *Daidalos and the Origins of Greek Art*. Princeton: Princeton University Press.

Morris, S. (1997) Greek and Near Eastern art in the Age of Homer. In *New Light on a Dark Age: Greek art in the Age of Homer*, edited by S. Langdon. Columbia, MO: University of Missouri Press, pp. 56–71.

Morris, S. (2001a) Potnia Aswiya: Anatolian contributions to Greek religion. In *Potnia: Deities and Religion in the Aegean Bronze Age*. Aegaeum 22. Annales d'archéologie égéenne de l' Université de Liège, pp. 423–34.

Morris, S. (2001b Artemis Ephesia: A new solution to the enigma of her 'breasts'? In *Das Kosmos der Artemis von Ephesus*. Österreichiches Archäologisches Institut Sonderschrift 37: Vienna, pp. 135–51.
Morris, S. (2003) Frogs around the pond: cultural diversity in the ancient world and the new millennium. *Syllecta Classica* 14:1–21.
Muhly, J. (1999) The Phoenicians in the Aegean. In *Meletemata: Studies in Aegean Archaeology Presented to Malcolm H. Wiener*. Aegaeum 20. Annales d' archéologie égéenne de l' Université de Liège, pp. 517–26.
Niemeier, W.-D. (1999) Die 'Zierde Ioniens': Ein archaischer Brunnen, der Jüngere Athenatempel und Milet vor der Perserzerstörung. *Archäologischer Anzeiger* 114:373–413.
Niemeier, W.-D. (2001) Archaic Greeks in the Orient: textual and archaeological evidence. *Bulletin of the American Schools of Oriental Research* 321:11–32.
Nylander, C. (1970) *Ionians at Pasargadae: Studies in Persian Architecture*. Boreas 1. Uppsala: University of Stockholm.
Parker, B. (2000) The earliest known reference to the Ionians in the cuneiform sources. *Ancient History Bulletin* 14(3):69–77.
Paspalas, S. (2001) The Late Geometric and Archaic Pottery. In *Torone I. The Excavations of 1975, 1976, and 1978*, edited by A. Cambitoglou, J. K. Papadopoulos, and O. Tudor Jones. Athens: Archaeological Society, pp. 309–29.
Patzek, B. (1996) Griechen und Phöniker in homerischer Zeit. Fernhandel und der orientalische Einfluss auf die frühgriechische Kultur. *Münstersche Beiträge zur Antiken Handelsgeschichte* 15:1–32.
Purcell, N. (1990) Mobility and the Polis. In *The Greek City from Homer to Alexander*, edited by O. Murray and S. Price. Oxford: Oxford University Press, pp. 29–58.
Quinn, J. D. (1961) Alcaeus and the fall of Babylon (604 B.C.), 48 (D16). *Bulletin of the American Schools of Oriental Research* 164:19–20.
Şahin, S. (1987) Zwei Inschriften aus dem südwestlichen Kleinasien. 1. Archaische Inschrift aus Priene, aus der Zeit des Psammetichos. *Epigraphica Anatolica* 10:1–2.
Schaps, D. (2001) The conceptual prehistory of money and its impact on the Greek economy. In *Hacksilber to Coinage: New Insights into the Monetary History of the Near East and Greece*, edited by M. Balmuth. Numismatic Studies 24. New York: American Numismatic Society, pp. 93–102.
Schaps, D. (2004) *The Invention of Coinage and the Monetization of Greece*. Ann Arbor: University of Michigan Press.
Schibli, H. (1990) *Pherekydes of Syros*. Oxford: Oxford University Press.
Senff, R. (2000) Die archaische Wohnbebauung am Kalabaktepe in Milet. In *Die Ägäis und das Westliche Mittelmeer. Beziehungen und Wechselwirkungen 8. bis. 5. Jh. v. Chr.*, edited by F. Kritzinger. Vienna: Österreichische Akademie der Wissenschaften, pp. 29–37.
Shipley, G. (1987) *A History of Samos, 800–188 B.C.* Oxford: Oxford University Press.
Skon-Jedele, N. (1994) 'Aigyptiaka': A Catalogue of Egyptian and Egyptianizing Objects Excavated from Greek Archaeological Sites, ca. 1100–525 B.C., with historical commentary. Unpublished Ph.D. thesis, University of Pennsylvania.
Snodgrass, A. (1964) Carian armourers: the growth of a tradition. *Journal of Hellenic Studies* 84:107–18.
Tadmor, H. (1986) Monarchy and the elite in Assyria and Babylonia: The question of royal accountability. In *The Origins and Diversity of Axial Age Civilizations*, edited by S. Eisenstadt. Albany: SUNY Press, pp. 203–24.
Thomas, N. (1991) *Entangled Objects. Exchange, Material Culture and Colonialism in the Pacific*. Harvard: Harvard University Press.
Thompson, C. (2003) Sealed silver in Iron Age Cisjordan and the 'invention' of coinage. *Oxford Journal of Archaeology* 22:67–107.
Tiverios, M. (1999) Κάρες στο μύχο του Θερμαϊκού κόλπου. *Archaia Makedonia* 6(2):1175–81.

Tsiafakis, D. (2000) On some East Greek pottery found at Karabournaki in Thermaic Gulf. In *Die Ägäis und das Westliche Mittelmeer. Beziehungen und Wechselwirkungen 8. bis. 5. Jh. v. Chr.*, edited by F. Kritzinger. Verlag der Österreichischen Akademie der Wissenschaften, pp. 417–23.

Tzanavari, K. and T. Christides (1995) A Carian graffito from the Levet table. *Kadmos* 34:13–16.

Vermeule, E. (1983) The Hittites and the Aegean world. 3. Response to Hans Güterbock. *American Journal of Archaeology* 87:141–3.

Villing, A. (2002) For whom did the bell toll in ancient Greece? Archaic and Classical Greek bells at Sparta and beyond. *Annual of the British School at Athens* 97:223–95.

Weiler, I. (1996) Soziogenese und soziale Mobilität im archaischen Griechenland. Gedanken zur) Begegnung mit den Völkern des Alten Orients. In *Wege zur Genese griechischer Identität. Die Bedeutung der früharchaischen Zeit*, edited by C. Ulf. Berlin: Akademie Verlag, pp. 211–39.

West, M. L. (1971) *Early Greek Philosophy and the Orient*. Oxford: Oxford University Press.

West, M. L. (1999) The Invention of Homer. *Classical Quarterly* 49:364–82.

Winter, I. (1995) Homer's Phoenicians: history, ethnography, or literary trope? [A Perspective on Early Orientalism]. In *The Ages of Homer: A Tribute to Emily Townsend Vermeule*, edited by J. Carter and S. Morris. Austin, TX: University of Texas Press, pp. 247–71.

6 Notes on the Phoenician Component of the Orientalizing Horizon

Eric Gubel

> The purple men are at the moment the most favoured Levantines, for various reasons, not all of them academic. (Boardman 1994:95)

Introduction

Until the early seventies, the importance of Greek mercantile activities in the Mediterranean has been overestimated at the expense of those of earlier and contemporary Levantine *entrepreneurs* active in the same area in the wake of the Mycenaean thalassocracy's apogee and subsequent decline. Nowadays, however, their contribution to Europe's cultural heritage is no longer underrated and the term 'Phoenician expansion' is widely acknowledged in history classes throughout Europe. The present paper will not deal with this phenomenon as a whole, as it rather concerns the identity of which Phoenicians in particular took part in this process coined the 'Phoenician expansion' by the late Sabatino Moscati, a process which in my view was bolstered by Aramaeans and other ethnic entities of the Levant as well, starting with the A of Ammonites down to the Z of Zemarites to paraphrase Old Testament sources. A non-exhaustive selection of testimonials illustrating this point would includes amongst others the Monte Sirai statue (Cecchini 1991) and the Vulci glass recipient (Rathje 1991:171–5), both referring to the art of Guzana; a group of Villanovian stelae from Padania inspired by North Syrian bronze work and ivories (Brussels 1981:110–11, cat. no. 59; Cerchiai 1988:227–38; Bologna 2000:338–9, cat no. 446); 'Lyre-Player' seals from Pithekoussai and Etruria reflecting Aramaean and Phoenician mercantile activities in Cilicia (Boardman and Buchner 1966; Boardman 1990); the anthropomorphic alabaster recipient from Tutugi, tumulus 20 near Galera signalling Phoenician interaction with the Ammonite culture along the Red Sea trade route (Gubel 1987:75–80; 1991: 131–8); Israelite seals from Cadiz and Carthage (Avigad and Sass 1997:128, cat. no. 267 and 107, cat. no. 185); the Phrygian lion-rhyton from Veio (Bologna 2000:128–9 cat. no. 78 with fig. p. 98, below) and a Babylonian inscribed bowl from Faleri (Bologna 2000: 130–2, cat. no. 83) or the engraved Tysckiewicz ivory sceptre ornament illustrating the symbiosis of Syrian, Phoenician, Greek, Cypriot and Etruscan art (Gubel 1999a).

The Phoenician expansion: early phases and protagonists

'Pre-colonization' phase (1200–850 BC)

As recently reiterated, the Homeric tradition prefers the term *Phoenician* wherever seafaring merchants from the Levant and their often ambiguous activities are concerned, reserving the term *Sidonian* for all things noble, either on the material (Ajax's *krater* for instance, or the embroidered textiles of Sidon in *Odyssey* XV.417; *Iliad* VI.28), or on a moral level (Phedymos, king of Sidon is qualified as a 'noble man': Tsirkin 2001:276). It is not without interest to linger on this subdivision, for if the term Phoenician indeed derives from the Old Kingdom Egyptian term *Fenkhw* which initially referred to foreign craftsmen specializing in woodwork and still situating the homeland of the latter on the Syro-Phoenician coastal strip in Ptolemaic sources (Dils 1992:170), the city of Sidon emerges as an important centre from the 18th dynasty onwards and even outranges Egypt's traditional commercial partner Byblos, not to mention Tyre which still had to rise into prominence. We learn from the report of Wenamon that around 1080 BC the Sidonian king or *armateur* Warkat-ili boasted no less than 50 vessels, assuring maritime traffic between Tanis in the Nile Delta and his home town, whereas trade between Egypt and Byblos was transported by no more than 15 ships (Leclant 1968:9–12). The same document also establishes that Byblos, all the while maintaining strong ties with Egypt, had regained its control over Amurru which it had lost in the Amarna period and which had since then gained the status of a petty kingdom marking the limits of both Egyptian and Hittite political influences in the Levant (Gubel 1999b:54–5). Our excavations at Tell Kazel/Sumur, key site of the Aakar plains which mark the core territory of Amurru, have brought to light a major Phoenician complex which materializes this drive northwards and explains the installation of the first harbour fit for long-distance trade at nearby Tabbat al-Hammam (Capet and Gubel 2000:425–57).

Bypassing the insular Phoenician city of Arwad, Byblos now had access to the Aramaean markets in North and Central Syria, at the same time disposing of a second bridge-head to ensure trade with Cyprus. Unlike the 'Table of Nations' (*Genesis* X.6) which acknowledges the economic boom brought about by Byblos within the borders of the former kingdom of Amurru by the explicit mention of the Arkite, the Sumarite and the Zemarite along with the Arwadite and the Sinnite, the identity of Byblos and its northern coalition partners was veiled in other biblical and classical sources by the general ethonym 'Phoenician'. The (re-)foundation of Batrun by Ittobaal I, presumed founder of the bicephalic Tyro-Sidonian kingdom in the early 9th century BC, may be regarded as an attempt to cut Byblos off from this profitable network—successfully so in the long run considering the period of gradual decline to follow in the next century marking the apogee of the Tyro-Sidonian bicephalic kingdom (Gubel 1995:341).

In projecting this distinction between 'Northern' and 'Southern' Phoenicians (the latter henceforth called Sidonians for the sake of convenience) on the distribution map of Oriental goods from east to west during the Dark Ages or early Iron Age I (c. 1200–800 BC), we find ourselves unable to credit either of these groups as the more active partner in this process. This is partly because of the actual paucity of material remains, as well as the interaction of both groups with the local population in Egypt, Cyprus and Crete and because of the fact that parallels to early imports in Italy are both attested along the Syro-Palestinian coast and occasionally in the Nile Delta as well. While awaiting more discriminating evidence allowing us to identify the production centres of individual types of, for example, metal wares within this area, it must be emphasized that Sidon is the only one of these centres where every single diagnostic type of the metal recipients characteristic of the first wave of exports to the Aegean and the western Mediterranean can be matched by local finds. The repertoire in question recently studied by H. Matthäus (2001:153–214) includes bowls with lotus (or rather lily handles), *situlae* with a spiralled handle attachment decoration reminiscent of the *Omega/uterus* pendant worn by the figurines from Khaldeh on the northern border of the Sidonian territory (Negbi 1976:186, cat. nos 1644–646), as well as bowls with bar-shaped attachments with swing handles. Sidon is the only site where the Egyptian-made juglets with lotus handles exported to the Aegean are attested to date (Matthäus 2000:520–3). The early first millennium BC 'smiting Ba'al' figurine recovered from the sea off Sciacca in Sicily ties in with an iconography common to all Levantine sites of this and the preceding Late Bronze age periods (Collon 1972), including Sidon where the icon represented the god Reshef in the local (royal) pantheon (Gubel 1993:104–105). Still as far as Sidon's initiative—or at least leading role—in this trade is concerned, we must of course be reminded of the results of recent soundings in the harbour of Sidon stressing both the importance of the local metal industry and its dependency on ores imported since the end of the Bronze Age from the Rio Tinto/Sierra Morena mines in Andalusia (Le Roux *et al.* 2003). The biblical accounts of king Hiram's tri-annual expeditions to Tarshish as well as the high date of the foundation of Cadiz (1104/3 BC) herewith gain in credibility (Bunnens 1979).

Before resuming the highlights of the second wave of Oriental imports in the western Mediterranean, we must now turn to the impact of Phoenician presence in the Egyptian Delta towns of Tanis and Bubastis, respectively the political capital and town of origin of the Libyan pharaohs of the 22nd and 23rd dynasties. It is here that foreign metalworkers had become familiar with the Egyptian lotus jugs during the New Kingdom, subsequently exported to the Aegean. It is more specifically in Bubastis that the prototype of the aforesaid swing-handled bowls had been conceived under later Ramessid rule (Gubel 2000:70–2; 2001:44). Shortly before or after 850 BC, the first 'classical' Phoenician bowl with narrative friezes representing the Bastet festival was produced here (and exported to Cyprus: Meyer 1987), as well as its sister-piece from the tomb of Shalmaneser III's Levantine queen Yaba recently found at Nimrud (Hussein and Suleiman 2000: pl. 48). Both these bowls highlight the Phoenicians' predilection for alabaster recipients produced at Bubastis under the aegis of the goddess Bast and (re-)used for the export of wine from the western oases. Probably as early as the reign of Herihor (1080–1074 BC), the input of foreign artists in the production of the blue glazed lotus chalices and amulets (Tuna el Gebel/Hermopolis) is betrayed by a decorative repertoire prefiguring that of Phoenician ivories and bowls, two artistic media which also owe a lot to Libyan-age Egyptian jewellery (Tait 1963). Under the reign of Osorkon II (874–850 BC), finally the interaction between Phoenicians and Libyan-age Egypt was consolidated by the construction of the Bast temple at Bubastis on an island between two canals (Kitchen 1986:318). The specific setting may have inspired the monumental *naiskoi* built in the middle of a sacred lake at Amrit in the Aakar plains under Gyblite control, as well as in Byblos itself as we have recently demonstrated (Gubel *et al.* 2002:63–4). Needless to add that both these buildings were the prototypes of shrines constructed in the West such as at Nora in Sardinia, along with other architectural features from the Bubastis temple including the Hathoric capitals favoured by the Cypro-Phoenician *koinai* and the palmetto-capitals of the 'Paradise flower' type as coined by B. Shefton (1988:97).

The 'colonization' phase (850–675 BC)

Considering the importance of the Egyptian Delta, it comes as no surprise that many exports illustrating the second phase of Phoenician expansion are intimately linked with the history of Phoenician activities there, instead of merely representing an eclectic choice of *aegyptiaca* or 'bazaar' viz. '*souq* stocks', picked up at random by *des marchands de bibelots*—traders of trinkets. The activities of Phoenicians in a geographical area which at one time formed the core territory of the Asiatic dynasties (24th and 25th), may admittedly explain the diffusion of antiquities such as a vase of Apophis I found in Andalusia (Padró I Parcerisa 1995: 101–106) or the anachronistic use of the scarab of Sheshi-Maaibre by the Carthaginian administration (Redissi 1999:7). On the other hand, the plundering of Sidon may have caused the diffusion of such heirlooms piously conserved previously to commemorate the city's longstanding ties with Egypt (Culican 1986:673–84). The maintenance of free-port facilities in the Delta, access granted to centres further south such as Memphis and Heracleopolis (Lopez Grande *et al*. 1995: pls 51, 61–4), as well as royal gifts sent to Byblos for instance (Gubel *et al*. 2002:61–3), all mirror the Libyan pharaohs' need for raw materials exclusively obtainable by way of maritime exploits they were themselves unable to accomplish. The remarkable boom of Egyptian bronze work under their rule, all too often still ascribed to the plundering of the temple of Jerusalem, is indeed rather due to imports shipped to the Delta by Phoenician middlemen as evidenced as well by incrustation techniques on the finished products (cf. Padró I Parcerisa 1995: 101–106).

Prima inter pares amongst the metal figurines of the second wave of expansion in the West is the Seville statuette representing the Sidonian goddess Astarte Hor, whether or not this is the pacified manifestation of the Hurrian Astarte, namely the 'Lady at the Window' (Bonnet 1996:127–32; Lipiński 1995:132–43). The wig, the so-called *Etagenperrücke* is typical for a contemporary Egyptian trend copied by the Phoenician artist. The Ptah statue from Cadiz, on the other hand, points to Memphis, where a 'Camp of the Tyrians' is still reported by Herodotos in the 5th century BC (Lipiński 1995:323–4). Whereas several names inscribed on the Phoenician bowls corroborate a Sidonian origin (Markoe 1985:72–4 for references), the alternation of Aramaean and Phoenician motifs on the Olympia bowl, or the Aramaic name figuring on the bowl found at Salerno, raise the question as to whether this indicates the cosmopolitan character of Tyro-Sidonian workshops or, alternatively, that of the different ethnic origins of the itinerant craftsmen participating in the Phoenician expansion process. Ribbed bowls of the type that had antecedents in Tanis also form one of the hallmarks during this second expansion phase, and it is not without interest to note that they survive as anachronisms both in the hinterland of Sidon itself as well as in Andalusia (Hachmann and Penner 1999:121–6, pls. 61–2), where the Cadiz sarcophagi will later mark a renewed Sidonian interest in the area (Lembke 2001:76–9).

Besides these bowls, the new generation of metal vessels includes piriform *oinochoai* with handle attachments in the form of a palmette or 'Paradise flower', well known from one of the most popular motifs in the Tyro-Sidonian ivory repertoire depicting the twin children of Eshmun, assimilated with Atum in the Sidonian pantheon (Gubel 2001). Petal stands, torch and lamp holders, often indiscriminately described as Cypriot, form another diagnostic group once again associated with the regional art of Tyre and Sidon (Matthäus 1999), in the latter case the only centre where *thymiateria* of this specific type survive into the Hellenistic period (Gubel 1987:260; Berlin 2002:138–41). Yet another category of bronze work includes chariot and equestrian bridle harness accoutrements, distributed from Cyprus via Crete to Huelva in

Andalusia. They remind us of the fact that these items of personal prestige of the *marryannu* or captains of the Late Bronze Age cavalry in the Levant had lost none of their distinguishable connotation to the captains of industry and navigation for whom they became heirlooms at the outset of the first millennium BC (Gubel 2003).

Other new articles marketed abroad by the protagonists of the second Phoenician expansion wave, also destined to disappear in the first quarter of the 7th century BC, reflect an extension of Phoenician marketing networks in Egypt and the Near East as illustrated by faiences from the emerging new centre Sais in the Delta, *tridacna squamosa* shells from the Red Sea route or ostrich eggs from inland Syria, if not Africa (Gubel forthcoming). The array also includes ivories (Huelva, Trayamar, Malaga, Praeneste), some of which reflect the art of the Tanis workshops as shown by the barque scene on a panel from Praeneste, where the shape of the alabastra is rather suggestive of the plumper examples represented by local finds than the slender ones depicted on the Golgoi bowl, also discovered *in situ* (von Bissing 1940: pl. 17.2 and 6 respectively).

Finally, mention must be made of the alabaster vessels from the Egyptian Delta widely distributed in Andalusia as well as in Mesopotamia later on, following the plundering of the royal storerooms in Sidon (Culican 1986). Besides the straightforward Egyptian recipients within the series, the awkward copies of Egyptian inscriptions and the fact that the majority of the Andalusian finds translate pottery forms current in the early first millennium BC Levant in alabaster and glass alabastra alike, once more exemplify the Phoenician take-over and product-marketing of local industries in the Delta during the 9th century BC. Whereas early Phoenician settlers in Andalusia re-used Third Intermediate Period Egyptian alabaster jars for cremation or funeral purposes in more general terms, the native (?) population of the Egyptian delta of the Tanite nome in its turn re-used Phoenician commercial amphorae for cat burials (Favard-Meeks 1999: fig. 3).

None of the types of bronzes or other luxurious objects diagnostic of the second wave of the Phoenician expansion westwards was to survive the crisis of the 670s. In our opinion, the abrupt halt in the export of these prestige articles to Cyprus, Crete, Malta and further West in the early 7th century BC cannot be explained but in terms of the situation in the homeland, where the bicephalic kingdom of the Tyro-Sidonian coalition dissolves shortly before the dramatic sack of Sidon in 685 BC by the Assyrians and the subsequent isolation of Tyre during the decades to follow.

Scarce as it is, material evidence as to the *northern Phoenician* participation in this phase of the expansion process must be looked for in deposits in the Aegean as well as in Etruria characterized by 'middlemen merchandise' including exotic ex-votos from Urartu and Luristan (e.g. Schmid 2001:11–34), or even Phrygia as a spouted vessel would imply (Bologna 2000:98, bottom; Winter 1973:402–403.) but which, significantly enough, are lacking in the focal points of the Sidonian expansion.

Sidonian impact on Orientalizing art: a few examples

Several motifs surviving in the Orientalizing art of the western Mediterranean corroborate the distinction between Phoenician—and more specifically Sidonian—influences which presumably reflect the different trade routes via which they had been introduced abroad. In the case of the four-winged scarab,[1] a ring from Khaldeh south of Beirut (Culican 1986:389–90) as well as a bowl fragment from the Idaean Cave in Crete (Matthäus 2000:529–31, fig. 9) establish that this design was devised in Phoenicia (where Khaldeh was part of the Sidonian kingdom) and propagated abroad before the late 9th century BC. In Cyprus the local elite was to become familiar with the four-winged scarab motif thanks to the *repoussé* decoration of slightly more recent Phoenician bowls and engraved designs on scarab(oid) seals, stimulating its occasional adoption in, for example, the local sculpture of the Chypro-Archaic period (Faegersten 2003:294, cat. no. 60, pl. 34). Imports such as the Tharros bracelet (Hölbl 1986: pl. 158.3) or, closer to the Etrurian periphery, a gold bowl from Palestrina may be put forward here as direct sources of inspiration to the Etruscan artists. The inscription of the latter item (Eshmunya'ad, a theonym referring to Sidon's chief deity) as well as several iconographical details straightforwardly refers to Sidon as the ultimate origin of this heraldic device (Hölbl 1979:154–5).

Such is, in my opinion, also the case for the Oriental influence which marks several stelae from Sesto Fiorentino (Fiesole) which I recently proposed to link with the Sidonian *naiskoi* and, presumably, ivories as well depicting the motif of acolytes of the cult of Eshmun holding *oinochoai* and Atum scepters (Gubel 2001). Here again, seals such as the well-known Tharros scarab (Hölbl 1986: pl. 153), or an example from Vulci, may be quoted as possible sources of inspiration (Hölbl 1979:74, cat. no. 350).

The motif of the nude maiden, sometimes represented as part of a twin, such as on the Baurat Shiller Crown (Culican 1986:495–515), or even in the context of a group of three nude maidens on a mid-7th century BC gold cloth ornament from Narce (Cristofani 2000: fig. on p. 174), suspiciously recalls the divine triad Anat-Astarte-Asiti venerated in Sidon as the spouses of Baal Horon, Eshmun and Reshef respectively and reproduced either individually, as a pair or even a threesome on horse blinkers in bronze and ivory (Gubel 2003). As established by older Egyptian sources, these three Sidonian goddesses were all connected with the royal chariot, with horses and stables as well as with wounded warriors because of their healing powers. It comes as no surprise therefore to note their popularity in Andalusia, North Africa and Etruria. Nor is it surprising that Asiti's companion Reshef as represented on Sidonian triangular horses' frontlets, recurs on similar elements of equestrian harnesses at Marsiliana d'Albenga, still holding his shield, spear, bow and arrows (Gubel 2003).

In this and similar chariot burials in Italy or Andalusia (Huelva), both Sidonian imports and the impact of Sidonian art concentrate on the discriminating paraphernalia of a horse-riding elite with an emphasis on its male members who were also furnished with bowls, *oinochai* and other utensils used during banquets.

The typology of imports forwarded by the 'Northern Phoenician' traders on the other hand seems, however vaguely defined as yet, of a more eclectic nature and concentrating—at iconographical level—on *passe-partout* motifs such as the cycle of the Sacred Tree or the theme of the *pothnia theroon*.

In answering the question raised by the organizers of the present symposium, both the quantity of imports of locally produced artefacts in the western Mediterranean displaying Phoenician influences, justifies the notion of an Orientalizing horizon. The term in question may nonetheless be specified in the context of regional or even supra-regional entities, once the identity of the external stimulating factors in this process can be more clearly defined. Since the days of Sir Boardman's statement, found at the head of this paper, the problem of the 'purple men' has been approached in a more critical way as shown by several studies used in this contribution. Further ethnic differentiation within the general Phoenician group, as agents active in the production and propagation of elements contributing to the Orientalizing horizon, may remain beyond the scope of academic research however, just as the identification of specific city-states and their impact on this process. Lastly, much more information may be gained in the future by studying individual objects in the broader context of their original cultural, social, religious and typological setting. In this respect, the concept of the recent Bologna exhibition *Principi etruschi* marks a giant step forward.

Acknowledgments

I would like to thank the organizers of this colloquium for their kind invitation to participate in the event, subsequently for their patience in awaiting my draft and finally, for their constructive critiques and corrections. Thanks are also due to Alessandro Naso for some new bibliographical references. Responsibility for the ideas expressed in this paper, as well as any shortcomings, remains, however, entirely mine.

Endnote

1. For Late New Kingdom Egyptian prototypes of cartouche rings, cf. Terrace 1963:273, pl. 58.16–17; on the Phoenician adoption of the type, cf. Culican 1986:547. See Boardman 1970:5–15 on the introduction of the type in Cyprus and Boardman 1967:3–31 for a review of cartouche and related types of rings in Phoenicia, Cyprus, Greece and Etruria.

References

Avigad, N. and B. Sass (1997) *Corpus of West Semitic Stamp Seals*. Jerusalem: Israel Exploration Society.
Berlin, A. M. (2002) Power and its afterlife: Tombs in Hellenistic Palestine. *Near Eastern Archaeology* 65(2):138–48.
Boardman, J. (1967) Archaic finger rings. *Antike Kunst* 10(1):3–31.
Boardman, J. (1970) Cypriot finger rings. *Annual of the British School at Athens* 65:5–15.
Boardman, J. (1990) The Lyre Player Group of seals: an encore. *Archäologischer Anzeiger*:1–17.
Boardman, J. (1994) Orientalia and Orientals on Ischia. *Annali di Archeologia e Storia Antica*. Ns 1:95–100.
Boardman, J. and G. Buchner (1966) Seals from Ischia and the Lyre-Player Group. *Jahrbuch des Deutschen Archäologischen Institut* 81:1–62.
Bologna 2000 = *Principe etruschi tra Mediterraneo ed Europa* (exhibition catalogue). Venezia: Marsilio Editori.
Bonnet, C. C. (1996) *Astarté. Dossier documentaire et perspectives historiques*. Roma: Centro Nazionale per le Ricerche.
Brussels 1981 = *Prima Italia. Arts italiques du Ier millénaire avant J.C.* (exhibition catalogue). Bruxelles: Musées royaux d'Art et d'Histoire.
Bunnens, G. (1979) *L'expansion phénicienne en Méditerranée*. Bruxelles and Rome: Academia Belgica.
Capet, E. and E. Gubel (2000) Tell Kazel. Six centuries of Iron Age occupation (c. 1200–612 BC). In *Essays on Syria in the Iron Age*, edited by G. Bunnens. Louvain, Paris and Sterling: Peeters Press, pp. 425–57.

Cecchini, S. M. (1991) La statua dell'acropoli di Monte Sirai. In *Atti del II Congresso Internazionale di Studi Fenici e Punici, Roma, 9–14 novembre 1987*. Roma: Centro Nazionale per le Ricerche, pp. 683–9.

Cerchiai, L. (1988) Le stele villanoviane. *Annali di Archeologia e Storia Antica* 10:227–38.

Collon, D. (1972) The Smiting God: A study of a bronze in the Pomerance collection in New York. *Levant* 4:111–34.

Cristofani, M. (ed.) (2000) *Etruschi: una nuova imagine*. Firenze: Giunti Gruppo Editoriale.

Culican, W. (1986) *Opera Selecta*. Göteborg: Paul Aströms Förlag.

Dils, P. (1992) Fenkhu. In *Dictionnaire de la civilisation phénicienne et punique*, edited by E. Lipiński (general director). Turnhout and Paris: Brepols, p. 170.

Favard-Meeks, C. (1999) Tell Suelin. In *Studies on Ancient Egypt in Honour of H.S. Smith*, edited by A. Leahy and J. Tait. London: The Egypt Exploration Society, pp. 83–96.

Faegersten, F. (2003) *The Egyptianizing Male Limestone Statuary from Cyprus*. Lund: University Press.

Gubel, E. (1987) *Phoenician Furniture. A Typology based on Iron Age Representations with Reference to the Iconographical background*. Leuven: Peeters.

Gubel, E. (1991) From Amathous to Zarephat and back again. In *Proceedings of the First International Conference of Cypriote Studies, Brussels-Liège-Amsterdam, 29 May–1 June 1989*, edited by F. Vandenabeele and R. Laffineur. Nicosia: Leventis Foundation, pp. 131–8.

Gubel, E. (1993) The iconography of inscribed Phoenician glyptic. In *Studies in the Iconography of Northwest Semitic Inscribed Seals*, edited by B. Sass and C. Uehlinger. Fribourg and Göttingen: University Press and Vandenhoeck & Ruprecht, pp. 101–29.

Gubel, E. (1995) Phoenician foundations in archaeological perspective. In *Nuove fondazioni nel vicino oriente antico: realtà e ideologia. Atti del colloquio 4–6 dicembre 1991*, edited by S. Mazzoni. Pisa: Università degli Studi di Pisa. Dipartimento di Scienze Storiche del Vicino Oriente, pp. 341–55.

Gubel, E. (1999a) Un chef-d'oeuvre de l'art orientalisant retrouvé: la pyxide Tyszkiewicz aux Musées royaux d'Art et d'Histoire de Bruxelles (A. 1161). *Bulletin des Musées royaux d'Art et d'Histoire* 70:103–21.

Gubel, E. (1999b) The Phoenicians: a nation of seafarers and merchants. In *The Levant. History and Archaeology in the Eastern Mediterranean*, edited by O. Binst. Cologne: Könemann, pp. 46–79.

Gubel, E. (2000) Das lybierzeitliche Ägypten und die Anfänge der phönizischen Ikonographie. In *Ägypten und der östliche Mittelmeerraum im 1. Jahrtausend v.Chr.*, edited by M. Görg and G. Hölbl. Wiesbaden: Harrassowitz, pp. 69–100.

Gubel, E. (2001) The Breath of Life or the riddle of the ram-headed sceptre. *Archaeology and History in Lebanon* 13:35–44.

Gubel, E. (2003) Phoenician and Aramean bridle-harness decoration: examples of cultural contact and innovation in the Eastern Mediterranean. In *Crafts and Images in Contact: Studies on Eastern Mediterranean Art of the First Mediterranean BCE*, edited by C. E. Suter and C. Uehlinger. Fribourg: Academic Press; Göttingen: Vandenhoeck and Ruprecht, pp. 111–47.

Gubel, E. (2005) Phönizische Kunst (Phoenician Art). In *Reallexikon der Assyriologie und der Vorderasiatische Archäologie 10-7/8*, edited by G. Frantz-Szabo and U. Hellwag. Berlin and New York: Walter de Gruyter, pp. 539–43.

Gubel, E., A. Caubet, E. Fontan, F. Baratte, F. Briquel-Chatonnet, P. Bordreuil, C. Deslandes, M. Etienne, P.-L. Gatier, A. Hermary, A. Kassis and M. Yon (2002) *Musée du Louvre. Département des antiquités orientales. Art phénicien. La sculpture de tradition phénicienne*. Paris and Gand: Réunion des Musées Nationaux and Snoeck.

Hachmann, R. and S. Penner (1999) *Kāmid el-Lōz, 3. Der Eisenzeitliche Friedhof und seine Kulturelle Umwelt*. Bonn: Habelt.

Hölbl, G. (1979) *Beziehungen der ägyptischen Kultur zu Altitalien*. Leiden: Brill.

Hölbl, G. (1986) *Ägyptisches Kulturgut im phönikischen und punischen Sardinien*. Leiden: Brill.

Hussein, M. M. and A. Suleiman (2000) *Nimrud. A City of Golden Treasures*. Bagdad: Al Huriyah Printing House.

Kitchen, K. A. (1986) *The Third Intermediate Period in Egypt (1100–650 BC)*. Warminster: Aris and Phillips.

Leclant, J. (1968) Les relations entre l'Égypte et la Phénicie. In *The Role of the Phoenicians in the Interaction of Mediterranean Civilizations*, edited by W. A. Ward. Beirut: American University of Beirut, pp. 9–31.

Lembke K. (2001) *Phönizische anthropoide Sarkophage*. Mainz: Philipp von Zabern.

Le Roux, G., A. Véron and C. Morhange (2003) Geochemical evidences of early anthropogenic activity in harbour sediments from Sidon. *Archaeology and History in Lebanon* 18:115–19.

Lipiński, E. (1995) *Dieux et déesses de l'univers phénicien et punique*. Leuven: Peeters.

Lopez Grande, M. J., F. Quesada Sanz and M. A. Molinero Polo (1995) *Excavaciones en Ehnasys el Medina (Heracleopolis Magna) II*. Madrid: Ministerio de Cultura.

Markoe, G. (1985) *Phoenician Bronze and Silver Bowls from Cyprus and the Mediterranean*. Berkeley, Los Angeles and London: University of California Press.

Matthäus, H. (1999) Zu Thymiateria und Räucherritus als Zeugnisse des Orientalisierungsprozesses im Mittelmeergebiet während des frühen 1. Jahrtausends v. Chr. *Cahier du Centre d'Études chypriotes* 29:9–31.

Matthäus, H. (2000) Die Idäische Zeus-Grotte auf Kreta. Griechenland und der Vordere Orient im frühen 1. Jahrtausend v. Chr. *Archäologischer Anzeiger*:520–3.

Matthäus, H. (2001) Studies on the Interrelations of Cyprus and Italy during the 11th to 9th Centuries B.C.: A Pan-Mediterranean Perspective. In *Italy and Cyprus in Antiquity 1500–450 B.C: Proceedings of an International Symposium held at the Italian Academy for Advanced Studies in America at Columbia University, November 16–18, 2000*, edited by L. Bonfante and V. Karageorghis. Nicosia: Costakis and Leto Severies Foundation, pp. 153–214.

Meyer, J.-W. (1987) Die Silberschale VA 14117—Ägyptisch oder phönizisch? In *Phoenicia and the East Mediterranean in the First Millennium B.C. Proceedings of the Conference held in Leuven from the 14th to the 16th of November 1985*, edited by E. Lipiński. Studia Phoenicia 5. Leuven: Peeters, pp. 167–80.

Negbi, O. (1976) *Canaanite Gods in Metal*. Tel Aviv: Publications of the Institute of Archaeology.

Padró I Parcerisa, J. (1995) *New Egyptian-Type Documents from the Mediterranean Littoral of the Iberian Peninsula before the Roman Conquest*. Barcelona: Université Paul Valéry and Societat catalana d'egiptologia.

Rathje, A. (1991) An Exotic Piece from Vulci: the Egyptian Blue Pyxis in Berlin. In *Stips Votiva. Papers Presented to C.M. Stibbe*, edited by M. Gnade. Amsterdam: Allard Pierson Museum, pp. 171–5.

Redissi, T. (1999) Étude des empreintes de sceaux de Carthage. In *Karthago III*, edited by F. Rakob. Mainz: Phillip von Zabern, pp. 4–92.

Shefton, B. (1988) The Paradise Flower, a 'Court Style' Phoenician Ornament: its history in Cyprus and the Central and Western Mediterranean. In *Proceedings of the Seventh British Museum Classical Colloquium April 1988*, edited by V. Tatton-Brown. London: British Museum, pp. 97–117.

Schmid, S. G. (2001) Neue Luristanbronzen aus Griechenland. *Mitteilungen des Deutschen Archäologischen Insitut. Athenische Abteilung* 116:11–34.

Tait, G. A. D. (1963) The Egyptian relief chalice. *Journal of Egyptian Archaeology* 49:93–139.

Terrace, E. L. B. (1963) Ancient Egyptian jewellery in the Horace L. Mayer collection. *American Journal of Archaeology* 67:267–74.

Tsirkin, J. B. (2001) Canaan. Phoenicia. Sidon. *Aula Orientalis* 19:271–9.

von Bissing, W. (1940) Die Alabastra der hellenistischen und römischen Zeit. *Studi Etruschi* 14:99–146.

Winter, I. (1973) *North Syria in the 1st millennium BC*. Ann Arbor: University Microfilms International.

7 On the Organization of the Phoenician Colonial System in Iberia

Maria Eugenia Aubet

Introduction

Southern Iberia is the area of the western Mediterranean about which most is known during the earliest period of Phoenician colonization (8th–6th centuries BC). Since 1964, almost uninterrupted excavations along the Mediterranean coast of Andalusia, in the bay of Cadiz and, more recently, in Portugal have furnished a substantial quantity of archaeological data (Fig. 7.1). The number of early Phoenician colonies exceeds that of any other region of the central and western Mediterranean. The area lying to the east of the Straits of Gibraltar may serve as an example: there, up to 10 colonial centres have been identified along some 100 km of coastline, that is to say, an average of one Phoenician settlement every 10 km. The best known include Cadiz (ancient *Gadir*), Cerro del Villar (probably *Mainake*), Málaga (ancient *Malaka*), Toscanos, Morro de Mezquitilla, Chorreras, Almuñécar (ancient *Sexi*) and Adra (ancient *Abdera*).

The main features of these settlements are their striking harbour possibilities, their siting on promontories or small islands in the mouth of rivers and the homogeneity of their material

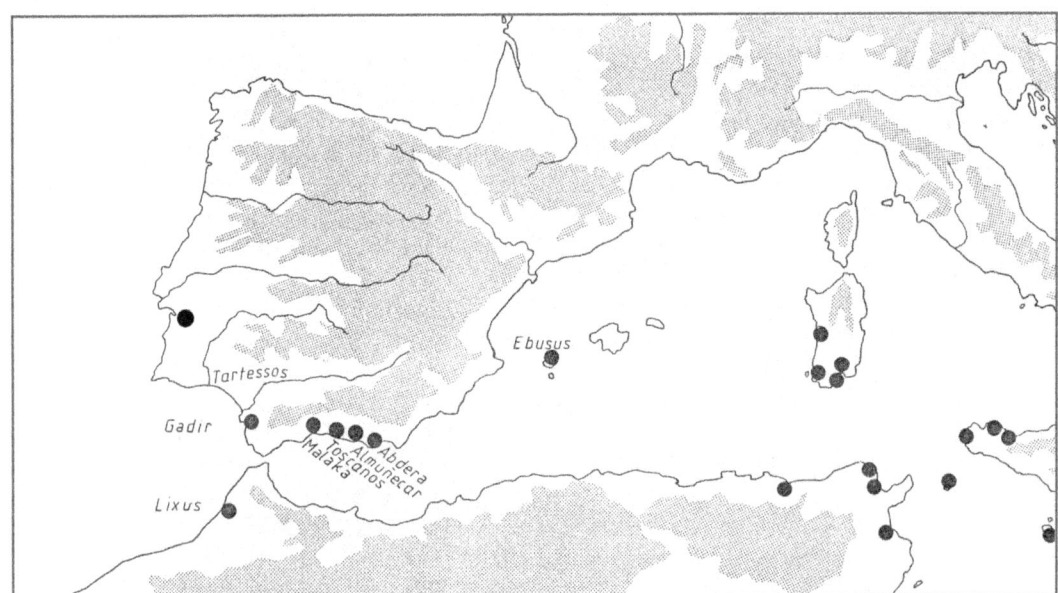

Figure 7.1   The Phoenician colonies in the West.

culture, mortuary practices, ritual and ideology, reflecting the arrival of clearly intrusive populations of Eastern origin.

From the outset, these colonies have yielded very ancient chronologies in comparison with the rest of the western Mediterranean. These chronologies, based on imports of Late-Geometric and Geometric Greek pottery, place the foundation of the earliest settlement (Gadir/Doña Blanca and Morro de Mezquitilla) around 760–750 BC. The application of calibrated radiocarbon dating now places this first colonial horizon at the end of the 9th century BC (Aubet 2001:372–7), and this, together with the downward revision of radiocarbon chronologies on Phoenician sites in the East (Gilboa and Sharon 2001), reduces the chronological distances between the metropolis and its colonies during the first period of expansion westwards.

Colonial models

The huge quantity of archaeological data acquired in southern Iberia made it possible in the 1980s to initiate a theoretical discussion about the nature, function and impact of the Phoenician colonies. One of the advantages offered by southern Iberia is that, at the time when the Phoenician centres began to be identified, the indigenous hinterland, in particular Tartessos and the Atlantic area, had been studied for a long time. Hence, the archaeological research mostly focused on questions such as the colonial impact on the indigenous peripheries and how they interacted, the 'Orientalizing' phenomenon and the mechanisms by which the Tartessian elites and population were manipulated. Moreover, the interaction between colonist and colonized in the area of Cadiz-Tartessos makes it clear that the commercial and political clout of the Phoenician colonies could have been in direct proportion to the degree of socio-economic integration of the indigenous groups in the interior. In Tartessos, 'Orientalizing' was a selective phenomenon which concerned only a minority, the indigenous aristocracy, and a limited area, where strong chiefdoms had existed in the previous Late Bronze Age period (Aubet 1982; Aubet *et al.* 1996; Frankenstein 1997).

Another question that has caught the interest of the researchers has revolved around the category and function of the colonies, analysis of which has come down in the end to a mere question of typology—trade colonies vs. settlement colonies—while the terminology in use, especially that of the French economists of the 19th century—*comptoirs, colonies de commerce, entrepôts, colonies de peuplement, colonies d'exploitation agricole*—has fostered the setting up of excessively rigid models. The tendency has generally been to resort to the classic Greek model within a debate, in which the idea that colonization, settlement, 'Orientalizing' and the occupation of agricultural land were synonymous has been dominant. This attitude, taken from the Greek *apoikia* (Finley 1976:169–78; Whittaker 1974; Boardman 2001:40), not only implies certain prejudices towards the Phoenicians in general, but takes no account of the Levantine and eastern antecedents of the Phoenician colonial expansion, which show a broad and solid tradition of founding trade colonies from at least the second millennium BC (Larsen 1976).

In southern Iberia, the first Phoenician colony in which the question of territory and land-use has been tackled seriously is that of Cerro del Villar, 4 km west from Malaka. The archaeological record, palaeo-botanical and soil analyses, the faunal record and pollen diagrams demonstrate that the inhabitants of the colony restricted themselves to consuming agricultural resources and stock raised by others. During the 8th and 7th centuries BC, not only have no agricultural and stockraising practices been observed in the immediate valley, but the region is little suited to agriculture and very poor in metals, so it is obvious that the objective in founding the colony was not the exploitation and control of the agricultural resources and raw materials of the hinterland (Aubet *et al.* 1999).

Lastly, and connected with the foregoing, the private and/or state origin of these trade emporia has been widely debated (cf. Bondì 1978). This debate tended to consider the concepts of private enterprise and institutional trade as mutually exclusive in the organization of the Phoenician colonial diaspora. The debate probably started from a mistaken approach, ignoring the eastern antecedents of the phenomenon. In reality, in the Near East, the two spheres—private and institutional—did not always act separately in international long-distance trade, so the debate is probably premature and superfluous, as has been demonstrated recently (cf. Bongenaar 2000).

The structure of the colonial system

As long as the concept of colonialism is associated with domination, intrusion, conquest, economic exploitation, oppression and asymetric relations of power, it is logical that analysis of a colonial system should prioritize the study of the forms and relationships of colonial interaction (cf. Finley 1976:167; Dirks 1992:12; Rowlands 1998:327–9). However, and contrary to the usual standpoint, Phoenician colonialism in Iberia has almost always been studied from the point of view of the colonized, that is to say, the Tartessian 'Orientalizing' world and the indigenous communities of the Late Bronze Age.

Overestimation of the indigenous side, which always tends to receive sympathy, has pushed a study of the internal structure of the colonies into the background; analysis has not gone beyond the level of description and taxonomy prevalent in the 1970s and 1980s. The result is that we know very little about the colonizers and the forms of their socio-political organization, despite the fact that the archaeological evidence points to relatively complex intra- and intercolonial relations.

We believe that the time has come to initiate a first approximation to the study of the internal dynamics of the colonies and the way they were organized during the early stages of the 8th and 7th centuries BC. For that we shall turn to the archaeological record of some of the best known colonial settlements, so as to establish a series of archaeological indicators which, in our opinion, may help to define significant features of the socio-political relations both within the colonies and between them.

1. Settlement size and demography

The area occupied by the Phoenician colonies is quite modest. They are generally small settlements with a high density of buildings and dwellings fitted into a relatively regular urban layout. The inhabited area of these centres ranges from the smallest colonies, occupying some 2 ha (Morro de Mezquitilla, Abdera), 2.5 ha (Toscanos) and 3 ha (Chorreras), to the biggest ones covering up to 8 ha (Cerro del Villar) and 10 ha (Gadir) respectively. One of the few colonies extensively excavated (Cerro del Villar/*Mainake*) has a potential capacity to house some 30 large dwellings with a colonial population estimated at 200 inhabitants (Fig. 7.2).

So it is clear that none of the Phoenician colonies attained the dimensions of some of

Figure 7.2 The island of Cerro del Villar, near Málaga (reconstruction).

the Greek colonies, like Himera in Sicily, which, in the 7th century occupied an area of some 80 ha. Consequently we might think that the origin, function and settlement size of the Phoenician colonies are radically different from those of the Greek colonies, with the possible exception of Pithekoussai, where the settlement pattern and commercial character are closer to the Phoenician than the Greek colonial world.

The cemeteries confirm the presence of a relatively limited colonial population in southern Iberia during the 8th–7th centuries. Thus, the two Phoenician cemeteries at Almuñécar, 'Laurita' (c. 730–625 BC) and Puente de Noy (c. 600), have produced a total of 22 early burials, while the monumental necropolis at Trayamar (c. 650–600 BC), associated with the settlement of Morro de Mezquitilla, has produced five chambered tombs containing a total of 12 burials. The remaining known cemeteries—Lagos (Chorreras), Montañez (Cerro del Villar) and Cerro del Mar (Toscanos)—contained even fewer burials.

Rather than cemeteries these are small clusters of burials and if we compare them with the cemeteries of the Punic period (6th–3rd centuries BC), containing hundred or thousands of burials—Jardín, Villaricos, Ibiza—we have to admit that the differences in the Phoenician population between one period and the other are considerable.

2. Domestic architecture

If anything is characteristic of the architecture in the Phoenician colonies it is the extraordinary size of the earliest dwellings and the careful layout of the towns. In Morro de Mezquitilla, the private houses constructed in the earliest occupation levels, from the first half of the 8th century—level B1b—are notable for their huge size and the luxury of the finishes (Fig. 7.3). These are large dwellings, some of them, like building K, as much as 15 m long, with a total of 16 rooms inside (Schubart 1983). Both the uniform orientation of the houses and the arrangement along regularly laid out streets denote considerable planning of the urban space.

The same may be said of Chorreras and Toscanos, which also reflect a rapid growth from the first days of their foundation. In Toscanos, the great concentration of dwellings during the first stages of its existence (strata I-III, 730–700 BC) in the central part of the promontory becomes apparent through the construction of buildings of considerable size—houses A, B and H—arranged along streets at different levels and linked by monumental staircases of ashlars (Niemeyer and Schubart 1968:80–1; Niemeyer and Schubart 1969:26).

In Cerro del Villar too, very big dwellings have been identified in levels of the 8th century BC. Outstanding among them are the ones excavated in sectors 2 and 8, notable for being very complex domestic structures on a rectangular plan and made up of 12 or more rooms, some around a central open courtyard. Their orientation, form and delimitation by more or less regular streets are identical to those of the big dwellings in the earliest phases in Carthage

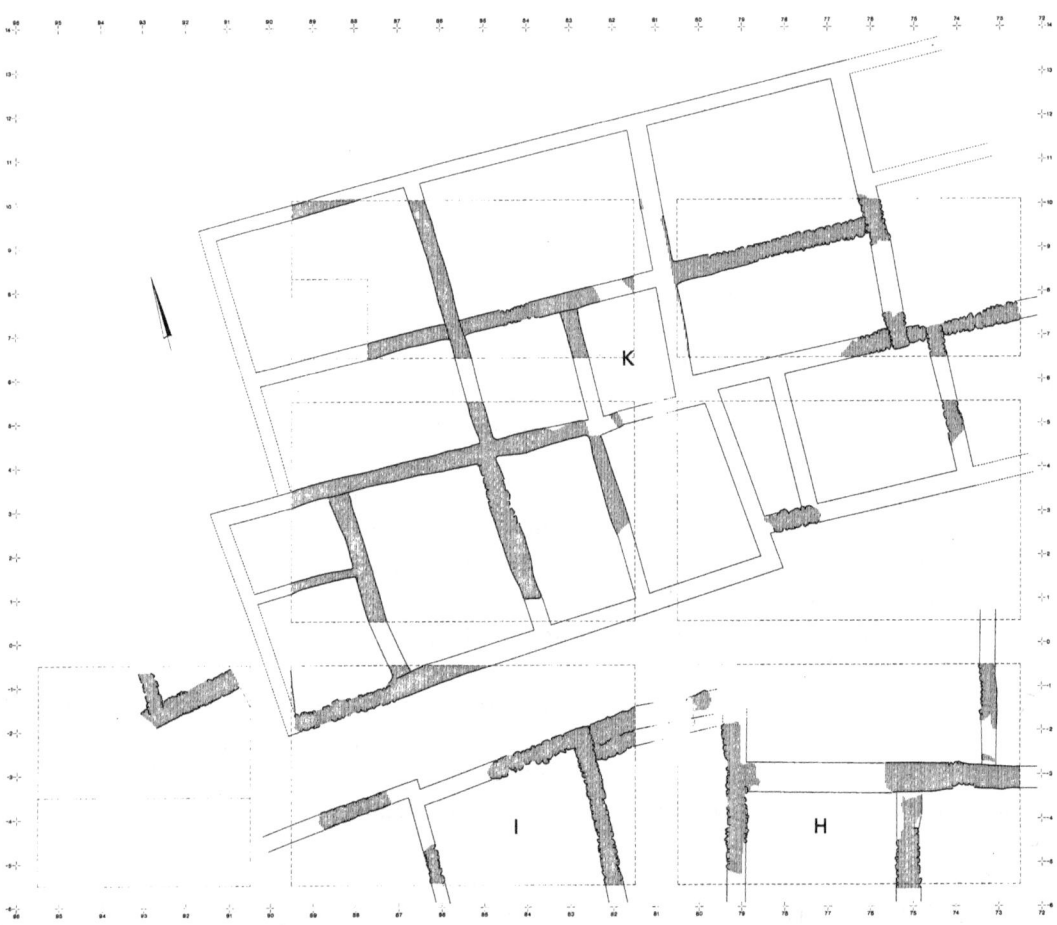

Figure 7.3 Phoenician dwellings at Morro de Mezquitilla (after Schubart).

(Niemeyer and Docter 1993:213; Niemeyer and Docter 1995:488–9) and Motya (Famà 2002:37–40), which would indicate the presence of rich merchants from the very beginning of the colonization.

The mortuary furniture of the Phoenician cemeteries confirms the presence of important elite groups among the first colonists in the West. The Egyptian alabaster urns used as cinerary urns in the cemeteries of Almuñécar, Toscanos and Lagos (Fig. 7.4), and the great monumental burial structures and hypogea in Trayamar, Jardín and Puente de Noy, built in ashlar masonry or cut into the rock, are exceptionally rich in terms of grave goods and labour investment, in comparison with other cemeteries of the same period, like those at Motya, Bithia or Tyre itself (Aubet 2001:329–37). The fact that the colonists of Almuñécar deposited their ashes in alabaster vases with royal inscriptions of the XXII Dynasty—the largest assemblage of Egyptian royal pieces so far found outside the Nile Valley—reveals the presence of some exceedingly acquisitive individuals able to engage technicians and professional architects to build their monumental tombs and dwelling houses.

At the other extreme of the social scale are some very modest dwellings like the ones identified at Toscanos—houses E, F and G (Niemeyer and Schubart 1968:80–1)—which contrast with the luxurious dwellings in the centre of the settlement, and are found in the area of a great storehouse edifice (Niemeyer 1972:20, 1982:199, 1985:117). The presence of a hearth inside house F denotes its domestic nature and both its size and characteristics

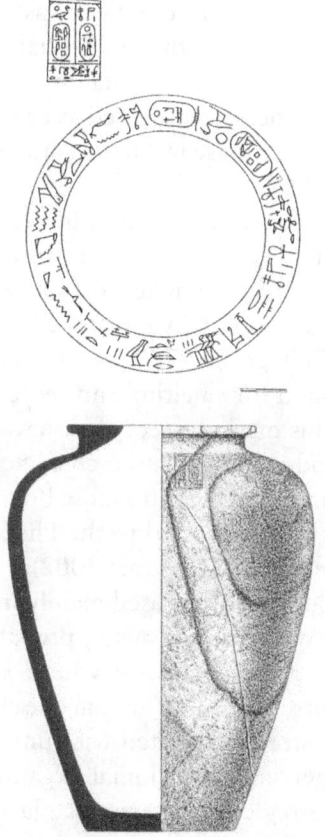

Figure 7.4   Alabaster urn from Almuñecar with inscription of pharaoh Apophis.

suggest that these are very simple dwellings, almost hovels, probably occupied by workers engaged in the activities of the harbour and the warehouse.

3. Public buildings

We still do not know for certain whether any public buildings existed in the Phoenician colonies. And yet some colonies, especially the more important ones, must have had some kind of administrative and management set up, like the ones the classical sources report for Carthage in the Punic period, where mention is made of houses for the senate, law courts and arcaded market buildings (Polybius X:10).

In Iberia, the only colonial building for which a public use has been attributed is the so-called "storehouse" or Building C in Toscanos (Maas-Lindemann and Schubart 1982:5–6; Niemeyer 1972:18–20, 1982:185–96; Schubart 1975:203, 1982:216). This building differs from all the rest in its monumental character and size (14 × 10.75 m), its tripartite plan, the orderly technique of its construction and its central position near the harbour (Fig. 7.5). With two entrances opening onto two streets and probably having two floors, it was built around 700 BC and was in use for almost the whole of the 7th century BC. Inside it, a vast quantity of storage jars and containers was found, amounting to 70% of all the pottery (Maas-Lindemann and Schubart 1982:27–9). There is every indication that the building was planned from the outset as a construction of huge proportions, with a space marked out in advance for depositing merchandise and commodities for export and import. The storehouse at Toscanos has clear parallels in the Near East (cf. Herr 1988), where this type of building with three aisles is associated with commercial and administrative activities of a private nature, concentrating large stocks of merchandise in transit inside it for purposes of speculation. In Al Mina these storehouses also served as centres for dealing and retail trading (Woolley 1953:157–60), like the storehouse in Motya, situated in the harbour area of the city (Isserlin and du Plat Taylor 1974:91).

In the neighbouring colony of Cerro del Villar, a mercantile sector has been discovered, similar to the one in Toscanos. In this case, it is a central street, lined by very large dwellings dating to the end of the 8th century BC, flanked on one side by small arcaded structures open to the street for use as shops, and in which storage jars containing fish and agricultural products were found (Aubet 1997) (Figs. 7.6–7.7). In the back room of one of these businesses a metallurgical workshop was found for smelting and recycling objects of silver, bronze and iron. To judge by the evidence, this market street must have been an important public place for the transit of people and goods; its mercantile character is confirmed by a find of lead weights inside some of the dwellings of merchants close by. Some of the weights are inscribed with Phoenician letters and they all correspond to the Phoenician standard, in particular to that of the southern cities of Tyre and Akko (Aubet 2002).

In the Near East, weights of this type were used mainly in retail trade, based on payments and transactions involving small quantities of metal, probably gold and silver, in which 'to weigh' was synonymous with 'to pay'. The places where weights of this type were usually found were market places, harbours, shops and 'bureaux de change' in palaces and sanctuaries, and so the existence of a market street associated with units of weight and measurement of Oriental origin implied a commercial and colonial organization stable enough to impose its own measuring system in the region. The market place must no doubt have attracted natives from the interior periodically in a deliberate process of integration and/or economic

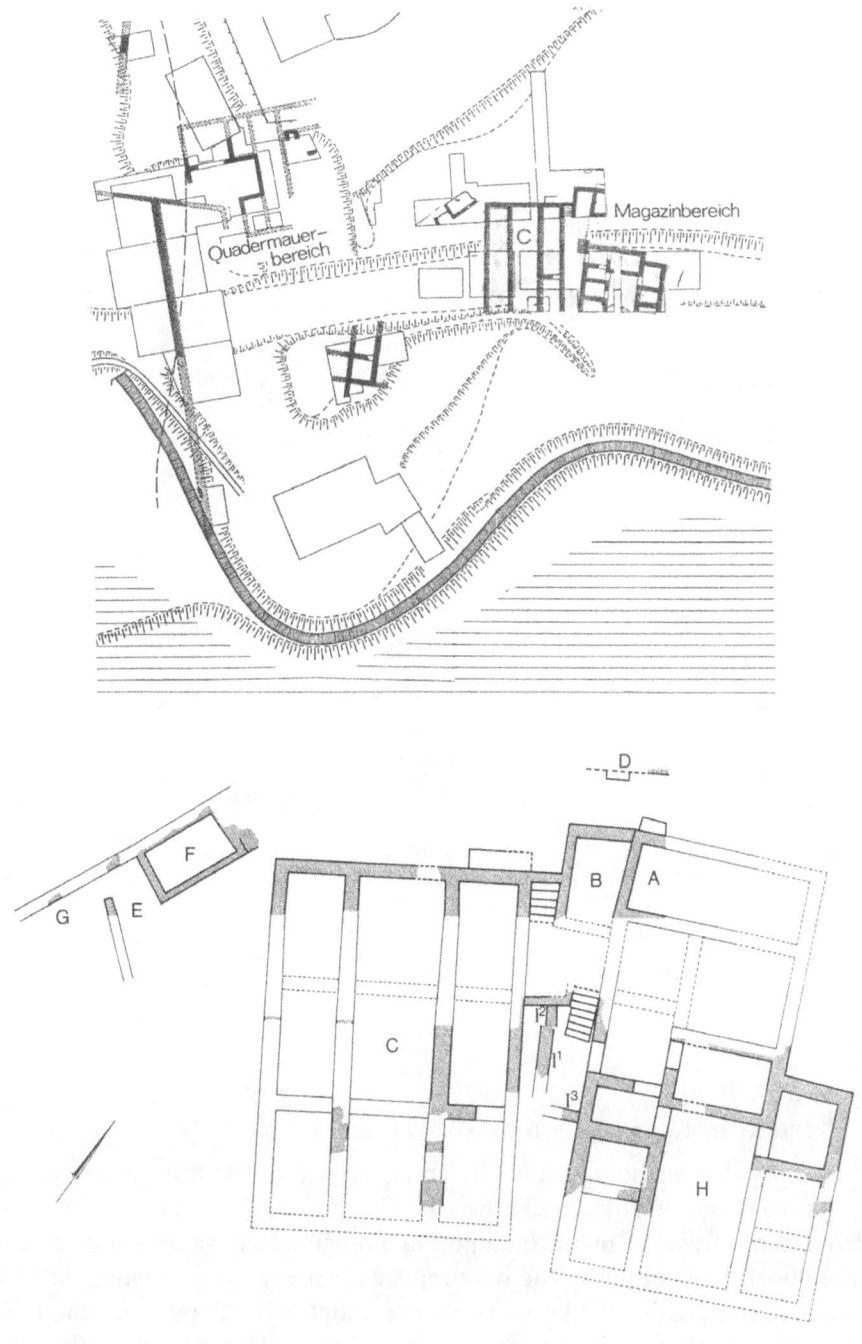

Figure 7.5 The central area at Toscanos and plan of the warehouse.

convergence based on recognition by the indigenous elites of a common system of prices and equivalences. From our point of view, this process may be considered 'Orientalizing'.

Other constructions that might be associated with public use are the harbour installations. They are poorly documented so far and only partial remains of a wharf at Toscanos (Arteaga

Figure 7.6   The market street at Cerro del Villar.

1988) and of a possible anchorage constructed at the end of the 8th century on the south-eastern side of the island of Villar are known.

Apart from Gadir, traces of public buildings of a religious nature have not so far appeared in any of the Phoenician colonies. The only remains that can be associated with temples or sanctuaries come from Gadir. We know very little about this colony, since the modern city is sitting on top of the Roman, Punic and Phoenician cities. Nevertheless, although we have only isolated remains, they reveal the existence in the 8th–7th centuries of monumental cult buildings. Outstanding, among others, is a proto-aeolian stone capital found in the sea to the north-west of the city, where the classical sources place the temple of Baal, as well as a host of bronze ex-votos representing a male individual, found with remains of great ashlars on the island of Sancti Petri, some 18 km south from the centre of Gadir, in the very place where the classical sources locate the famous temple of Melqart (Perdigones 1991; Aubet 2001:269).

Figure 7.7   Cerro del Villar: reconstruction of the market street.

4. Industrial installations and specialized activities

The finding of several kilns for producing pottery in the far north of the island of Cerro del Villar—Sector 9—betrays the presence of a peripheral industrial zone in the early days of occupation of the colony, at the end of the 8th century (Fig. 7.8). From the second half of the 7th century a significant change in the economic activity of the settlement can be observed with a surge in the production, storage and transport of goods; this is reflected in the proliferation of potters' workshops specializing in the standardized production of receptacles for transport and storage (Aubet *et al.* 1999:157–285). Everything indicates that the economy of the centre specialized from then on in trading in manufactured products and products obtained from the periphery—cereals, grapes, fish, wine and olive oil. This economic restructuring, which affected the whole of the bay of Malaga, coincides with an important change in the economic strategy of the indigenous groups in the interior, who were intensifying agricultural activity and trading a large part of the surplus products after the mid-7th century (Aubet 1995). The creation of an agricultural hinterland around Cerro del Villar is thus a late and post-colonial phenomenon, when the ancient colony was transformed at the end of the 7th century into an industrial periphery dependent on neighbouring Malaka.

In Toscanos a similar change is to be seen in the second half of the 7th century, when the habitat was extended to cover an area of 12 ha and its periphery turned to pottery and metal production.

In the earliest occupation levels at Morro de Mezquitilla, in the first half of the 8th century, we see the existence of a district of metallurgical workshops outside the habitat and made up of

Figure 7.8   8th-century pottery kilns at Cerro del Villar.

small blacksmith's forges (Schubart 1998). Most of these kilns predate the construction of the great dwellings of phase B1b, like the big building K, and appear to be associated with dwellings and temporary wooden structures (Schubart 1999:242). The presence of small furnaces for smelting iron in the first level of Phoenician occupation at Morro not only reveals the presence of the earliest centre for iron production known in western Europe, but indicates that one of the primary activities of the Phoenicians on arrival in Iberia, before erecting permanent installations, was small-scale smelting of iron and probably silver as well, in a temporary context appropriate to a harbour or port of call on the shipping route to the Atlantic.

From all this it can be inferred that alongside the major sector of the colonial population, made up of merchant elites living in the big dwellings in Toscanos, Morro, Chorreras and Cerro del Villar and buried in the rich mausoleums of Trayamar and Almuñécar, a sector of society existed devoted both to craft and industrial activities—potters, smelters, architects—and to the retail sale of local products. This sector, relatively modest at first, acquired considerable influence from 650 BC in response to a restructuring of the colonies and the appearance of a centralized trade coordinated from new urban centres—the Punic cities—which gradually replaced the ancient colonies.

Together with these specialists and craftsmen, mention should be made of another social group, associated with the modest dwellings E, F and G in Toscanos (Niemeyer 1985:117). Their location near the great warehouse and close to a pier or jetty reveals the presence of a few families employed in activities connected with the warehouse and the harbour and whose social status—dockers, fishermen, freight transporters—cannot have been very different from that of the crew members of the ships that anchored in the colonies.

Conclusions: specialization and colonial hierarchies

All the archaeological indications suggest the existence of a hierarchy of colonies in the 8th–7th centuries based on two main categories: a majority made up of the trading ports on the Mediterranean coast and another consisting of just one colony, Gadir, which is clearly superior in status. It is undoubtedly an organizational system responding to a trading hierarchy. The main features of this colonial system are:

1. The group of early colonies consisting of Cerro del Villar, Toscanos, Morro, Chorreras and Almuñécar is distinguished by their modest size and by being dominated by elite groups, consisting in all likelihood of associations of merchants and entrepreneurs enjoying a high social status, whose members can be defined as belonging to a specialized mercantile bourgeoisie, very close to political power. Unfortunately their archives and correspondance are not available, not having been preserved. Their establishment in small trading colonies, each one specializing in particular and different economic activities, suggests the possibility that these establishments were originally founded by merchant groupings of firms based on family bonds. That is the only explanation for the unitary character of the archaic cemetery at Almuñécar or the content of the chambered tombs of Trayamar, veritable collective and family pantheons that were reopened periodically to receive some of their members (Niemeyer and Schubart 1975:59–90). In the case of Trayamar we are speaking of some five or six ruling families at the head of the government of the colony during the second half of the 7th century BC. Something similar can be deduced from the 21 burials at Almuñécar, staggered over a period of some 100 years (730–625 BC), which would imply the presence of two or three principal rulers per generation at the head of the colony.

These were merchants who travelled to the West with their sets of weights, settled in places enjoying excellent harbour conditions to serve as a support base for shipping, and developed complementary and specialized activities there. Thus, the colony at Morro, the earliest, is located at the entrance to a small valley with virtually no access to the interior. Apart from the small ironworks of its early days, no specific economic activity is known there other than having served as a place of residence for a wealthy community of merchants who, at a certain point in time, spread out towards neighbouring Chorreras.

The reasons for the choice of Cerro del Villar appears to have been its excellent island and harbour situation, its location at the entrance to the great overland route of the Guadalhorce valley, which linked the coast of Malaga with Tartessos, and its function as a market place for interregional exchange. Profit was not derived from control of local resources but from price fluctuations and differences between the local market area and the markets the goods were destined for. This may be considered also as typical 'Orientalizing'.

The initial economic activity at Toscanos seems to have revolved around its harbour warehouse, a monumental building, which, to judge by its content, served as a repository and display case for goods and probably also as a place for deals and transactions.

In any case, no signs of the existence of buildings or installations devoted to administration or the management of trade are found in any of the colonies, so we must envisage a degree of economic autonomy and local management in the hands of private commercial firms linked in turn to a central colonial administration, which must have been located in Cadiz. Finally, the somewhat irregular spacing of these centres, with some, such as Toscanos, Morro de

Mezquitilla and Chorreras, located within a few kilometers of one another, argues against a centrally determined settlement hierarchy in this area.

2. All we know about Cadiz comes from indirect testimony. It consists of scattered data, but significant in relation to the status of the colony, that of a single, tightly integrated colonial polity. We shall set out below its three chief characteristics:

a) Only Gadir has produced monumental remains belonging to cult buildings, certainly two in the ancient period, both featuring monumental architecture as inferred from the presence of ashlar buildings and stone capitals. Most noteworthy is the famous temple of Melqart, lying at the southern tip of the Cadiz archipelago; its prestige and importance in antiquity relates to one of the mechanisms habitually used in commercial diasporas: the construction of sanctuaries which combined the cults of the natives and the colonists (Kition in Cyprus, Kommos in Crete, Tas-Silg in Malta). In this sense, the temple served simultaneously as guarantor of the 'good intentions' of the colonists, as a representative of the Phoenician state and as a common place where transactions could be effected, coordinated and centralized. It is not by chance that the temple in Cadiz was built in honour of Melqart, the symbol of the monarchy and state of Tyre. As the representative of the Tyrian political institutions, Melqart could sanction trade agreements and political alliances subscribed to by the colonial authorities and the local rulers.

b) Gadir's sphere of influence was enormous and extended over the whole region of Tartessos, with its large scale production of silver during the 8th and 7th centuries. That production required a considerable infrastructure consisting of an extensive maritime and overland trading network to ensure a continuous flow of the metal—the production has been estimated at several tons—from the mines in the interior to the ports of Cadiz and Huelva (Aubet 2001:279–85). For almost 150 years, this activity required a very sophisticated and extensive organization, ranging from the mine, the extraction of the mineral in the mountains, its processing and transformation into ingots to its transport to the coast. Furthermore, it implied the supervision of specialized, perfectly coordinated officials and administration at each of the stages of production—miners, metallurgists, carriers, for the most part natives—and consequently the existence of pacts and agreements with the local elites. From its location and the needs of the market, it is obvious that Gadir had need of a socio-political organization that was much more complex and centralized than that of the colonies along the Mediterranean coast, and both the scope of its commercial traffic and its administrative structures would have demanded the direct involvement of the political institutions of Tyre.

c) Of all the Phoenician colonies in Iberia, only Cadiz shows enough power and capacity to impose its commercial domination overseas. The archaeological evidence and the Gaditanian character of the material culture of a number of secondary colonies founded from the West give a measure of the political and economic power of the government of the colony between 650 and 600 BC (Fig. 7.1). The establishment of fishing installations in Morocco (Mogador) dates from this period, as do riverside warehouses on the coast of Portugal (Abul), centres of transhipment and transit trade in Lixus and Ibiza and probably small trading posts in Oran (Algeria) as well (cf. Gómez Bellard 1990; Mayet and Tavares da Silva 2000; Arruda 1999–2000; Aranegui 2001).

The importance attributed by the classical tradition to Gadir rests on the prestige of its principal institution, the temple of Melqart, which, as the representative and agent of the state of Tyre, was perfectly capable of channelling the aspirations of the metropolis, combining the quest for profit on the part of a free enterprise system, centered in Toscanos or Cerro del Villar, and the political control of the silver and metal trade in the west through the colonial authority and administration in Cadiz. As synonymous with colonialism, 'Orientalizing' in Iberia would mean centralized silver production and deliberate economic integration, and above all, an affair between elites.

References

Aranegui, C. (2001) *Lixus. Colonia fenicia y ciudad púnico-mauritana*. Saguntum 4. Valencia: Universidad de Valencia, Laboratorio de Arqueología.

Arruda, A. M. (1999–2000) *Los fenicios en Portugal: Fenicios y mundo indígena en el centro y sur de Portugal (siglos VIII-VII a.C.)*. Cuadernos de Arqueología Mediterránea 5–6. Barcelona: Laboratorio de Arqueología, Universidad Pompeu Fabra de Barcelona.

Arteaga, O. (1988) Zur phönizischen Hafensituation von Toscanos. In *Forschungen zur Archäologie und Geologie im Raum von Torre del Mar 1983/84*, edited by H. Schubart. Madrider Beiträge 14. Mainz: P. von Zabern, pp. 127–41.

Aubet, M. E. (1982) Zur Problematik des Orientalisierenden Horizontes auf der Iberischen Halbinsel. In *Phönizier im Westen: die Beiträge des Internationalen Symposiums über 'Die Phönizische Expansion im Westlichen Mittelmeerraum' in Köln vom 24. bis 27. April, 1979*, edited by H.G. Niemeyer. Madrider Beiträge 8. Mainz: P. von Zabern, pp. 309–35.

Aubet, M. E. (1995) From trading post to town in the Phoenician-Punic world. In *Social Complexity and the Development of Towns in Iberia from the Copper Age to the Second Centruy AD*, edited by B. Cunliffe and S. Keay. Proceedings of the British Academy 86. Oxford: Oxford University Press, pp. 47–65.

Aubet, M. E. (1997) A Phoenician market place in Southern Spain. In *Ana šadî Labnāni lū allik: Beiträge zu alt Orientalischen und mittelmeerischen Kulturen. Festschrift für Wolfgang Röllig*, edited by B. Pongratz-Leisten, H. Kühne and P. Xella. Vluyn: Neukirchener Verlag Neukirchen, pp. 11–21.

Aubet, M. E. (2001) *The Phoenicians and the West: Politics, Colonies, and Trade*. 2nd edn. Cambridge: Cambridge University Press.

Aubet, M. E. (2002) Notas sobre tres pesas fenicias descubiertas en el Cerro del Villar (Málaga). In *Da Pyrgi a Mozia: studi sull'archeologia del Mediterraneo in memoria di Antonia Ciasca*, edited by M. G. Amadasi Guzzo, M. Liverani and P. Matthiae. Vicino Oriente Quaderno 3/1. Roma: Università di Studi di Roma 'La Sapienza', pp. 29–40.

Aubet, M. E., J. A. Barceló and A. Delgado (1996) Kinship, gender and exchange: the origins of Tartessian aristocracy. In *The Iron Age in the Mediterranean Area: Archaeological materials as Indicator of Social Structure and Organization (with particular reference to the Early Iron Age)*, edited by A. M. Bietti Sestieri and V. Kruta. XIII International Congress of Prehistoric and Protohistoric Sciences, Forlì, Italy, 8/14 September 1996. Colloqium XXIII. Forlì: ABACO, pp. 145–59.

Aubet, M. E., P. Carmona, E. Curiá, A. Delgado and M. Párraga (1999) *Cerro del Villar I. El asentamiento fenicio en la desembocadura del río Guadalhorce y su interacción con el hinterland*. Sevilla: Junta de Andalucia, Consejería de Cultura.

Bongenaar, A. C. V. M. (2000) Introduction. In A. C. V. M. Bongenaar (ed.), *Interdependency of Institutions and Private Entrepreneurs: proceedings of the second MOS Symposium (Leiden 1998)*. Istanbul: Nederlands Historisch-Archaeologische Instituut, Leiden: Nederlands Instituut voor het Nabije Oosten, pp. 1–4.

Boardman, J. (2001) Aspects of 'Colonization'. *Bulletin of the American Schools of Oriental Research* 322:33–42.

Bondì, S. F. (1978) Note sull'economia fenicia: impresa privata e ruolo dello stato. *Egitto e Vicino Oriente* 1:139–49.

Dirks, N. B. (1992) Introduction. In *Colonialism and Culture*, edited by N. B. Dirks. Ann Arbor: University of Michigan Press, pp. 1–25.

Famà, M. L. (2002) *Mozia. Gli scavi nella 'Zona A' dell'abitato*. Bari: Centro Internazionale di Studi Fenici, Punici e Romani di Marsala.

Finley, M. I. (1976) Colonies: an attempt at a typology. *Transactions of the Royal Historical Society* 26:167–88.

Frankenstein, S. (1997) *Arqueologia del colonialismo*. Barcelona: Crítica.

Gilboa, A. and I. Sharon (2001) Early Iron Age radiometric dates from Tel Dor. In H. J. Bruins, I. Carmi and E. Boaretto, Near East Chronology: Archaeology and Environment. *Radiocàrbon* 43(3):1343–351.

Gomez Bellard, C. (1990) *La colonización fenicia de la isla de Ibiza*. Madrid: Ministerio de Cultura.

Herr, L. G. (1988) Tripartite pillared buildings and the market place in Iron Age Palestine. *Bulletin of the American Schools of Oriental Research* 272:47–67.

Isserlin, B. S. J. and J. du Plat Taylor (1974) *Motya. A Phoenician and Carthaginian City in Sicily*. Leiden: Brill.

Larsen, M. T. (1976) *The Old Assyrian City-state and its Colonies*. Copenhagen: Akademisk Forlag.

Maas-Lindemann, G. and H. Schubart (1982) *Toscanos. Die westphönizische Niedrlassung an der Mündung des Río de Vélez. Grabungskampagne 1971*, Madrider Forschungen 6. Berlin: Walter De Gruyter.

Mayet, F. and C. Tavares da Silva (2000) *L'établissement phénicien d'Abul, Portugal: comptoir et sanctuaire*. Paris: E. de Boccard.

Niemeyer, H. G. (1972) Orient im Okzident. Die Phöniker in Spanien. *Mitteilungen der Deutschen Orient-Gesellschaft zu Berlin* 104:5–44.

Niemeyer, H. G. (1982) Die phönizische Niederlassung Toscanos: eine Zwischenbilanz. In *Phönizier im Westen: die Beiträge des Internationalen Symposiums über 'Die Phönizische Expansion im Westlichen Mittelmeerraum' in Köln vom 24. bis 27. April, 1979*, edited by H.G. Niemeyer. Madrider Beiträge 8. Mainz: P. von Zabern, pp. 185–204.

Niemeyer, H. G. (1985) El yacimiento de Toscanos: urbanística y function. *Aula Orientalis* 3:109–26.

Niemeyer, H. G. and R. F. Docter (1993) Die Grabung unter dem Decumanus Maximus von Karthago. *Römische Mitteilungen* 199:201–44.

Niemeyer, H. G. and R. F. Docter (1995) Die Grabung unter dem Decumanus Maximus von Karthago. *Römische Mitteilungen* 202:475–502.

Niemeyer, H. G. and H. Schubart (1968) Toscanos und Trayamar. *Madrider Mitteilungen* 9:76–105.

Niemeyer, H. G. and H. Schubart (1969) *Toscanos. Die altpunische Faktorei an der Mündung des Río de Vélez: Grabungskampagne 1964*. Madrider Forschungen 6. Berlin: Walter de Gruyter.

Niemeyer, H. G. and H. Schubart (1975) *Trayamar: Die phönizischen Kammergräber und die Niederlassung an der Algarrobo-Mündung*. Madrider Beiträge 4. Mainz: P. von Zabern.

Perdigones, L. (1991) Hallazgos recientes en torno al santuario de Melkart en la isla de Sancti-Petri (Cádiz), *Atti del II Congresso Internazionale di Studi Fenici e Punici*. Centro Nazionale delle Ricerche, Roma, pp. 1119–132.

Rowlands, M. (1998) The archaeology of colonialism. In *Social Transformations in Archaeology: Global and Local Perspectives*, edited by K. Kristansen and M. Rowlands. London: Routledge, pp. 327–33.

Schubart, H. (1975) Las excavaciones de Torre del Mar y el panorama arqueológico de las fundaciones fenicias en la costa mediterránea de la Península Ibérica. *Papeles del Laboratorio de Arqueología* 11. Valencia: Universidad de Valencia, pp. 199–206.

Schubart, H. (1982) Phönizische Niederlassungen an der Iberischen Südküste. In *Phönizier im Westen: die Beiträge des Internationalen Symposiums über 'Die Phönizische Expansion im Westlichen Mittelmeerraum' in Köln vom 24. bis 27. April, 1979*, edited by H.G. Niemeyer. Madrider Beiträge 8. Mainz: P. von Zabern, pp. 207–34.

Schubart, H. (1983) Morro de Mezquitilla. Vorbericht über die Grabungskampagne 1982 auf dem Siedlungshügel an der Algarrobo-Mündung. *Madrider Mitteilungen* 24:104–31.

Schubart, H. (1998) Phönizische Eisenschmiede auf dem Morro de Mezquitilla. *Veröffentlichung Joachim Jungius, Universität Hamburg* 87:545–57.

Schubart, H. (1999) La forja fenicia del hierro en el Morro de Mezquitilla. In *La cerámica fenicia en Occidente: centros de producción y áreas de comercio. Actas del I seminario internacional sobre temas fenicios, Guardamar del Segura, 21–24 de noviembre de 1997*, edited by A. González Prats. Alicante: Diputación Provincial, pp. 241–56.

Whittaker, C. R. (1974) The Western Phoenicians: colonisation and assimilation. *Proceedings of the Cambridge Philological Society* 200, n.s. 20:58–79.

Woolley, C. L. (1953) *A Forgotten Kingdom*. London: Parrish.

8 The Orientalizing Period in Etruria: Sophisticated Communities

Corinna Riva

Introduction

Poulsen's art-historical definition of 'Orientalizing' was formulated with Etruscan objects that were being excavated from the second half of the 19th century, and subsequently had a deep-seated influence in shaping the artefactual studies that followed on the style and iconography of Eastern imports and their influence upon 'indigenous' material in Etruria. Since then, scholarship on Orientalizing Etruria has greatly advanced beyond those artefactual studies of the 19th and 20th century.

Yet, today, two key extant intellectual trends are crippling the opportunity for refining our comprehension of the 7th century in Etruria. Firstly, current interpretations of the 'Orientalizing phenomenon' or 'movement' as the assimilation of a 'way of life' by Etruscan elites are the outcome of a significant departure from an art-historical towards a more conceptual approach. Yet, in reality, they still staunchly uphold a superficial, object-oriented notion of the Orientalizing phenomenon which has also hindered the art-historical approach. To be exact, the adoption of a new 'way of life' by Etruscan elites is conceptualized in similar ways to the embracing of stylistic and iconographic motifs on Etruscan and imported objects, and primarily in a diffusionist fashion. A particular lifestyle was selected by the elites via the same means and channels through which particular objects reflecting that very lifestyle were imported from the East. It was subsequently 'transmitted' by the Etruscans themselves to other regions in Central Italy via aristocratic channels of communication such as gift-exchange and search for raw material (Naso 2000c:95–179). The second key problem with current research stems from the first. The 'way of life' approach predicates the prominence of elites in such a totalizing fashion that the Orientalizing phenomenon is seen as exclusively aristocratic exactly because all those elements that characterize it have to do with a 'princely' culture. In its scholarly treatment, Orientalizing Etruria has thus become in all respects a culture of princes or *basileis*. Other concurrent cultural, historical and socio-political events of this period are drawn aside, and often moved forward as more momentous occurrences in the following Archaic period, largely seen as a phase of Hellenic influence over Etruria (Torelli 2000b).

The term 'Orientalizing' indicating a discrete chronological phase in the first millennium BC has recently come under serious scrutiny in scholarship on Mediterranean antiquity. It has been set in a new light by some conceptually (Morris in this volume), and has been reasserted by others both archaeologically and chronologically (Murray 1993). Yet it has also been outright rejected both on the basis of the Orientalist nuances that its semantics imply, and for setting apart the

7th century as the one and only Orientalizing phase in Mediterranean antiquity (respectively, Purcell in this volume and Osborne 1993). By contrast, scholarship on ancient Etruria has not followed suit. Recent trends in research indicate quite the opposite: the so-called Orientalizing phenomenon in Etruria is more popular than ever, and the idea of a discrete chronological phase (750–650 BC) characterized by distinct historical and socio-political developments prompted by contacts with and influence from the Eastern Mediterranean continues to appeal in an ever more vigorous fashion (Naso 2000a; Dore *et al.* 2000).

This paper sets out to fulfil two ambitious aims. Firstly, it aims to take a critical look at current research on the Orientalizing period in Etruria as outlined above. In particular, it will attempt to downplay, if not question, the arguments around kingship that current scholarship supports. Secondly, and more importantly, it aims to see whether we can still speak of an Orientalizing phenomenon or movement in Etruria and if so in what ways this is possible.

Current approaches to the 'Orientalizing phenomenon or movement': funerary symbolism and the diffusion of a culture of princes

In the post-war era, new developments in Etruscan studies contributed to a new conceptualization of the Orientalizing phenomenon. In 1939, Pallottino established a chronological framework still firmly in place today (Pallottino 1939). More importantly, this framework illustrated the undeniable continuity in the material culture of Etruria through time, which provided crucial proof to the autochthony of Villanovans/Etruscans, and ended all controversy on the question of the origins of the Etruscans. This shift required a re-evaluation of a phase of change that could no longer be explained in terms of immigration from the East. In 1965, the entry 'Orientalizing' in the *Encyclopedia of World Art* was published, and it is not by accident that an etruscologist, Pallottino himself, undertook the task. Orientalizing was no longer purely conceived as an artistic expression, a style or an iconography, despite the art-historical forum that Pallottino was entertaining. In his own words, 'the phenomenon can be explained essentially in the light of the development on the waters of the Meditarranean basin of an immense commercial activity fostered by a happy combination of historical and economic circumstances' (Pallottino 1965:784). These circumstances, he perceptively surmised, were largely determined by the taste and demands of an elite, in Etruria, as in Greece, Cyprus, the Levant and the Near East.

Today, scholars of Mediterranean antiquity have widely recognised that during the late phases of the Iron Age intensification of contacts—commercial or otherwise—throughout the Mediterranean basin was not simply a catalyst for the transmission of artistic styles and skills upon the material culture and the societies of single regions (Murray 1993:80–4). The matter of this exchange was also non-material: ideas, religious beliefs, ritual knowledge, literacy, manners and customs, or, in one word, lifestyles (de Polignac 1992; Strøm 1992; Burkert 1992). In Etruria, as in Latium, the Orientalizing phenomenon conceived as assimilation of a way of life by local elites has become an increasingly fertile avenue of research (Cristofani and Martelli 1994; Martelli 1995; Murray 1993:81–101, 1994; Morris 1997; d'Agostino 1999; Dore *et al.* 2000; Ridgway 2000; Naso 2000a, 2000b). This has been mostly examined in the funerary realm of material culture, through artefacts that are found in wealthy graves and that relate to this way of life: banqueting and drinking vessels denoting feasting and wine-drinking;

spits, firedogs, axes, knives and other tools for the preparation and consumption of meat, as well as other ritual equipment, prestige items, and specific objects indicating status—the chariot, the sceptre, the throne. From the late 1960s through the 1970s and later, excavations of non-funerary contexts have shown that this lifestyle was not only simulated to express status and reproduced as funerary ideology. The 7th-century aristocratic house at Ficana in Latium Vetus (Pavolini 1981; Rathje 1983), and the 'palatial' structures or *regiae* of Murlo south of Siena (Phillips 1992; Stopponi 1985:64–8, 74–98), Casale Marittimo in Val di Cecina near Volterra (Esposito 1999; Torelli 1999), and the residential quarters of Acquarossa near Viterbo (Östenberg 1975; Wikander and Roos 1986:40–72), as well as other smaller similar residential centres—Poggio Buco (Bartoloni 1992), Castelnuovo Berardenga (Talocchini 1980), Tuscania (Ricciardi 1982; Gualtier 1990), and now Roselle (Bartoloni and Bocci Pacini 2002)—indicate that a princely life was also practised in domestic contexts whether of a private or public, sacred or secular nature. The rich figurative repertoire applied to the friezes and other architectural decorative elements of these residences testifies to an overt and conscious display of this life (Torelli 1992, 1997:87–121, 2000a; Sassatelli 2000). Scholars have seen wine drinking and banqueting as appropriate customs to this new lifestyle, an expression of a socially exclusive ideology within death and within the *regiae* (in Italy and Etruria: Torelli 1988:57–63; Rathje 1990, 1995; Naso 2000a, 2000b; Cristofani 1995; in Greece: Dentzer 1982:429–52; Morris 1999; in Iberia: Almagro Gorbea 1991; 1996; Ruiz Delgado 1989). Besides wine drinking and banqueting, uses of writing and adoption of particular funerary rituals are further prominent components of this lifestyle and ideology (Cristofani 1975; Bagnasco Gianni 1996:446–52; 1999; Lazzarini 1999:63–6; d'Agostino 1977; 1999). Ultimately, scholars argue, display of specific status symbols and funerary trappings served the purpose of collective self-representation (*Selbstdarstellung*) of the elites as socially defined groups within increasingly larger and politically more complex communities (Naso 2000b).

In all this reasoning, particular attention has been paid to the sophisticated ways in which this aristocratic lifestyle and ideology were manifested. To be sure, the archaeological evidence fully warrants this vision: however closely one may trace a sequence of developments leading up to the end of the 8th century BC, a scenario of rather rapid change in the material culture after the end of the century is unequivocally apparent. In the course of the 7th century, visible transformations on the plateaux of the future coastal urban centres included the appearance of earthen ramparts and new architectural structures such as ashlar stone masonry buildings, as exemplarily seen at Tarquinia (Bonghi-Jovino and Chiaramonte-Treré 1997), but contemporary to these changes is the appearance of 'palatial' structures in various inland locations from southern to northern Etruria, as described above. In funerary contexts, the adoption of new grave types and funerary rituals are contemporary to the appearance of new sets of grave-goods. Cremation is replaced by inhumation as the construction of the grave changes to welcome multiple depositions: the pit and trench graves reserved for single or double depositions gave way to larger trench graves, which, in some cases, were built into architecturally complex structures until they reached monumental dimensions as in Cerveteri and in Tarquinia. As the remains of ritual activities, the grave-goods indicate that funeral performances became complex affairs within the community, as single members of the burying group were being laid in collective burials over successive interments. The monumental *necropoleis* of the south Etruscan coastal centres, particularly Cerveteri and Tarquinia, provide exemplary case studies for these spectacular transformations (for Caere: Colonna 1986:396–423; Prayon

1989:441–9). Yet, recent new discoveries, particularly in northern Etruria, as in the territory of Volterra with Casale Marittimo (Esposito 1999; Bruni 2000) and the area of Valdarno with Pisa (Bruni 2000), are showing an increasingly richer picture of these transformations across Etruria, and one should cautiously take into account the regional variations in the pattern of change, particularly between south Etruria and northern Etruria and the area of the Colline Metallifere. Such variations, however, have more to do with the time-scale over which change took place and the different types of grave structures or rituals adopted over this time-scale, rather than the nature of change itself.

Indeed, the transformations in the material culture of this period are not as abrupt or uniform as one might expect: they occur at different time-scales in different areas. What was rather immediate, as I hope to demonstrate, is a process of political authority becoming visible in death, an attempt at the institutionalization of political power. This was the result of the swift formation of communities as well as cause for the appearance of new and sophisticated forms of material culture in funerary contexts. For instance, the adoption of the burial chamber reserved for multiple depositions took place in the Colline Metallifere in very distinct locations much earlier, and over a longer time span than in south Etruria, possibly under the impetus of contacts with Sardinia where the use of hypogea for collective burials was a widespread and continuous practice since the Bronze Age (Bartoloni 2000:27–9; 2003:57–63; Lo Schiavo 2000). Similar influences from Nuragic Sardinia have also been considered for explaining the slightly later appearance of *tholos* tombs in northern Etruria, namely in the Val d'Arno (Bartoloni 2000:27; 2003:65). Even within the same burial ground, we sometimes witness the use of different types of grave and ritual; one such case is Populonia, an important centre for metallurgy and exceptionally open to the outside world in the Colline Metallifere, where inhumation and cremation coexisted from the 9th century BC, and the collective burial in chamber tombs with both inhumed and cremated individuals appeared side by side with single inhumations in *fossa* graves at the end of the 9th century, in the cemeteries of Granate and Poggio del Molino (Bartoloni 2000, 2003:57–63). Certain traits of the funerary ritual were adopted more slowly and in a more progressive way, or indeed in a very distinct way from one area to another. For example, the 7th-century shift from cremation to inhumation is not at all a linear phenomenon: cremation was practised for the treatment of the body of exceptional deceased individuals well into the late 7th century, both in coastal south Etruria and in smaller inland centres, as in the Molinello *tumulus* at Asciano near Siena (Mangani 1993, 2000). In Cerveteri, the inhumation rite is adopted along with cremation during the 9th century (Pohl 1972). At Tarquinia, the chamber tomb was reserved mainly for single or double burials rather than multiple depositions. At the *necropolis* of Pisa, in the Valdarno, northern Etruria, the recent discovery of a monumental tumulus has shown the complexity of burial ritual adopted there (Bruni 2000). Furthermore, certain combinations of grave-goods occur in certain cemeteries only. The cemeteries in the Colline Metallifere, for example, preserve stronger funerary associations with warfare in the type of the warrior grave (d'Agostino 1999), and this may well indicate a deliberate choice of funerary representation in opposition to an emphasis on mercantile activities in the tomb groups of south Etruria, particularly seen at Cerveteri.

In spite of all these variations within Etruria, however, we notice that what is occurring from the end of the 8th century consistently throughout Etruria is the rapid development of high levels of sophistication in the exploitation of funerary symbolism and the manipulation of the funerary ideology. How are we to explain some complex associations of symbols of power that appear suddenly with little or no precedent? What is the significance of the deposition of chariots and sceptres or axes, in exceptional burials in both south and northern Etruria? Surely, this must be the core of the matter in this Orientalizing phenomenon, yet one which has not yet been fully answered by current research. Assigning certain grave goods the function of symbols of political power is hardly an adequate explanation. We need to ask ourselves where this symbolism originates from in order to understand the nature of political power which these objects communicate. More importantly, we must seek to understand why these symbols of political power were buried with the aristocratic group in the first place. We might be able to work backwards and trace certain symbols in earlier archaeological contexts, without necessarily arguing purely in terms of historical continuity of certain practices. Yet, it is clear that the reasons why recent research has not been able to answer these questions are to be found in the object-oriented and diffusionist perspective to which the lifestyle approach is still shackled.

The complexity of the Orientalizing funerary ideology or way of life is recognized with reference to the Homeric epics on the basis of objects that relate to a whole series of practices—wine drinking, banqueting, gift-exchange—that underlay the aristocratic lifestyle (Ampolo 2000). Yet, consideration of these objects is often restricted to an artefactual analysis, where the original function and/or the prototype of the object being studied whether from a stylistic, iconographic or even functional point of view provide the answer to the value and meaning that the object would have acquired in Etruria (Rathje 1979; 1980; Naso 2000a). Detailed analyses comparing various classes of objects, particularly luxury goods, have created the backdrop against which the elite way of life is investigated. The motif of the paradise flower (Shefton 1989), the architectural features of monumental *tumuli* in South Etruria (Naso 1996), or the bronze fan (Guldlager Bilde 1994) are significant thematic examples of this research: they incorporate careful analysis in comparing the style, iconography or function of the motif or object, but they lack consideration of the local context of use and its significance in this context—whether archaeological, historical, or simply funerary. This remarkable lack of contextualization of the object being analysed means that the architectural features of monumental *tumuli* are carefully studied, but in isolation, with little or no equally careful attention to relating them to the interior of the *tumuli*—the space and the contents of the burial; that objects adorned with the paradise flower are simply classified according to this particular ornament with no attention to any possible relations between them other than the ornament itself; that, similarly, the bronze fan, recognized as a status symbol reserved to female individuals, is significant purely for its association with the Eastern imagery of the fan, and hardly because of some possible significant funerary association or use in their local context. The result is an unrefined view of a rather refined type of material culture: 'the princes invested the surplus of their resources in the purchase of luxury goods in order to imitate the lifestyle in fashion at the courts of Ionia in western Asia Minor and of the Near East, based on opulence and material comfort' (Naso 2000a:122).

Imitation implies a clear diffusionist view: the Orientalizing phenomenon is essentially a process of transmission from the East, and of emulation in the West.

Limiting this diffusionist and object-oriented perspective purely to the borrowing of objects and luxury goods would not make the standpoint adequate. It becomes even more dubious when the argument is extended to ideas, ideological, cultural, and, more importantly, political models, namely monarchic features of political power. The mode in which the transmission of such models is conceptualized is unequivocal and is made explicit in the ultimate compilation of the latest scholarship on Etruria:

> The discovery of imports ... implies direct or indirect trade with the peoples who produced them: contacts were not limited to the exchange of goods, but also comprised ideological and cultural models ... [T]he custom of consuming wine and meat together was transmitted ... from the eastern Mediterranean ... (Naso 2000a:116)

And again:

> Deriving from the centres of the interior ... and the emporia of Syria ... these models brought to the West, via Cyprus, the ideology and the most evident attributes—the luxury goods—of the area, from which the monumental style of the palaces and tombs was also borrowed. (Naso 2000a:122)

The most perplexing and debatable point of this perspective regards forms of political power, namely the ways in which material culture is held to reflect the adoption of the Oriental monarchy: 'Undoubtedly of Oriental origin, perhaps dating to before a period exchanges began with the Greeks, are several Oriental features in the Etruscan culture; one of these can be discerned in vestiges of the archaic connection between kingship and hierogamic practice' (Torelli 2000b:145). And again: 'Another important aspect of the ideology of power lies in its reference to Oriental monarchies: it cannot be denied that the western aristocrats ... were fascinated by them, and this explains the adoption of all the insignia of Oriental power: palace and throne, but also collective tumuli ...' (Gras 2000:20).

These observations would be an easy target for allegations of strong Orientalist undertones, particularly insofar as the concept of Oriental hierocratic dynastic forms is concerned in relation to the formation of modern western identities: this is a theme fully analysed by David Wengrow in this volume. Yet more urgent is to resist the definition of the Orientalizing phenomenon or movement in Etruria purely as a princely culture along with the related diffusion of Oriental monarchic models on the grounds that it ignores the local context of use of the material culture under study. Analysis of the strictly archaeological context of the objects as I have described above, however, is not sufficient. To contextualize the objects and material symbols in their own historico-cultural space also involves an appreciation of the local material culture of earlier periods, together with a careful integration of different types of evidence—not just of an aristocratic nature like the wealthy tomb or the palace.

Questioning the aristocratic model: the visibility of new forms of political power in funerary representation and ritual

As we shift our gaze to the periods immediately preceding the late 8th century, there is no historical break that we can account for in the ways in which a sudden visibility of elites may be noticed. As recent research in prehistory has cogently demonstrated, the final phases of the Late Bronze Age, that is, the second half of the second millennium BC, mark the point in time for a re-organization of the landscape of south and northern Etruria, prefiguring the geographical and spatial arrangement of the future cities (Pacciarelli 2000:98–114). Even before then, settlements that were later abandoned show growing levels of complexities: Luni sul Mignone, San Giovenale, Monte Rovello and Sorgenti della Nova (Negroni Catacchio 1995) in south Etruria (di Gennaro 1986); Bosco Malenchini and Poggio alle Fate (Zanini 1997:81–93),

Livorno-Stagno (Zanini 1997:103–115) near Livorno, the area of Monte Cetona (Cipolloni 1971; de Angelis 1979), and Radicofani (Rossi 1998) in northern Etruria. Economic relations with the wider Mediterranean world and accumulation of wealth are visible at some of these settlements, namely Luni and Monte Rovello (Pacciarelli 2000:103). Others, Sorgenti della Nova and Le Sparne di Poggio Buco, acted as cult centres (Negroni Catacchio 1995; Zanini 1998). Following the abandonment of all these sites for reasons that can only be surmised, and the concurrent occupation of the plateaux of the future urban centres in the course of the final phases of the Late Bronze Age (Pacciarelli 2000: fig. 60), these new centres developed into large settlements (Pacciarelli 2000:128–36) in the course of the 9th century, and this spatial development goes hand in hand with the enlargement of areas designated to funerary use. Here, the swift increase of single burials indicate a larger nucleus, within the community, of individuals being granted a burial rite with a specific funerary characterization: women were offered objects related to spinning and weaving activities, and men were buried with weapons and other equipment of military accoutrement. It is more than likely that new forms of political power emerged at this stage as a result of the need for socio-political organization of these much larger communities. And the locus where this became visible was death, the same ritual space where socio-economic roles as well as isolated forms of prestige had been expressed through material symbols since the final phases of the Late Bronze Age (Pacciarelli 2000:212). Differentiations in the ritual and objects reserved for the deceased are already visible in the 9th but become even more so during the 8th century. The grave now becomes a space for ritual action both for the deceased who is given a more complex funerary representation, and the burying group performing cultic rites around the grave. This is evident at some *necropoleis* like Tarquinia and Vulci (Iaia 1999), and Populonia and Vetulonia in northern Etruria where the contents of some tomb-groups, particularly those that include distinctive goods, reveal multiple levels of ritual performance of which cremation represents only an initial stage of the rite (Iaia 1999:113). It is less visible at other *necropoleis* like Cerveteri (Pohl 1972; Merlino and Mirenda 1990:8–10) where cremation and inhumation rites coexisted and the graves were comparatively poor of grave-goods. This might either reflect a lack of hierarchy and a slow process of socio-political development at Cerveteri (Delpino 1987:22–23; Peroni 1989:505–508) which is unlikely, or a different way of expressing socio-political interaction in death, which might include a fictitious egalitarian form of funerary treatment or, much more simply, indicate that certain groups were buried elsewhere, outside the vicinity of the central settlement, and this is more likely (Carandini 2003:475–6). Yet, it is clear that these communities were constituting themselves around distinct human groups, whether family or otherwise, as spatial analyses of several *necropoleis* have amply demonstrated (Peroni 1989:462–532; 1994:267–78; 1996:478–94; Iaia 1999:121–2; Boiardi and von Eles 2002), and this is a turning point and crucial first fingerprint of the nature of political authority in Etruria. Special sets of grave-goods that the scholarship identifies as 'status symbols' (Naso 2000a:111) marked some tomb groups and created visible differentiations within the burying community as well as within these distinct groups. At the same time, the cremation rite intended as an act of sacrifice conveyed a sacred value to the world of the dead (Peroni 1996:224–6). It is unlikely that any individual, regardless of his/her standing within society, was given this rite, as a simple calculation of the ratio between the likely number of inhabitants at any large Villanovan centre and the number of the buried ones would show (Peroni 1989:429; Mandolesi 1999: fig. 84): the burying groups were already a community within the community, and the privilege to be in the vicinity of the divinity through cremation, as Peroni (1996:224–6) puts it, would not have been granted to anybody. This cultic quality of death and its social exclusivity are both confirmed by the only known votive deposit dated to the first phase of the Iron Age, perhaps to the 9th century BC, at Banditella near Vulci, which included a series of miniaturized biconic urns, the very same urns reserved for the dead (d'Ercole and Trucco 1992; Iaia 1999:113–14).

That all these developments from the final phases of the Late Bronze Age onwards were decisive for changes taking place in the following centuries has now been positively recognized by classical archaeologists and etruscologists alike, and an explosion of Orientalizing elites is looking more and more like an art-historical chimera (Naso 2000a:111; Menichetti 2000a:207; Peroni 2000). Yet, scholars are nevertheless unhesitantly unanimous in attributing a royal or princely character to those few tomb groups characterized by special objects and increasing in number in the course of the 8th century with little or no explanation of how such forms of political authority came about. Warrior graves are the earliest instances of these so-called princely tomb groups: Tomb 871 at Veii Grotta Gramiccia containing a spectacular parade panoply made of thin metal sheet including a helmet with a long crest, a round shield, iron sword and bronze spear as well as other distinctive goods such as a tripod, a wheeled incense burner, and various bronze vessels (Müller Karpe 1974:94, table 24, 5; Strøm 1971:140–1); Tomb 1036 at Veii Casal del Fosso, also containing a full panoply with spear, swords, as well as a bronze axe, an iron 'sceptre' with amber and laminated gold decoration, and a heavy iron club (still unpublished; Colonna 1991:69–82). The contents of Tomb 1036 have led Colonna to define the context as princely without doubt and to link the combination of club, double shield and pectoral to the dress of the Roman *Salii*, a *sodales* group associated to the war-god (Colonna 1991:82). Other well-known examples of warrior graves include the slightly later Tomba del Guerriero at Tarquinia (Hencken 1968:201, 573; Strøm 1971:141–5; Kilian 1977), and Tomb 21 at Castel di Decima (Bedini 1977:287–8; Stary 1981:190; Bartoloni *et al.* 1982:263; the tomb is still unpublished).

That individuals were given a special cultic treatment through cremation, but some individuals were distinguished by the deposition of symbols of political power referring to some sort of authority, whether sacred, social or strictly political, evidently suggests that the grave represented a focus of socio-political action for the community from the Villanovan period onwards. Yet, the formation of elite groups within Iron Age communities was a long-growing process, as I have described, and can in no adequate way account for the appearance of princes in the archaeological record, even less for individuals invested with royal forms of political authority unless we wish to apply these terms, elite, princely and royal, to the material record interchangeably and uncritically. We cannot furthermore systematically apply the term royal to the material record simply because later literary traditions define the Archaic history of Etruria as a royal age (Torelli 1988:57–8; Menichetti 2000a:205). The famous Tomb of the Statues at Ceri, near Cerveteri, dated to around 650 BC, is perhaps the most misunderstood funerary context of all (Colonna and von Hase 1984): the amalgamation of a passage from the *Aeneid* (VII, 177–191) on the royal palace of king Picus with close stylistic parallels of north-Syrian models in the craftsmanship of the statues has led scholars to talk of oriental-style Archaic kingship (Menichetti 2000a:206; Figure 8.1). That the statues carved at the sides of the entrance to the tomb appear to be holding a sceptre-like object and the curved staff, the *lituus*, has been used as a direct argument for calling these two objects regal insignia. This term has subsequently been used to call similar objects found in the foundation deposits of a sacred building on the Civita at Tarquinia, and dated to the first quarter of the 7th century BC (Bonghi Jovino 1987; 2000; Bonghi Jovino and Chiaramonte Trerè 1997:169–79, 217–20; Carandini 2003:457–87). Although 6th-century evidence points to the *lituus* as an emblem of distinction, and later Etruscan iconographic sources do show the *lituus* in the hands of priests and magistrates (Jannot 1993), in no sense can this symbol of power allude to royalty in the 7th century other than in much later Roman accounts on legendary kings (Livy 1.18.7). As a religious instrument, the *lituus* may have later acquired the quality of instrument for the exercise of political authority; yet, to extend this route back to 7th-century burials is, I think, too far-fetched. The same applies to the axe, originally an instrument for sacrifice (Carancini 1984:285; Tassi Scandone 2001:203).

Furthermore, recent hypotheses regarding early ownership of land and the related sociopolitical institutions from family to genos have conceived of the head of the aristocratic group as a *rex* with absolutist powers (Carandini 2003:467–71). This assumption can hardly be warranted, given that these hypotheses are ultimately deriving from the funerary record. If we want to understand the symbolism of political authority in Etruria as expressed in death, we must stick to the symbolic language of death. Any attempt to extrapolate social reality directly from the context of ritual is futile because rituals are mis-statements of reality, and ritual action always bears a disconnection from reality, as anthropological studies have widely demonstrated (Bloch 1989:43). Other, more sociologically oriented studies on the manipulation of reality as a form of power relation, namely Bourdieu (1977:164, 171–83, 195–6) on the notions of *habitus* and misrecognition, have forcefully argued for a self-reproductive system of society's structure

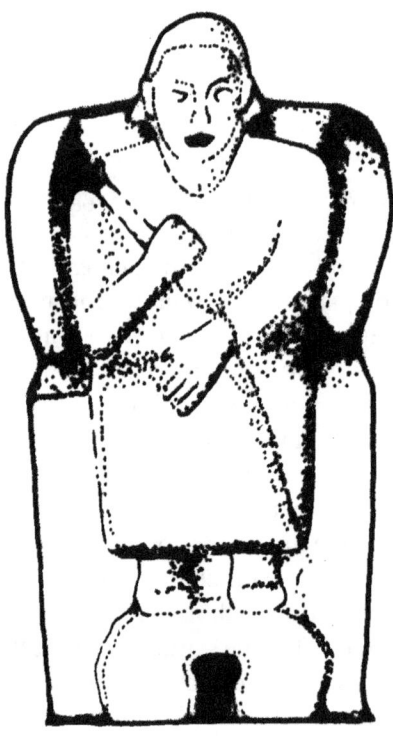
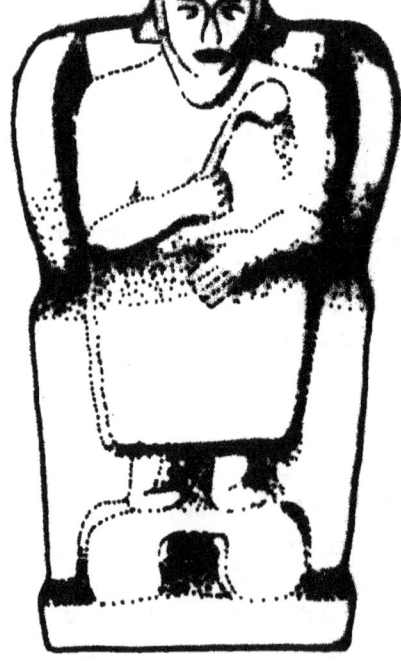

Figure 8.1 Tomba delle Statue, Ceri near Cerveteri.

and its power relations that is acknowledged and recognized by all social groups through the practice of *habitus*. The notion of misrecognition is in this case enlightening: in any specific field or arena for social interaction, social practices are carried out according to the schemes of *habitus*, yet *habitus* itself produces a sense of (false) reality that is naturalized through strategies of power relations by certain groups. Hence, *habitus* is both imposed and imposing. Reality thus produced is not simply forced on the dominated groups, but (mis)recognized as such by those very groups. Misrecognition of reality can thus be institutionally organized and guaranteed through sets of practices and rituals, as seen in practices of gift-exchange and in relations of reciprocity (Bourdieu 1977:171). This process of naturalization of reality through which power relations are euphemized is all the more effective in a field where *habitus* is practised within a ritual sphere as around the tomb.

Other studies specifically devoted to death rituals have noted how the value in examining any funerary record lies in the ways in which the collective consciousness of a society is revealed to us, through an organized collective discourse of death that becomes repetitive and unconscious in the course of time (Vovelle 1990:64–80). During the Villanovan phase, however, at a time of profound socio-political change, a discourse of death was being established by newly formed communities expanding at a fast pace. Similarly, new forms of political authority were just taking shape, and this timely coincidence in the socio-political growth of the community ushered in the world of the dead as an appropriate space, a collective *mise-en-scène*, for the manipulation of ritual symbols underlying new ideas about political authority. Multi-layered rituals thus gave way to complex representation(s) of political authority and reality. Yet it is not the simple deposition of status-symbols that revealed such representation(s), but, more crucially, the funerary associations of these symbols. Nor can we assume that only one way of expressing political authority took place at a time of transition. We must expect the diversity of funerary associations to reflect competing forms of power rather than attempt to draw out a single model of aristocratic power in Etruria. One-dimensional visions of aristocratic power in Etruria are purely the result of the attitudes by Roman authors towards Etruscan elites and their insistence on the polarity *domini-servi* (Colonna 1985). Thus, for example, how would we interpret some early Villanovan cremations at Tarquinia covered by an *impasto* lid in the shape of a helmet, yet relatively poor in grave contents (Hencken 1968:147–343)? Special military connotations were not necessarily associated with distinct grave goods as one would expect from other types of warrior burials. Whether or how such competing forms of power were then materialized within society is another matter and goes beyond the symbolic language I wish to discuss.

Some recent studies have established that material symbols of power found in the grave have a long history of ritual meaning evolving into the 8th century and later. Colonna's analysis of the funerary deposition of double bronze shields from proto-historic to Orientalizing graves is a compelling account of this (Colonna 1991). In this paper, I would like to give the account of yet another, more pervasive symbol, which began being manipulated through a whole range of funerary associations in Villanovan *necropoleis*, and through which funerary discourses of power began taking shape during the 9th century, and crystallized in the 7th century through burgeoning forms of material display: the symbol of the house.

I hope that focus on the house as an element of funerary symbolism will shed a more nuanced light on the contexts and material that the scholarship insists on calling princely.

The house: conceiving political authority in the symbolic language of death

The house, and its related aspects the family and land ownership, have been fully explored in all their socio-political and economic significance, particularly insofar as the nature of socio-political interaction within emerging Etruscan cities is concerned (Carandini 2003:457–87). Yet, there has been a surprising neglect about reading the house as a funerary discourse on political authority. Studies that have come closest to such a reading have laid emphasis on the symbol of the house as expression of a claim to the original *oikos*, hence, to ancestry and genealogy for the family at first, and for the *genos* later on (Menichetti 1988:79–80; Carandini 2003:35–84). I would like to direct attention to some funerary associations that are related to the symbol of the house: some of these have not been noticed by scholars or have been underestimated because they lack explicit or strict reference to the house, such as representations of the door, of the hut and so forth. By drawing these associations out, I hope it will become clear that the house was, in fact, the fulcrum of a discourse on political power in death, and that there was nothing Oriental, royal or princely about it. In fact, the idea of the house as locus of political authority was a distinctly Etruscan trait, and originated from the abrupt formation of large living communities, as I have described above, and the socio-political consequences of this.

Two interrelated features of the funerary record denote the idea of the house not simply as the centre of socio-economic activity and wealth of the group, the family and the *genos*. Rather, they indicate that the house became the symbolic language through which political authority was conceived. These are, firstly, the symbolic integration of the warrior and military leadership within the house, and secondly the integration of female domestic roles within a politically charged framework that was itself ultimately denoted as military. These two features underlie various correlations in the grave that I would like to explore.

The earliest of these correlations pertains to the representation of the hut in some Villanovan burials. Either the cremation urn was itself shaped as a miniature hut, a burial tradition that is likely to have originated in Latium but was contemporaneously adopted in Etruria (Bartoloni *et al.* 1987; Figure 8.2), or the hut was represented on the top of some *impasto* helmets that were the lid of urn vessels reserved for the male deceased as found at Vulci and Veii (Bartoloni *et al.* 1987: table LXI). The representation of the hut as urn was rare, and most cremations were placed in the so-called biconical urn. The biconical urn symbolically replaced the cremated human body, as indicated by the special treatment of several of these vessels that were either decorated with human features, adorned with personal ornaments or dressed in cloth (d'Agostino 1977:57–61; Toms 1992–93; Torelli 1997:27; Iaia 1999:114; Boiardi 2002:22–5). Although it may have acquired different ritual meanings in different areas, the hut-shaped urn was always reserved for a very few individuals, who were buried with distinctive objects, and sometimes military equipment or other items related to the male sphere (Bartoloni *et al.* 1987:223–4). That these hut urn burials were exceptional is confirmed by isolated examples made of precious material, as the laminated bronze hut urn from Vulci dated to the 8th century (D'Atri 1987a:170).

The choice of assigning the hut urn to a specific gender varied from centre to centre. At Vetulonia, for example, the grave-goods in hut-shaped urns were mostly prestige items. Hence, determining the gender of the deceased has proven difficult, yet one particular hut

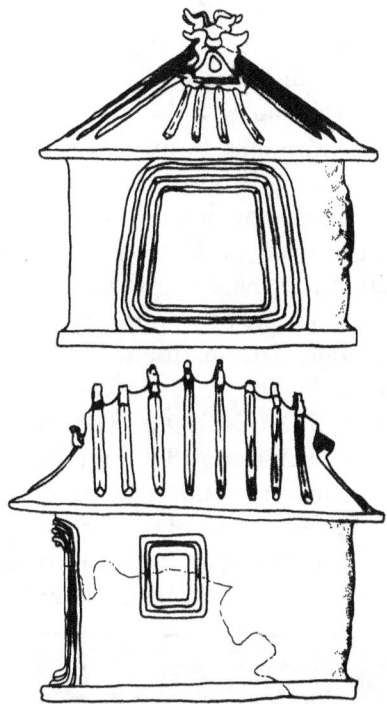

Figure 8.2   Hut-shaped urn, Monterozzi, Arcatelle necropolis, Tarquinia (Scavi comunali 27/II-4/III).

urn burial had been marked by a stone lid in the shape of a shield (Cygielman 1987:151). At Vulci, Vetulonia and Veii, we have examples of double cremations where the male and female deceased were placed, respectively, in the hut-shaped urn and in the biconical urn (D'Atri 1987a:167). Association of the hut urn with male armed individuals is most visible at Tarquinia, where a total of seven hut urns were found (D'Atri 1987b). All the five hut urns with grave-goods at Tarquinia were combined with weapons and/or other male objects such as the razor, an item probably connected to the rite of passage from male youth to warriorhood (Iaia 1999:117), and, sometimes, with a bronze tripod or sacrificial table, which was used for very special funerary rites such as ritual banquets (D'Atri 1987b:174).

That military leadership of these individuals could be designated by the symbol of the house implies that the earliest form of political authority in the community was imagined in death as integration of military supremacy with the domestic realm. The contrast between the more widely spread biconical urn assimilating the human body and the miniaturized hut assimilating the house is significant: it stands between emphasis upon the single member of the burying community, and emphasis upon the embodiment of distinct members with the space that underscores the community itself. This integration endured in the symbolic language of death of the following centuries. Use of hut-shaped urns continued into the 8th century, particularly at Vetulonia (Bartoloni et al. 1987:222). At Veii, a local tradition of *cippi* in the shape of hut roofs developed in the course of the 8th century to mark *fossa* inhumation graves. Widely found in the local cemeteries, these funerary markers could reach up to three meters in length (Buranelli 1987:180). Another local tradition developed at Caere during the second half of the 7th century BC. Here, a small group of red *impasto* cinerary urns reproducing the house with a pitched roof is found in some small chamber tombs at the cemeteries of Bufolareccia, Monte Abatone and Laghetto (Buranelli 1985; Coen 1991). Similar to these urns are some small tufa *sarcophagi* dated to the 8th century coming from Veii, Bisenzio and Tarquinia (Buranelli 1985:56).

By the 7th century, the idea of the house as locus of the warrior's political authority was made more poignantly through burgeoning forms of display, namely in the chamber tomb, a communal space where members of the burying group were inhumed together. From the beginning, the chamber tomb imitated the house in the structural and decorative details of the interior space, as seen most distinctly at Caere (Figure 8.3). In these tombs, despite the widespread use of the inhumation rite some individuals were cremated, and were given the accoutrement of the warrior. It is no coincidence that this occurred in some of the richest and monumental chamber tombs in south Etruria: Tomb 5/Monte Michele (Boitani 1982; 1985; Buranelli 1985:57; Coen 1991:121), and Tomb V/Riserva del Bagno at Veii (unpublished, Bartoloni 1984:21; Boitani 1985:536, n. 2); the Regolini Galassi Tomb at Caere (Pareti 1947:251–82; Colonna and Colonna di Paolo 1997); the Tomb of the Bronze Chariot at Vulci (Emiliozzi 1997: no. 195); the Bernardini Tomb at Praeneste (Camporeale 1967:143; Boitani 1985:551; Coen 1991:121–2), but also in one of the earliest chamber tombs at Tarquinia (Iaia 1999:127, n. 34). In Veii's territory, at Malagrotta, three other wealthy burials dated to 7th century contained a male cremation and female inhumation (Bartoloni 1984:21). In northern

Figure 8.3   Interior space, Tomba degli Animali Dipinti I, Caere.

Etruria, use of the chamber tomb was never fully established, and cremation was widely practised well into the 7th century, except for Populonia where the earliest chamber tombs with circular plan appeared as early as the 9th century (Fedeli 1983:370). Here, the chamber tombs were used for single depositions that were also characterized by military equipment, and only towards the end of the century did they begin to receive multiple depositions (Fedeli 1983:85–6, 2000; Bartoloni 2000). Exceptional male incinerations in bronze urns, however, are found in northern Etruria as well: Tomba del Duce/V (Camporeale 1967:141; Strøm 1971:73, no. S.54, 180; Buranelli 1985:54, 57; Steingräber 1985:285, no. 462) and Circolo dei Lebeti (Falchi and Pernier 1913:429) at Vetulonia, and Circolo della Fibula at Marsiliana d'Albegna (Minto 1921:81, 277; Strøm 1971:192; Bartoloni 1984:14; Buranelli 1985:54; Coen 1991:120–1; Emiliozzi 1997: no. 112). The custom of male incineration in 7th-century burials is also attested in the Faliscan area, at Narce/Falerii (Bartoloni 1984:13; Boitani 1985:536, n. 2, 551, n. 43), and in Campania, at Pontecagnano (d'Agostino 1977; Bartoloni 1984:14). In some instances, the bronze urn was a miniature hut: Tomb 5/Monte Michele at Veii, Circolo della Fibula at Marsiliana, and Tomba del Duce/V at Vetulonia where the hut urn was made of silver. Other isolated examples of bronze laminated house urns dated to the 7th century come from Civita Castellana and from Orvieto (Buranelli 1985:57).

In these chamber tombs, affirmation of political authority in death as indissoluble link between military prowess and the household was incontestable: the warrior was given the ultimate rite in his own funerary house. This symbolic correlation can, however, also be discerned in a distinct class of burials which contained, among the grave-goods, a chariot. The earliest chariot burials are dated to the end of the 8th century, and are found at the Casal del Fosso and Vaccareccia cemeteries of Veii, the Banditella cemetery of Marsiliana d'Albegna, and at the cemeteries of Bologna and Verucchio further inland. Chariot burials grow in number throughout Etruria to reach their peak towards the mid-7th century, attesting to a wider choice of this rite (Emiliozzi 1997:336). The key aspect of these burials is that this special rite was reserved to distinguished individuals, regardless of their gender. This represents a crucial shift in the symbolic language of death, where women had been buried with spinning and weaving equipment throughout the Villanovan period, and had thus been distinguished by their role within the household. Military connotation in death had distinguished male burials only. With the deposition of the chariot, however, female graves, too, were marked by reference to military leadership. Yet, this characterized exceptional members of the burying group only, hence recognition of military status coincided with assertion of political authority for *both* men and women. The inclusion of women in the representation of military leadership may be a consequence of a new focus on the gentilicial group rather than on the single male warrior (d'Agostino 1990:71–5).

That women in Etruria enjoyed a public status outside the private realm of the household is confirmed by the appearance, in later periods, of the matronymic next to the patronymic to mark filiation in inscriptions (Rallo 2000). Furthermore, during the 7th century, evidence related to writing and literacy places women in a prominent position within society as holders of the handicraft of writing that had sacred and religious connotations (Pandolfini and Prosdocimi 1990; Bagnasco Gianni and Cordano 1999:85–106). Chariot burials reveal yet another dimension of women's position in society, namely, a political role that is defined by military status, but is, at the same time, very much linked to the household. In fact, female burials were still denoted by items of domestic equipment. Indeed, the richer the contents of the grave, the more emphasis on the domestic role through the deposition of large quantities of spinning and weaving items. A good example is seen in Tomb 1/San Cerbone at Populonia, dated to the 7th century, which contained 24 spools and 16 spindle whorls (Minto 1934:360). Some female graves were also distinguished by the depositions of particular spinning and weaving objects made in precious or non-functional material such as bone, amber or bronze, as shown by the contents of the female chariot burial Tomb 2/Banditella from Marsiliana (Minto 1921:34–9; Woytowitsch 1978: no. 38; Strøm 1971:191; Emiliozzi 1997: no. 105). Thus, the more powerful was the military status that women enjoyed in death through the deposition of the chariot, the more prominent their domestic role appeared to be within the grave.

All this evidence places emphasis, once again, on the conceptualization, in the symbolic language of death, of political authority as the incorporation of the warrior within the house. In death, political authority as military leadership within the house was also granted to women, holders of the household's insignia *par excellence*.

Other grave-goods that further indicate a woman's political role in death were sceptre-like poles, the fan and the axe. Sceptre-like objects were deposited in female burials between the end of the 8th and the mid-7th centuries BC (Guidi 1993:83, fig. 6.16; von Eles 2002:132). The fan with the handle made of either bronze, ivory or wood was found in both wealthy male and female depositions, most conspicuously in Tomb 89/Lippi at Verucchio (von Eles 2002) and the Tomba del Duce/III at Vetulonia (Camporeale 1967), both of which are male chariot burials. Yet, iconographic evidence associates the fan with women, as seen on the *tintinnabulum* from the Tomba degli Ori in the cemetery of Arsenale Militare at Bologna (Figure 8.4). On the engraved scene of this famous bronze-laminated pendant, the fans are hanging from the wall behind two enthroned women who are occupied with spinning and weaving activities (Morigi Govi 1971; Guldlager Bilde 1994:13).

Axes are mostly found in male burials throughout the Iron Age, and are interpreted as a tool of sacrifice with strong sacred and cultic connotations (Carancini 1984:240–4). They

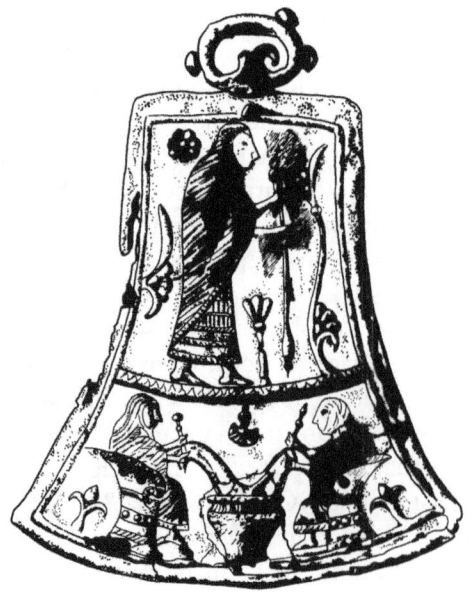

Figure 8.4   *Tintinnabulum*, Tomba degli Ori, Bologna.

are also interpreted as weapons, particularly those that appear to have been functional, but in some wealthy warrior burials they were distinctly ritual objects and highly decorated, as seen in the specimens from Casale Marittimo (Esposito 1999:53, 60). Some of these non-functional axes did start appearing in female depositions as well from the middle of the 7th century at Bologna, and were combined with the so-called votive spatula, which was probably used for collecting the burnt remains of sacrifice (Carancini 1984:242). Carancini (1984:243), however, has noted that funerary associations that concern the axe differed from area to area within Etruria, and this prevents us from making general statements about the association of these axes with female burials.

Despite this difficulty about making secure funerary associations, the evidence discussed so far is reasonably consistent in expressing an idea which we can trace in death from the 9th century onwards, that is, from the time when communities came together on large settlements and this is the embodiment of political authority defined as military status in the house. That women were represented in death as holders of this political authority makes this argument even more compelling since women played a crucial role for the maintenance and successful well-being of the household.

The iconography of political authority: the Verucchio throne

Perhaps the object that most conclusively supports these arguments is the wooden throne with engraved decoration found in the previously mentioned male warrior grave 89/Lippi at Verucchio (Torelli 1997:52–81; von Eles 2002). The burial is a male cremation dated to the middle of the 7th century, and contained the remains of a chariot. The cremated remains were contained in a laminated bronze situla that was wrapped in a cloth, covered by a shield, and placed inside a wooden casket where other personal items of the deceased warrior had been deposited. On top of this casket stood the throne.

The throne is magnificently decorated with engraved scenes set onto two distinct registers (Figure 8.5). The scenes on the upper registers illustrate activities related to the production of wool and textiles, sheep shearing, spinning and weaving in front of houses. In the lower register, three distinct scenes show different activities. Two scenes portray the transport of two figures, one male on the left-hand side, and one female on the right-hand side, both seated on a throne, on a four-wheeled chariot accompanied by other figures: a solemn and ceremonial image (von Eles 2002: figs. 120, 123). The other, much more complex scene is located between these two chariot scenes and depicts a series of human figures, some enthroned at the edges of the scene, some armed wearing a helmet and holding a shield and spear, and two female figures at the centre handling a knife and cutting an unidentified object, above whom are represented flying birds (von Eles 2002: fig. 121). Female figures dominate all of these images. Torelli (1997:52–86) has thus seen the imagery as pertaining to the female sphere and, in particular, to marriage. The chariot scene would represent the ceremonial transport of the bride, and the final complex scene would represent the exchange of marriage gifts: the object that is handled by the two women in the centre would be a piece of textile. He has furthermore suggested that the throne belonged to a woman, and, in particular, the mother of the male deceased, who handed over her symbol of power, the throne, to the descendant. Von Eles (2002:261–3) has rejected Torelli's interpretation, and argued that the object being cut by the two female figures cannot be identified. She has noted the juxtaposition between the two

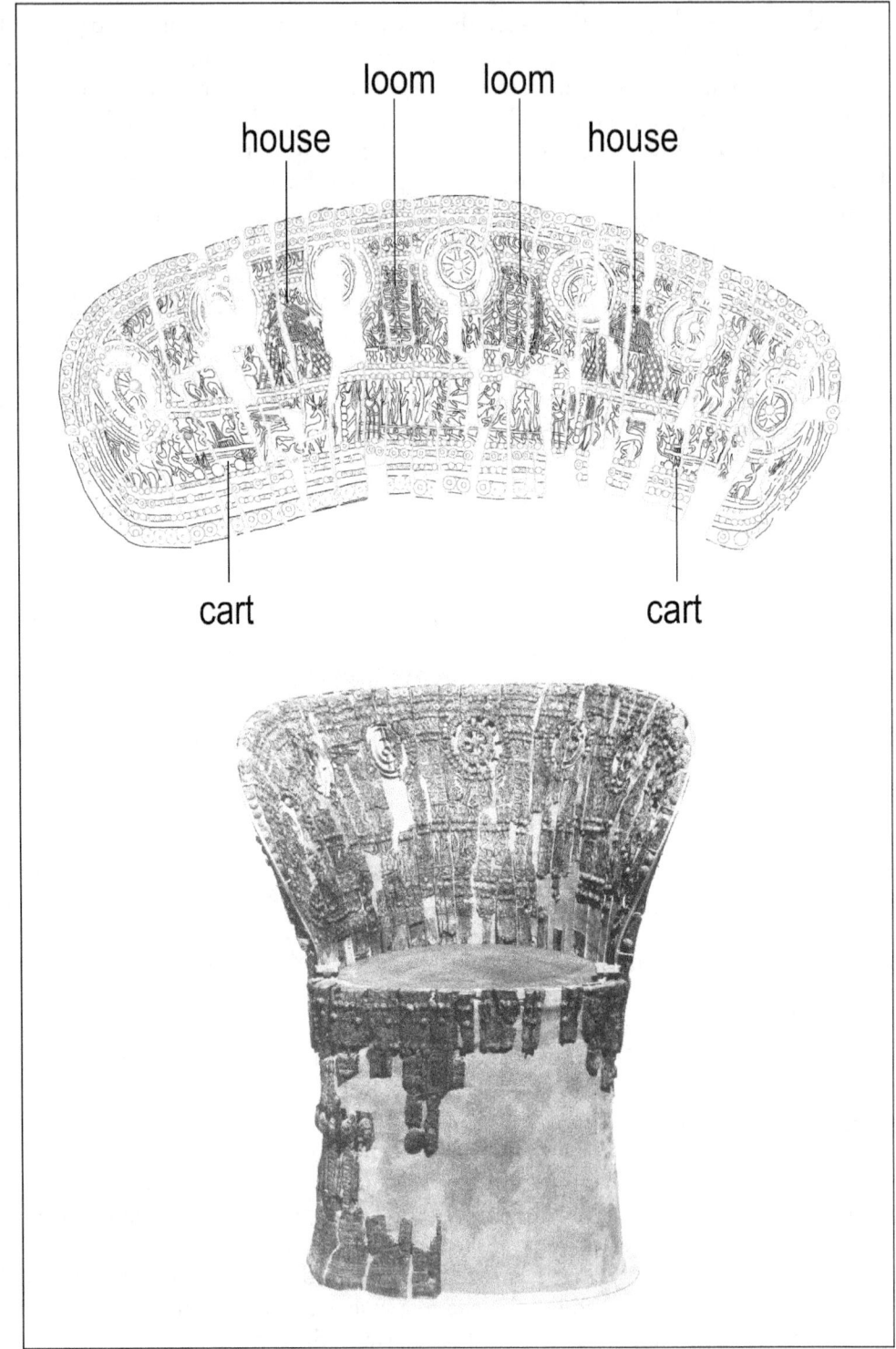

Figure 8.5 Verucchio throne and engraved scenes.

similar chariot scenes that are gender specific. Her suggestion is that this is a very public scene, and perhaps of a ritual nature: the object being cut in the centre may be sacrificial meat, and the images may refer to religious sacrifice (von Eles 2002:264).

Despite disagreement on the identification of objects and figures, two traits of the engraved scenes are nevertheless evident: firstly, the ritual and ceremonial nature of the imagery, and, secondly, the focus on the female world, and, more importantly, on the key role of women in the public sphere. If these aspects enhance the suggestions that I have made regarding the nature of political authority in Etruria, what further corroborates these suggestions is the centrality of the house that is depicted in the upper register of the throne's decoration. Here, on either side of two scenes depicting women sitting in front of gigantic looms are placed two similar scenes representing a house in fine detail (von Eles 2002: figs. 126, 128). By these houses are represented female figures among which are women holding what appears to be a pole, and carrying out activities to do with food preparation such as cereal milling (von Eles 2002:267). The two images of women weaving are emphasized by the exceptionally large size of the loom and of the women themselves. These are no ordinary scenes of daily life; emphasis on the house is achieved through the ritualization of household activities.

The arrangement within the same decorative register of detailed representations of the house and of ritualized domestic activities on a throne that was deposited to be seated upon a warrior chariot burial stands as further convincing evidence of the nature of political authority in Etruria that I have argued for.

The wooden throne stood inside the burial of an exceptional member of the community at Verucchio; the grave-goods indicate that his status may have been susbstantiated by a sacerdotal role, as well as military leadership. Yet, manipulation of funerary symbolism was not an exclusive claim in distinguished and wealthy funerary contexts.

Focus on the house as discourse on political authority in death is also relevant for promoting a more comprehensive view of Orientalizing Etruria through a wider variety of funerary contexts than those upon which the scholarship has concentrated solely for their princely characteristics. Some material and contexts that have been discussed demonstrate this, particularly those burials that show the development of local funerary traditions in the representation of the house: the *cippi* on inhumation graves at Veii, the red *impasto* cinerary urns at Caere, and the small tufa sarcophagi from Veii, Tarquinia and Bisenzio. Although these burials are limited in number, their grave contents disclose similar strategies in the manipulation of funerary symbolism as those found in princely contexts, which scholars would readily define as expression of the Orientalizing phenomenon. This evidence, in other words, suggests that these strategies had nothing to do with princely claims, or with traits about royalty. Rather, they were the expression of a discourse on political authority in death that permeated different social groups within growing communities.

Can we thus still speak of an Orientalizing phenomenon or movement in Etruria?

Sophistication in death ritual: not a princely claim

The material and tomb groups discussed above give us the impression that in the late 8th and 7th centuries in Etruria there is a marked advance of political complexity in newly formed communities within large settlements. This is mostly visible in the death realm of material culture where growing sophistication in the manipulation of symbols and funerary associations represents a way of expressing political authority by distinct social groups within the community. What are we to make of this picture in relation to the so-called Orientalizing movement? Can this picture accommodate the idea of an Orientalizing movement?

The late 8th and 7th centuries were a period of escalating change that had a strong cultural, economic, social and political impact. It is also a period of equally crucial change in other Mediterranean regions, as the papers in this volume demonstrate. Yet, a brief analysis of the evidence from the final phases of the Late Bronze Age onwards in Etruria has highlighted that a fundamental cause of change was the accelerated rate at which communities formed and grew in size. These new communities required a re-organization of increasingly and inevitably more complex socio-political relations within themselves. A result of this was the early appearance of competing forms of political power and the experience of new forms of authority, and this was most visible in the death realm. Yet, as the archaeological evidence shows, these new ways of expressing political authority were not restricted to 'princes', but concerned all the burying groups, who were an elite within the living community. Nor were they restricted to certain individuals within the group: an important shift from the previous phase was the inclusion of women in the display of military leadership which substantiated power relations. Among these groups, strategies for negotiating political authority took various material forms, yet, we can trace a continuity in the use of certain material symbols for expressing these strategies. The use of the house as symbol with all its socio-political and economic implications exemplifies how new, gender-inclusive forms of power could be represented under claims of legitimacy through continuity.

In all this, the only way in which we can retain the phrase of Orientalizing movement or phenomenon for Etruria is that we understand it as the manifestation of funerary sophistication in which objects and symbols, old and new, were being appropriated, used, and given new meanings for new experiences of social and political interaction within dominant groups and society at large. Contact with the world outside gave an impulse to the exploration of untrodden modes of funerary symbolism not simply in the appropriation of imported objects, but, more importantly, in the re-interpretation of unfamiliar objects vis-à-vis a recognized discourse of death. The result was an ever richer collective *mise-en-scène* for the expression of political authority.

Acknowledgments

I am indebted to Robin Osborne for reading my contribution thoroughly and offering interesting comments on earlier versions of the paper. I would like to thank Dr Patrizia von Eles from the Soprintendenza per i Beni Archeologici dell'Emilia Romagna for giving me permission to publish the figure of the Verucchio throne.

References

Almagro Gorbea, M. (1991) El mundo orientalizante en la peninsula iberica. In *Atti del II congresso internazionale di studi fenici e punici*, Roma 9–14 novembre 1987, edited by E. Acquaro, P. Bartoloni, M. T. Francisi, L. I. Manfredi, F. Mazza, G. Montalto, G. Petruccioli, S. Ribichini, G. Scandone and P. Xella. Roma: CNR, pp. 573–99.

Almagro Gorbea, M. (1996) *Ideología y poder en Tartessos y el mundo ibérico*. Madrid: Real Academia de la Historia.

Ampolo, C. (2000) Il mondo omerico e la cultura orientalizzante mediterranea. In *Principi etruschi tra Mediterraneo ed Europa*, edited by A. Dore, M. Marchesi and L. Minarini. Bologna: Museo Civico Archeologico, pp. 27–35.

Bagnasco Gianni G. (1996) *Oggetti iscritti di epoca orientalizzante in Etruria*. Firenze: Leo S. Olschki Editore.

Bagnasco Gianni G. (1999) L'acquisizione della scrittura in Etruria: materiali a confronto per la ricostruzione del quadro storico e culturale. In *Scritture mediterranee tra il IX e il VII secolo a. C.*, edited by G. Bagnasco Gianni and F. Cordano. Milano: Edizioni Et, pp. 85–106.

Bagnasco Gianni, G. and F. Cordano (1999) *Scritture mediterranee tra il IX e il VII secolo a.C.* Milano: Edizioni Et.

Bartoloni, G. (1984) Riti funerari dell'aristocrazia in Etruria e nel Lazio. L'esempio di Veio. *Opus* 3: 13–29.

Bartoloni, G. (1992) Palazzo o tempio? A proposito dell'edificio arcaico di Poggio Buco. *Annali di Archeologia e Storia Antica Istituto Orientale di Napoli* 14:9–33.

Bartoloni, G. (2000) La prima età del ferro a Populonia: le strutture tombali. In *L'architettura funeraria a Populonia tra IX e VI secolo a.C. Atti del Convegno. Castello di Populonia, 30–31 ottobre 1997*, edited by A. Zifferero. Roma: CNR and Università degli studi di Siena, pp. 19–36.

Bartoloni, G. (2003) *Le società dell'Italia primitiva. Lo studio delle necropoli e la nascita delle aristocrazie*. Roma: Carocci Editore.

Bartoloni, G., M. D. Cataldi and F. Zevi (1982) Aspetti dell'ideologia funeraria nella necropoli di Castel di Decima. In *La mort, les morts dans les sociétés anciennes*, edited by G. Gnoli and J. P. Vernant. Cambridge: Cambridge University Press, pp. 256–73.

Bartoloni, G., F. Buranelli, V. D'Atri and A. De Santis (1987) *Le urne a capanna rinvenute in Italia*. Roma: Giorgio Bretschneider.

Bartoloni, G. and P. Bocci Pacini (2002) Roselle: una rilettura dei dati di scavo nell'abitato arcaico. In *Città e territorio in Etruria. Per una definizione di città nell'Etruria settentrionale*, edited by M. Manganelli and E. Pacchiani. Colle di Val d'Elsa: Grafiche Boccacci, pp. 187–212.

Bedini, A. (1977) L'ottavo secolo nel Lazio e l'inizio dell'Orientalizzante antico. Alla luce di recenti scoperte nella necropoli di Castel di Decima. *La Parola del Passato* 32:274–309.

Bloch, M. (1989) *Ritual, History and Power. Selected papers in anthropology*. London: Athlone Press.

Boiardi, A. (2002) La rappresentazione simbolica del defunto. In *Guerriero e sacerdote. Autorità e comunità nell'età del ferro a Verucchio. La Tomba del Trono*, edited by P. von Eles. Firenze: All'insegna del giglio, pp. 22–9.

Boiardi, A. and P. von Eles (2002) I sepolcreti: organizzazione dello spazio e gruppi familiari. Caratteristiche della necropoli Lippi. In *Guerriero e sacerdote. Autorità e comunità nell'età del ferro a Verucchio. La Tomba del Trono*, edited by P. von Eles. Firenze: All'insegna del giglio, pp. 5–12.

Boitani, F. (1982) Veio: nuovi rinvenimenti nella necropoli di Monte Michele. In *Archeologia nella Tuscia I, Primo Incontro di Studio Viterbo 1980*, edited by G. Bonucci Caporali and A. M. Sgubini Moretti. Roma: Istituto di Studi Etruschi ed Italici, CNR, pp. 95–103.

Boitani, F. (1985) Veio: la tomba 'principesca' della necropoli di Monte Michele. *Studi Etruschi* 51 [1983]:535–56.

Bonghi Jovino, A. M. (1987) Gli scavi dell'abitato di Tarquinia e la scoperta dei 'bronzi' in un preliminare inquadramento. In *Tarquinia: ricerche, scavi e prospettive. Atti del Convegno Internazionale di studi, Milano 24–25 giugno 1986*, edited by A. M. Bonghi-Jovino and C. Chiaramonte-Treré. Roma: Edizioni ET, pp. 60–77.

Bonghi Jovino, A. M. (2000) Il complesso 'sacro-istituzionale' di Tarquinia. In *Roma. Romolo, Remo e la fondazione della città*, edited by A. Carandini and R. Cappelli. Milano: Electa, pp. 265–7.

Bonghi-Jovino, A. M. and C. Chiaramonte-Treré (eds.) (1997) *Tarquinia. Testimonianze archeologiche e ricostruzione storica. Scavi sistematici nell'abitato. Campagne 1982–1988*. Roma: L' 'Erma' di Bretschneider.

Bourdieu, P. (1977) *Outline of a Theory of Practice*. Cambridge: Cambridge University Press.
Bruni, S. (2000) L'architettura tombale dell'area costiera dell'area costiera dell'estrema Etruria settentrionale. Appunti per l'Orientalizzante antico e medio. In *L'architettura funeraria a Populonia tra IX e VI secolo a.C. Atti del Convegno. Castello di Populonia, 30–31 ottobre 1997*, edited by A. Zifferero. Roma: CNR and Università degli studi di Siena, pp. 151–72.
Buranelli, F. (1985) *L'urna Calabresi di Cerveteri*. Roma: L' 'Erma' di Bretschneider.
Buranelli, F. (1987) Veio. In *Le urne a capanna rinvenute in Italia*, edited by G. Bartoloni, F. Buranelli, V. D'Atri and A. De Santis. Roma: Giorgio Bretschneider, pp. 177–80.
Burkert, W. (1992) *The Orientalising Revolution. Near Eastern Influence on Greek Culture in the early Archaic Age*. Harvard: Harvard University Press.
Camporeale, G. (1967) *La tomba del Duce*. Firenze: Leo S. Olschki Editore.
Carancini, G. L. (1984) *Le asce nell'Italia continentale*. Prähistorische Bronzefunde IX. München: Beck.
Carandini, A. (2003) *La nascita di Roma. Dei, Lari, eroi e uomini all'alba di una civiltà*. Torino: Einaudi.
Cipolloni, M. (1971) Insediamento 'protovillanoviano' sulla vetta del monte Cetona. *Origini* 5:149–91.
Coen, A. (1991) *Complessi tombali di Cerveteri con urne cinerarie tardo-orientalizzanti*. Firenze: Leo S.Oschki Editore.
Colonna, G. (1985) Le forme ideologiche della città. In *Civiltà degli etruschi*, edited by M. Cristofani. Milano: Electa, pp. 242–89.
Colonna, G. (1986) Urbanistica e architettura. In G. P. Carratelli (ed.), *Rasenna. Storia e civiltà degli etruschi*. Milano: Credito Italiano, pp. 369–530.
Colonna, G. (1991) Gli scudi bilobati dell'Italia centrale e l'ancile dei *Salii*. *Archeologia Classica* XLIII:55–122.
Colonna, G. and F. W. von Hase (1984) Alle origini della statuaria etrusca: la Tomba delle Statue presso Ceri. *Studi Etruschi* 52:13–59.
Colonna, G. and E. Colonna Di Paolo (1997) Il letto vuoto, la distribuzione del corredo e la 'finestra' della Tomba Regolini-Galassi. In *Etrusca et italica. Scritti in ricordo di Massimo Pallottino*, edited by G. Nardi and M. Pandolfini. Roma: Università degli studi di Roma 'La Sapienza' and CNR Istituto per l'Archeologia Etrusco-Italica, pp. 131–68.
Cristofani, M. (1975) Il 'dono' nell'Etruria arcaica. *Parola del Passato* 161:132–52.
Cristofani, M. (1995) Italica, Arte. *Enciclopedia dell'Arte Antica*, Secondo Supplemento 1971–1974, 3:136–47.
Cristofani, M. and M. Martelli (1994) Lo stile del potere e i beni di prestigio. In *Storia di Europa II, Preistoria e antichità*, edited by J. Guilaine and S. Settis. Torino: Giulio Einaudi, pp. 1147–166.
Cygielman, M. (1987) Vetulonia. In *Le urne a capanna rinvenute in Italia*, edited by G. Bartoloni, F. Buranelli, V. D'Atri and A. De Santis. Roma: Giorgio Bretschneider, pp. 147–51.
d'Agostino, B. (1977) Tombe 'principesche' dell'orientalizzante antico da Pontecagnano. *Monumenti Antichi Accademia dei Lincei* 49, Serie Miscellanea, 2, 1:1–110.
d'Agostino, B. (1990) Military organisation and social structure in Archaic Etruria. In *The Greek City from Homer to Alexander*, edited by O. Murray and S. Price. Oxford: Clarendon Press, pp. 59–82.
d'Agostino, B. (1999) I principi dell'Italia centro-tirrenica in epoca Orientalizzante. In *Les princes de la protohstoire et l'émergence de l'état Actes de la table rone internationale organisée par le Centre Jean Bérard et l'École française de Rome, Naples, 27–29 octobre 1994*, edited by P. Ruby. Naples-Rome: Centre Jean Bérard and École Française de Rome, pp. 81–88.
de Angelis, M. C. (1979) Il Bronzo finale in Umbria e Toscana interna. In *Il Bronzo finale in Italia, Atti della XXI riunione scientifica dell'I.I.P.P., Firenze 1977*. Firenze: Istituto Italiano di Preistoria e Protostoria, pp. 221–47.
D'Atri, V. (1987a) Vulci. In *Le Urne a capanna rinvenute in Italia*, edited by G. Bartoloni, F. Buranelli, V. D'Atri and A. De Santis. Roma: Giorgio Bretschneider, pp. 167–71.
D'Atri, V. (1987b) Tarquinia. In *Le Urne a capanna rinvenute in Italia*, edited by G. Bartoloni, F. Buranelli, V. D'Atri and A. De Santis. Roma: Giorgio Bretschneider, pp. 172–6.

Delpino, F. (1987) Etruria e Lazio prima dei Tarquini. Le fasi protostoriche. In *Etruria e Lazio arcaico Atti dell' Incontro di studio (10–11 novembre 1986)*, edited by M. Cristofani. Roma: CNR, pp. 9–36.

Dentzer, J. M. (1982) *Le motif du banquet couché dans le Proche-Orient et le monde grec du VIIe au IVe siècle avant J.-C.* Rome: L' 'Erma' di Bretschneider.

de Polignac, F. (1992) Influence extérieure ou évolution interne? L'innovation cultuelle en Grèce Géométrique et archaïque. In *Greece between East and West: 10th–8th Centuries BC*, edited by G. Kopcke and I. Tokumaru. Mainz: Verlag Phillipp von Zabern, pp. 114–27.

d'Ercole, V. and F. Trucco (1992) Canino (Viterbo), località Banditella. Un luogo di culto all'aperto presso Vulci. *Bollettino di Archeologia*:13–15.

di Gennaro, F. (1986) *Forme di insediamento tra Tevere e Fiora dal Bronzo finale al principio dell'età del ferro*. Firenze: Leo S. Olschki Editore.

Dore, A., M. Marchesi and L. Minarini (eds.) (2000) *Principi etruschi tra Mediterraneo ed Europa*. Bologna: Museo Civico Archeologico.

Emiliozzi, A. (ed.) (1997) *Carri da guerra e principi etruschi. Catalogo della mostra, Viterbo, Palazzo dei Papi, 24 maggio 1997–31 gennaio 1998*. Roma: L' 'Erma' di Bretschneider.

Esposito, A. M. (1999) *Principi guerrieri. La necropoli etrusca di Casale Marittimo*. Milano: Electa.

Falchi, I. and L. Pernier (1913) Vetulonia. Il corcolo del monile d'argento e il circolo dei lebeti di bronzo. *Notizie degli Scavi* 10:425–37.

Fedeli, F. (1983) *Populonia. Storia e territorio*. Firenze: All'insegna del giglio.

Fedeli, F. (2000) Le Tombe a camera della necropoli villanoviana di Poggio del Mulino o del Telegrafo. In *L'architettura funeraria a Populonia tra IX e VI secolo a.C. Atti del Convegno. Castello di Populonia, 30–31 ottobre 1997*, edited by A. Zifferero. Roma: CNR and Università degli studi di Siena, pp. 37–46.

Gras, M. (2000) Il Mediterraneo in età Orientalizzante: merci, approdi, circolazione. In *Principi etruschi tra Mediterraneo ed Europa*, edited by A. Dore, M. Marchesi and L. Minarini. Bologna: Museo Civico Archeologico, pp. 15–26.

Gualtier, F. (1990) À propos de quelques éléments de décor architectural archaïques en terre cuite conservés au Musée du Louvre. In *Die Welt der Etrusker. Internationales Kolloquium 24.-26. Oktober 1988 in Berlin*, edited by H. Heres and M. Kunze. Berlin: Akademie-Verlag, pp. 271–76.

Guidi, A. (1993) *La necropoli veiente dei Quattro Fontanili nel quadro della fase recente della prima età del ferro italiana*. Firenze: Leo S. Olschki Editore.

Guldlager Bilde, P. (1994) Ritual and power: the fan as a sign of rank in Central Italian society. *Analecta Romana Instituti Danici* 22:7–34.

Hencken, H. (1968) *Tarquinia, Villanovans, and early Etruscans*. Cambridge MA: The Peabody Museum.

Iaia, C. (1999) *Simbolismo funerario e ideologia alle origini di una civiltà urbana. Forme rituali nelle sepolture villanoviane a Tarquinia e Vulci, e nel loro entroterra*. Firenze: All'insegna del giglio.

Jannot, J. R. (1993) Insignia potestatis. Les signes du pouvoir dans l'iconographie de Chiusi. In *La civiltà di Chiusi e del suo territorio. Atti del XVII Convegno di studi etruschi ed italici, Chianciano Terme, 28 maggio - 1 giugno 1989*, edited by G. Maetzke and L. T. Perna. Firenze: Leo S. Olschki Editore, pp. 217–37.

Kilian, K. (1977) Das kriegergrab von Tarquinia. *Jahrbuch Deutsche Archäologische Instituts* 92: 24–98.

Lazzarini, M. L. (1999) Questioni relative all'origine dell'alfabeto greco. In *Scritture mediterranee tra il IX e il VII secolo a. C.*, edited by G. Bagnasco Gianni and F. Cordano. Milano: Edizioni Et, pp. 53–66.

Lo Schiavo F. (2000) L'ambiente nuragico. In *L'architettura funeraria a Populonia tra IX e VI secolo a.C. Atti del Convegno. Castello di Populonia, 30–31 ottobre 1997*, edited by A. Zifferero. Roma: CNR and Università degli studi di Siena, pp. 101–22.

Mandolesi A. (1999) *La 'prima' Tarquinia. L'insediamento protostorico sulla Civita e nel territorio circostante*. Firenze: All'insegna del giglio.

Mangani, E. (1993) Diffusione della civiltà chiusina nella valle dell'Ombrone in età arcaica. In *La civiltà di Chiusi e del suo territorio. Atti del XVII Convegno di studi etruschi ed italici, Chianciano Terme, 28 maggio–1 giugno 1989*, edited by G. Maetzke and L. T. Perna. Firenze: Leo S. Olschki Editore, pp. 422–37.

Mangani, E. (2000) Le strutture del tumulo del Molinello. In *L'architettura funeraria a Populonia tra IX e VI secolo a.C. Atti del Convegno. Castello di Populonia, 30–31 ottobre 1997*, edited by A. Zifferero. Roma: CNR and Università degli studi di Siena, pp. 137–50.

Martelli, M. (1995) Circolazione dei beni suntuari e stile del potere nell'Orientalizzante. In *Viaggi e commerci nell'antichità. Atti VII Giornata archeologica*, edited by Bianca Maria Giannattasio. Genova: Facoltà di Lettere, Università di Genova, pp. 9–26.

Menichetti, M. (1988) Le aristocrazie tirreniche: aspetti iconografici. In *Storia di Roma, I, Roma in Italia*, edited by A. Schiavone and A. Momigliano. Torino: Einaudi, pp. 75–124.

Menichetti, M. (2000a) Political forms in the Archaic Period. In *The Etruscans*, edited by M. Torelli. London: Thames and Hudson, pp. 205–25.

Menichetti, M. (2000b) Carello cerimoniale da Bisenzio. In *Roma. Romolo, Remo e la fondazione della città*, edited by A. Carandini and R. Cappelli. Milano: Electa, pp. 228–9.

Merlino, M. and T. Mirenda (1990) La Protostoria. In *Caere e il suo territorio. Da Agylla a Centumcellae*, edited by A. Maffei and F. Nastasi. Roma: Istituto poligrafico e Zecca dello Stato, pp. 4–11.

Minto, A. (1921) *Marsiliana d'Albegna. Le scoperte archeologiche del Principe Don Tommaso Corsini*. Firenze: Istituto di edizioni artistiche.

Minto, A. (1934) Populonia: scoperte archeologiche fortuite dal 1931 al 1934. *Notizie degli Scavi* 1934:351–428.

Morigi Govi, C. (1971) Il tintinnabulo della 'Tomba degli Ori'. *Archeologia Classica* 23:210–35.

Morris, I. (1997) The art of citizenship. In *New Light on a Dark Age. Exploring the Culture of Geometric Greece*, edited by S. Langdon. Columbia and London: University of Missouri Press, pp. 9–43.

Morris, I. (1999) Iron Age Greece and the meanings of 'princely tombs'. In *Les princes de la protohstoire et l'émergence de l'état. Actes de la table ronde internationale organisée par le Centre Jean Bérard et l'École française de Rome, Naples, 27–29 octobre 1994*, edited by P. Ruby. Naples-Rome: Centre Jean Bérard and École Française de Rome, pp. 57–80.

Müller Karpe, H. (1959) *Beiträge zur Chronologie der Urnenfelderzeit nördlich und südlich der Alpen*. Berlin: De Gruyter.

Müller Karpe, H. (1974) *Beiträge zu italienischen und griechischen Bronzefunden*. Präistorische Bronzefunde XX Band 1. München: Beck.

Murray, O. (1993) *Early Greece*. London: Fontana Press.

Murray, O. (1994) Nestor's cup and the origin of the Greek *symposion*. ΑΠΟΙΚΙΑ *I piu' antichi insediamenti greci in occidente: funzioni e modi dell'organizzazione politica e sociale Scritti in onore di Giorgio Buchner. Annali dell'Istituto Orientale di Napoli* n.s. 1:47–54.

Naso, A. (1996) Osservazioni sull'origine dei tumuli monumentali nell'Italia centrale. *Opuscola Romana* 20:69–85.

Naso, A. (2000a) The Etruscan aristocracy in the Orientalizing Period: Culture, economy, relations. In *The Etruscans*, edited by M. Torelli. London: Thames and Hudson, pp. 111–39.

Naso, A. (2000b) Aspetti del tema 'Gesellschaft und Selbstdarstellung'. In *Akten des Kolloquiums zum thema Der Orient und Etrurien. Zum Phänomen des 'Orientalisierens' in westlichen Mittelmerraum (10.-6. Jh. v. Chr.). Tübingen 12.-13. Jun 1997*, edited by F. Prayon and W. Röllig. Pisa and Roma: Istituti Editoriali Poligrafici Internazionali, pp. 227–32.

Naso, A. (2000c) *I Piceni. Storia e archaeologia delle Marche in epoca preromana*. Milano: Longanesi.

Negroni Catacchio, N. (1995) *Sorgenti della Nova. L'abitato del Bronzo Finale*. Firenze: Istituto Italiano di Preistoria e Protostoria

Osborne, R. (1993) À la grecque. *Journal of Mediterranean Archaeology* 6(2):231–6.

Östenberg, C. E. (1975) *Case etrusche di Acquarossa*. Roma: Multigrafica editrice.

Pacciarelli, M. (2000) *Dal villaggio alla città. La svolta protourbana del 1000 a.C. nell'Italia tirrenica*. Firenze: All'insegna del giglio.

Pallottino M. (1939) Sulle facies culturali arcaiche dell'Etruria. *Studi Etruschi* XIII:85–129.
Pallottino M. (1965) Orientalizing style. *Encyclopedia of World Art* X:782–96.
Pandolfini, M. and A.L. Prosdocimi (1990) *Alfabetari e insegnamento della scrittura in Etruria e nell'Italia antica*. Firenze: Leo S. Olschki Editore.
Pareti, L. (1947) *La tomba Regolini-Galassi del Museo Gregoriano Etrusco e la civiltà dell'Italia centrale nel VII sec a C*. Città del Vaticano: Tipografia Poliglotta Vaticana.
Pavolini, C. (1981) Ficana. Edificio sulle pendici di Monte Cugno. *Archeologia Laziale* 4:258–68.
Peroni, R. (1989) *Protostoria dell'Italia continentale. La penisola italiana nelle età del bronzo e del ferro*. Popoli e civiltà dell'Italia antica 9. Roma: Biblioteca di Storia patria.
Peroni, R. (1994) *Introduzione alla protostoria italiana*. Roma-Bari: Editori Laterza.
Peroni, R. (1996) *L'Italia alle soglie della storia*. Roma-Bari: Editori Laterza.
Peroni, R. (2000) Formazione e sviluppi dei centri protourbani medio-tirrenici. In *Roma. Romolo, Remo e la fondazione della città*, edited by A. Carandini and R. Cappelli. Milano: Electa, pp. 26–30.
Phillips Jr., K. M. (1992) *In the hills of Tuscany. Recent excavations at the Etruscan site of Poggio Civitate (Murlo, Siena)*. Philadelphia: University Museum, University of Pennsylvania.
Pohl, I. (1972) *The Iron Age Necropoli of Sorbo at Cerveteri* Skrifter Utgivna av Svenska Institutet i Rom 4; 32. Stockholm: Paul Åströms Forlag.
Prayon, F. (1989) L'architettura funeraria etrusca. La situazione attuale delle ricerche e problemi aperti, In *Atti Secondo Congresso Internazionale Etrusco Firenze 26 maggio–2 giugno 1985 Supplemento di Studi Etruschi*, edited by G. Maetzke. Roma: Giorgio Bretschneider, pp. 441–9.
Rallo, A. (2000) The woman's role. In *The Etruscans*, edited by M. Torelli. London: Thames and Hudson, pp. 131–9.
Rathje, A. (1979) Oriental imports in Etruria in the 8th and 7th centuries BC: their origins and implications. In *Italy before the Romans. The Iron Age, Orientalising and Etruscan periods*, edited by D. Ridgway and F. R. Ridgway. London New York San Francisco: Academic Press, pp. 145–83.
Rathje, A. (1980) Silver relief bowls from Italy. *Analecta Romana Instituti Danici* 9:7–20.
Rathje, A. (1983) A banquet service from the Latin city of Ficana. *Analecta Romana Instituti Danici* 22:7–29.
Rathje, A. (1984) I *keimelia* orientali. *Opus* 3: 341–51.
Rathje, A. (1990) The adoption of the Homeric banquet in Central Italy in the Orientalizing period. In *Sympotica. A symposium on the symposion*, edited by O. Murray. Oxford: Clarendon Press, pp. 279–88.
Rathje, A. (1995) Il banchetto in Italia Centrale: quale stile di vita? In *In vino veritas*, edited by O. Murray and M. Tecusan. London: British School at Rome, pp. 167–75.
Ricciardi, L. (1982) Nota in margine alle terrecotte architettoniche. In *Archeologia nella Tuscia I, Primo Incontro di Studio Viterbo 1980*, edited by G. Bonucci Caporali and A. M. Sgubini Moretti. Roma: CNR Istituto di Studi Etruschi ed Italici, pp. 140–48.
Ridgway, D. (2000) The Orientalizing phenomenon in Campania: sources and manifestations. In *Akten des Kolloquiums zum thema Der Orient und Etrurien. Zum Phänomen des 'Orientalisierens' in westlichen Mittelmerraum (10.-6. Jh. v. Chr.). Tübingen 12.-13. Jun 1997*, edited by F. Prayon and W. Röllig. Pisa and Roma: Istituti Editoriali Poligrafici Internazionali, pp. 233–44.
Rossi, S. (1998) Lo scavo della fortezza. La fase protostorica (XII-X a.C.). In *La citta' fortificata di Radicofani, Siena*. Siena, pp. 149–53.
Ruiz Delgado, M. M. (1989) Las necrópolis tartésicas: prestigio, poder y jerarguías. In *Tartessos: arqueología protohistórica del bajo Guadalquivir*, edited by M. E. Aubet Semmler. Barcelona: Sabadell, pp. 247–85.
Sassatelli G. (2000) Il palazzo. In *Principi etruschi tra Mediterraneo ed Europa*, edited by A. Dore, M. Marchesi and L. Minarini. Bologna: Museo Civico Archeologico, pp. 145–53.
Shefton, B. (1989) The Paradise Flower, a 'Court Style' Phoenician Ornament: its History in Cyprus and the Central and Western Mediterranean. In *Cyprus and the East Mediterranean in the Iron Age. Proceedings of the Seventh British Museum Classical Colloquium, April 1988*, edited by V. Tatton Brown. London: British Museum Publication, pp. 97–117.

Stary, P. F. (1981) *Zur eisenzeitlichen Bewaffnung und Kampfesweise in Mittelitalien (ca. 9. bis 6. Jh. v. Chr.)*. Mainz am Rhein: P. von Zabern.
Steingräber, F. (1985) *Etruskische Möbel*. Roma: Giorgio Bretschneider.
Stopponi, S. (ed.) (1985) *Case e palazzi d'Etruria*. Milano: Electa.
Strøm, I. (1971) *Problems Concerning the Origin and Early Development of the Etruscan Orientalizing Style*. Odense: Odense Universitets Forlag.
Strøm, I. (1992) Evidence from the sanctuaries. In *Greece between East and West: 10th–8th Centuries BC*, edited by G. Kopcke and I. Tokumaru. Mainz. Verlag Phillipp von Zabern, pp. 46–60.
Talocchini, A. (1980) Castelnuovo Berardenga. *Studi Etruschi* 48:550.
Tassi Scandone, E. (2001) *Verghe, scuri e fasci littori in Etruria. Contributi allo studio degli insignia imperii*. Pisa: Istituti editoriali e poligrafici internazionali.
Toms, J. (1992–93) Symbolic expression in Iron Age Tarquinia: the case of the biconical urn. *Hamburger Beiträge zur Archäologie* 19–20:139–61.
Torelli, M. (1988) Le popolazioni dell'Italia antica: società e forme di potere. In *Storia di Roma, I, Roma in Italia*, edited by A. Schiavone and A. Momigliano. Torino: Einaudi, pp. 53–74.
Torelli, M. (1992) I fregi figurati delle regiae latine ed etrusche. Immaginario del potere arcaico. *Ostraka* 1:249–74.
Torelli, M. (1997) *Il rango, il rito e l'immagine. Alle origini della rappresentazione storica romana*. Milano: Electa.
Torelli, M. (1999) I principi guerrieri di Cecina. Qualche osservazione di un visitatore curioso. *Ostraka* 8(1):247–59.
Torelli, M. (2000a) Le regiae etrusche e laziali tra orientalizzante e arcaismo. In *Principi etruschi tra Mediterraneo ed Europa*, edited by A. Dore, M. Marchesi and L. Minarini. Bologna: Museo Civico Archeologico, pp. 67–78.
Torelli, M. (2000b) The Hellenization of Etruria. In *The Etruscans*, edited by M. Torelli. London: Thames and Hudson, pp. 141–55.
von Eles, P. (ed.) (2002) *Guerriero e sacerdote. Autorità e comunita' nell'età del ferro a Verucchio. La Tomba del Trono*. Firenze: All'insegna del giglio.
Vovelle, M. (1990) *Ideologies and Mentalities*. Cambridge: Polity Press.
Wikander, Ö. and P. Roos (1986) *Architettura etrusca nel viterbese. Ricerche svedesi a San Giovenale e Acquarossa, 1956–1986*. Roma: De Luca.
Woytowitsch, E. (1978) *Die Wagen der Bronze- und frühen Eisenzeit in Italien Prähistorische Bronzefunde* XVII. 1. München: C.H. Beck'sche Verlagsbuchhandlung.
Zanini, A. (ed.) (1997) *Dal Bronzo al Ferro. Il II millennio a. C. nella Toscana centro-occidentale, Catalogo della mostra*. Livorno: Comune di Livorno.
Zanini, A. (1998) Evidenze della tarda età del bronzo alla Selva del Gaggio in rapporto con l'abitato protostorico delle Sparne (Pitigliano-GR). In *Preistoria e protostoria in Etruria. Atti del terzo incontro di studi, Manciano Farnese 1995*, edited by N. Negroni Catacchio. Firenze: Octavo, pp. 433–42.

9 The Orientalizing Phenomenon: Hybridity and Material Culture in the Western Mediterranean

Peter van Dommelen

Orientalizing culture

Despite its more prominent stylistic and chronological connotations, Orientalization has long been implicitly understood in terms of culture contact and cultural change. This is particularly obvious in the central and western Mediterranean, where the cultural implications of 'eastern influence' are widely regarded as of fundamental significance for understanding local developments. The Orientalizing phenomenon has accordingly been characterized in explicitly cultural terms as a 'cultural transformation' rather than a mere stylistic influence or a chronological phase (Barker and Rasmussen 1998:117–20). In other words, Orientalization is not regarded as denoting change but as actually *causing* cultural change.

Explicit attempts to conceptualize Orientalization in the western Mediterranean have always remained few and far between. A recurring feature, the significance of which has usually been taken for granted rather than spelled out, is the close relationship between Orientalization and the Greek colonization of southern Italy and Sicily and, to a lesser extent, the Phoenician presence throughout the western Mediterranean basin: the implicit implication is that the (nearby) presence of a supposedly 'higher' culture would inevitably 'rub off' on the less developed Italic tribes. It is surely no coincidence that in regions without a colonial presence such as Etruria, there has always been much attention to the possible influence of travelling Greek craftsmen. The numerous attempts to associate the (semi-) mythical figure of Demaratos with cultural changes in Etruria constitute another telling case in point.

From a theoretical perspective, the assumptions underlying the term Orientalization as commonly used are akin to those of the concept of acculturation. Whilst this particular word has rarely figured in discussions of Orientalization, if indeed at all, direct contacts between Greek or Levantine settlers and traders on the one hand and Italic tribesmen on the other hand have consistently been highlighted as symptomatic of a wider 'meeting' between eastern Mediterranean and Italic cultures. Instead of examining the contact situations in and around the Greek and Phoenician colonial settlements on the Italian mainland or the islands and evaluating these in their own right, however, attention is always focused on the wider and 'higher' cultural encounter. More particularly, Orientalization is generally, if implicitly, presented as a classic instance of culture contact, in which exposure to a 'higher' culture somehow naturally triggers cultural change. This view is entirely consistent with the dominant conception of culture during much of the 20th century (Friedman 1990:14–24; Cusick 1998; cf. Jones 1997:45–51).

In recent decades, there has been much discussion of the theoretical premises and biases of the notions of acculturation and colonialism and of contact situations in general, but little attention has been given in these debates to the Orientalizing phenomenon in the western Mediterranean (Lightfoot 1995; Cusick 1998). It is my intention to explore in this paper whether and, if so, how recent insights regarding situations of culture contact can be used to understand Orientalization. An important feature of these debates is the notion of 'cultural hybridity', which has been a prominent concept in so-called postcolonial studies. In practical terms, I will limit my discussion of Orientalization to the western Mediterranean and in particular to the island of Sardinia.

More specifically, I will first of all turn to the notion of cultural hybridity and consider its theoretical background and recent usage of the term in postcolonial studies. I will then discuss the archaeological relevance of this concept in general with particular reference to classical Sardinia before moving on to the question whether the Orientalizing phenomenon can be understood as a case of cultural hybridity, using Iron Age Sardinia as a concrete case study.

Hybrid cultures and contexts

Hybridity has emerged as a research theme in cultural and postcolonial studies over the past decade. In recent handbooks on postcolonial theory, it is defined somewhat generically as 'the creation of new transcultural forms within the contact zone produced by colonialism' (Ashcroft *et al.* 1998:118) or as involving 'processes of interaction that create new social spaces to which new meanings are given' (Young 2003:79). The main proponent of hybridity is the postcolonial theorist Homi Bhabha who has developed the concept in his discussions of colonialism.

The term 'hybridity' is however much older and carries a laden conceptual background. The term emerged in the mid-19th century in biological and evolutionary debates to indicate a cross between two animal or plant species but it quickly developed into a social and cultural metaphor with heavily racist overtones: it basically came to denote a lack of racial purity (Young 1995:1–89). Because recent postcolonial usage of the term has been very much aware of these connotations and has been at pains to redefine it, there is good reason to accept the claim that these racist connotations have now been superseded (Papastergiadis 1997:257–8).

Ambivalence and subversion

The notion of cultural hybridity has been propagated by Bhabha as a means to break through dualist conceptions of colonial situations in which distinctions between colonizers and colonized are seen to be straightforward and stable. In contrast to the conventional view that the inhabitants of a colonized region are either colonial or indigenous, postcolonial theorists have highlighted the 'in-betweenness' of people and their actions in colonial situations and it explores the mixture of differences and similarities that relates many people to both a colonial and an indigenous background without equating them entirely to either one (Bhabha 1985). In Bhabha's own—and usually rather abstruse—words, cultural hybridity is 'the effect of an ambivalence produced within the rules of recognition of dominating discourses as they articulate the signs of cultural difference' (1985:110). This means that by complying with colonial norms and standards and by simultaneously hanging on to certain indigenous perceptions, people develop new cultural norms of their own and effectively 'invent' new traditions that are peculiar to each specific contact situation. It is important to note that this means that neither colonial norms nor indigenous traditions somehow survive in the new colonial context 'in disguise' but that both give way to an entirely new way of doing things and perceiving meanings and that this 'new way' is peculiar to each specific colonial situation.

As theorised by Bhabha, cultural hybridity is inherently associated with the twin notions of ambivalence and ambiguity, because these are the reason for the in-betweenness of many colonial subjects, who have links with both colonizers and colonized but are yet not fully part of either group. Their ambivalent status roots in the ambiguous gaps and fissures that result from constant negotiations over the differences and similarities between the various communities that make up any given colonial situation. According to Bhabha, ambivalence is a particularly prominent and recurrent phenomenon of modern Western colonialism, because it represents the inevitable consequence of a profound tension between the civilizing mission of the European colonizers and their deeply felt need to maintain a clear distinction between colonizers and colonized. While the ambition to 'civilize the natives' and to transform them to the European image of modern civilization motivated large numbers of missionaries to go out to the colonized areas and to establish schools for literally educating the natives and helping them to meet colonial standards, the conviction of European superiority led colonizers at the same time to insist that 'to be anglicized is *emphatically* not to be English' (Bhabha 1984:87; original emphasis; cf. Young 1990:141–56). As a consequence, no matter how good the education and transformation of the colonized natives were, the best they could do was to become *'almost the same, but not quite'* (Bhabha 1984:86; original emphasis): they would always and invariably remain the colonial Other.

Because Bhabha's views rely heavily on the tension between the civilizing vision of European colonizers and their strong sense of superiority that characterized modern European colonialism, they are not automatically relevant to pre-modern colonial situations. 'In-betweenness' and boundary-crossing are not specifically modern and Western, however, since intermarriage and indeed being born into colonial families as well as indigenous involvement in colonial administration and education inevitably blur the distinctions between colonial and indigenous inhabitants: second or third-generation descendants of colonial families are after all 'native' to the colonized region in a very basic sense and will inevitably develop a perspective on their colonial context that is different from the metropolitan one. I would therefore suggest that ambiguity is not so much an exclusively modern or Western phenomenon, even if European attitudes may have made it more pronounced in modern contexts, but rather one that will occur in most colonial situations in many but various ways. If ambiguity can thus be seen as an inherent feature of colonialism, it follows that hybridization is likely to have occurred in pre-modern colonial situations in one way or another, including those of the ancient Mediterranean (cf. van Dommelen 2002).

The key point that Bhabha makes is that articulating the differences between the original meanings of colonial representations results in their being uprooted and becoming unsettled. Eventually, he claims, the ambivalence of the hybrid actions and representations threatens to undermine the colonizers' discourse and thereby ultimately colonial authority itself. It is through the creation of this 'third space' that hybridity displaces the histories that constitute it in the first place and through which it sets up new and potentially alternative structures of authority. Hybridity is thus potentially both liberating and subversive and can lay the basis for silent resistance (Bhabha 1989).

In the wake of Bhabha's work, postcolonial studies now routinely invoke hybridity as a conceptual tool for implementing the postcolonial critique of dualist concepts of colonialism. In this view, hybridity explains the existence of many ambiguous groups and communities as a consequence of

> the process by which the discourse of the colonial authority attempts to translate the identity of the Other within a singular category, but then fails and produces something else. The interaction between the two cultures proceeds with the illusion of transferable forms and transparent knowledge, but leads increasingly into resistant, opaque and dissonant exchanges. It is in this tension that a 'third space' emerges which can affect forms of political change that go beyond antagonistic binarisms between rulers and ruled. (Papastergiadis 1997:279)

From this point of view, cultural hybridity draws attention to the mixed character of colonial situations, which constitute a metaphorical 'energy field of different forces' out of which hybrid cultures emerge (Papastergiadis 1997:258). These should not simply be understood as the result of a straightforward fusion, reordering or synthesis of a range of features of both colonial and indigenous background but rather as new creations in their own right. As such, hybrid identities represent more than merely 'the sum of the parts' and must be seen as having a unity and coherence in their own right (Nederveen Pieterse 1995:60–3, 2001: 230–9).

Culture and identity

While Bhabha's work may have overcome the racist background of hybridity, current postcolonial usage of the concept has brought to light two other major theoretical flaws. First and foremost among these is the fundamental critique that the notion of cultural hybridity is based on 'the presumption of the existence of once pure cultures' (Friedman 1995:73; 1997:72–7). Such a point of view first of all betrays a nostalgic yearning for a coherent and authentic precolonial past and a lack of historical contextualization (cf. below). Both attitudes underlie and are best illustrated by the common occurrence of stereotypical images of mostly the colonized such as 'the lazy native'. This point of view furthermore suggests that culture is understood in essentialist terms as constituting a well-defined, coherent and autonomous entity.

All this harks back to a well-known but well outdated holistic concept of culture in which cultures flow and mix and people's identities are determined by their culture. This fundamentally flawed notion continues to be surprisingly widely held in postcolonial studies and underlies repeated assertions such as 'the clash of cultures that colonialism invariably provoked ... encouraged the formation of new cultural hybrids' (Papastergiadis 1997:264): as is obvious in this particular phrase, it is cultures and not people who are assumed to be the protagonists of cultural encounters. The actual colonizers and the people who were colonized are thus ignored or at best reduced to passive and weak-willed objects of culture change (Friedman 1995:80–5, 1999:234–6). It is ironic that much postcolonial writing shares the same conceptual ground as the dualist representations it intends to criticise.

The second objection that has repeatedly been held against hybridity is its fluidity and lack of authenticity. Qualifications such as 'multiculturalism lite' and 'superficial spaghetti culture' and the claim that hybridity 'glosses over deep cleavages that exist on the ground' (Nederveen Pieterse 2001:221) are based on this view. Such criticisms result from the exclusive reliance of much postcolonial scholarship on literature and related forms of 'high art' and their concomitant failure to take into account the political and socio-economic contexts of the phenomena observed in those works of art. The much celebrated hybridity of Chris Ofili's art, for example, is no doubt part of cultural life in London but, despite the centrality of ethnicity in his work, one may wonder whether it provides a solid basis for understanding everyday life and racism in South London (Ratnam 1999). This is symptomatic of the general lack of contextualization, both historical and social, that has repeatedly been highlighted as one of the major shortcomings of postcolonial theory in general (cf. Parry 1994).

The allegation of inauthenticity is moreover dependent on an essentialist understanding of culture as discussed above, in which only cultures with 'pure' origins can be authentic (Friedman 1997:82–3). From a constructivist point of view, by contrast, the link between meaning and origins is not an intrinsic one, because '[cultural] forms become separated from existing practices and recombine with new forms in new practices' (Nederveen Pieterse 1995:49). Hybrid cultures are therefore no less authentic to their participants than 'pure' ones (if these exist at all), because the various 'cultural traits' are combined into a new and internally equally coherent culture (Friedman 1999:245–51). There is furthermore good reason to suspect that 'the contrast between hybrid/creole identifications and the essentialisation that is common to lower-class and marginalised populations ... is a contrast in social position', which implies that the distinction between hybrid and pure identities is a false one (Friedman 1997:88).

Hybridization as cultural practice

The basic idea of cultural hybridity as cultural mixture in one way or another is clearly an attractive one and not without relevance to archaeology and other social sciences, but it is equally obvious that it may easily lead into substantial conceptual pitfalls.

These shortcomings can be circumvented to some extent with the associated term 'hybridization', as the active form refers not so much to reified cultures as to the social actors who make up the colonial situation, while retaining the notion of 'mixture'. Social interaction among the inhabitants of colonial situations gives substance and shape to new traditions and 'hybridization' denotes precisely these processes of interaction and negotiation between various social groups. In short, hybridization captures the processes underlying the 'cultural mixture [which] is the effect of the *practice* of mixed origins' (Friedman 1995:84; emphasis added).

Because social actors living in contact situations have the 'transgressive power ... to create the conditions for cultural reflexivity and change' (Werbner 1997:1) and because identities as situated social constructs represent a major feature in ongoing social negotiations, the focus of hybridity must shift culturally predetermined identities towards the active construction of local identities on the ground in contact situations. Since the usually ambiguous meanings and perceptions that emerge from identification processes help to bridge cultural differences and to construct at least temporarily or seemingly stable identities, these local identities represent a primary means for social actors to work out the relationships in new and evolving contact situations (Werbner 1997:16–19; Friedman 1997:88). Ambivalence is thus paradoxically a major factor for strengthening the coherence and authenticity of hybrid cultures.

Instead of taking a 'top-down' view of hybridization, attention must be firmly focused on the local contexts of the contact situation and emphasize the local roots and local interests of at least part of the colonial community, while also acknowledging their extra-regional networks. Such an approach is not only much more in line with another basic tenet of postcolonial theory that calls for 'a conceptual reorientation' towards alternative histories and knowledges, in particular those 'from below' (cf. Young 2003:6). It also realigns the concept of hybridity with current social theory, since Bourdieu's practice theory matches a focus on hybrid practices particularly well. Hybrid practice can therefore be considered as a particularly useful conceptual tool to approach and 'fill in' the so often ignored grey areas that straddle the colonial divide.

On the whole, therefore, it is localized instances of 'hybrid practice' that are key to understanding local contexts as made up by their wider conditions. Since material culture, and the archaeological record by extension, is inevitably and variously implicated in these hybridizing processes and practices, meanings given to and perceptions of objects in these particular contexts must similarly be regarded as hybrid constructs.

Hybrid practices and objects of orientalization

The relevance of postcolonial theory in general and of the notion of hybridity in particular to the archaeology of the ancient Mediterranean follows quite readily from the prominent role of colonialism in the first millennium BC. Precisely because colonial situations became a common feature of many west Mediterranean regions during this period, as numerous colonial settlements were established by Phoenicians, Greeks, Carthaginians and Romans alike, and because Mediterranean-wide commercial contacts had been intensifying ever since the Mycenaean period, people from across the Mediterranean Sea met and mingled and no doubt exchanged many ideas and views alongside their trading goods.

Although Orientalization is not necessarily related to colonialism, the emphasis on cultural change and the indigenous adoption of Oriental elements clearly suggest that the concept may well be understood in terms of hybridization and, in particular, hybrid practices. In order to explore how the foregoing theoretical considerations can guide interpretations of concrete archaeological contexts, I will first focus on a classic colonial situation to consider hybridity from an archaeological point of view before turning to the Orientalizing phenomenon proper. In order to maintain some coherence between the two case studies, both are taken from the island of Sardinia.

The Mediterranean island of Sardinia provides a good case study for studying the theme of hybridization, because the island has long been intensively involved in long-distance exchange contacts and, from the first millennium BC, experienced a long series of colonial exploits and occupations (van Dommelen 1998:11–13). The Sardinians of the 'Nuragic' Bronze Age period maintained regular contacts with the eastern Mediterranean, Cyprus in particular, from at least the late Bronze Age (13th century BC). Their descendants subsequently saw the establishment of a series of permanent Phoenician settlements on the southern and western shores of the island (later 8th century BC), at a time when indigenous society was already undergoing significant social changes. This period (9th to 6th centuries BC) is conventionally referred to as the Nuragic Iron Age and includes an Orientalizing phase (later 8th–7th century). In the later 6th century BC, the erstwhile Phoenician colony of Carthage took over the Phoenician coastal settlements and gradually expanded its rule into the interior regions of the island, introducing Punic culture to the furthest reaches of the southern Sardinian countryside.

Hybridization in Punic Sardinia

The Carthaginian occupation of southern Sardinia represents a classic colonial situation, in which the North African city held sway over southern Sardinia in both economic and political terms. According to ancient literary sources, Carthaginian power was established in the central decades of the 6th century BC with extensive military force. Fierce local resistance, however, allegedly led to the defeat of the first military expedition and although a second campaign some time later was eventually successful, the Carthaginians still suffered heavy losses, loosing one of their commanders-in-chief on the battlefield. By the end of the 6th century, Carthaginian rule appears nevertheless to have been firmly established in the southern regions of Sardinia (Figure 9.1).

From an archaeological point of view, the Carthaginian occupation can readily be recognized in the archaeological record, as new types of pottery, houses and burials of an exclusively Punic, i.e. colonial, appearance replaced the indigenous Sardinian material culture of Bronze and Iron Age traditions. Large-scale adoption of Punic material culture in the countryside of southern Sardinia from the later 5th century BC has accordingly usually been interpreted as signalling the disappearance of the indigenous Nuragic inhabitants from these regions. It is mostly assumed that they either lost their cultural identity by becoming Punic or were forced out of southern Sardinia altogether and replaced by Punic immigrants from North Africa. In short, the combined archaeological and historical evidence has been interpreted as demonstrating both the profound impact of Carthaginian colonial domination and the fierce but eventually futile resistance of the indigenous Sardinians. Domination, exploitation and resistance are thus the key notions of the conventional representation of Punic Sardinia.

Detailed scrutiny of the archaeological evidence now available suggests however that the Punic appearance of the archaeological record for the 5th to 3rd centuries BC was less exclusive than it would seem. Many of the rural settlements in the interior regions have for instance been noted as being closely associated with indigenous settlements, in most cases *nuraghi*, the prehistoric Bronze Age tower settlements of Sardinia. At the same time, however, all portable material culture used in these settlements was unmistakably Punic in appearance (van Dommelen 1998:129–51).

An even more complex mixture of cultural elements of variable provenance is provided by a series of modest rural shrines that have been attested in the western areas of southern Sardinia. While the Greek goddess Demeter would appear to have been the focus of worship at these sites, the Punic characteristics of the rituals performed clearly demonstrate the Carthaginian origins of the cult practices. The recurrent presence of incense-burners in various shapes, including that of the conventional Demeter *kernophoros*, silver ears of grain and animal and food remains indicate that this rural cult included most of the Greek and Punic characteristics of Demeter worship. This is of course entirely fitting in the colonial context, as we can safely assume that this cult was introduced via the colonial connections of these Sardinian regions with Carthage, where the Demeter cult was officially inaugurated in 396 BC and a number of Punic features were incorporated alongside the conventional Greek traditions (Lancel 1995:345–6).

A far more unusual aspect of the Sardinian cult, however, was the location of the shrines in abandoned *nuraghi* and the presence of large numbers of oil-lamps that no doubt had been offered to the goddess to be lit in her honour. These elements are significant, because they can both be traced back to the precolonial Iron Age; *nuraghi* had become prominent symbols of power by the Iron Age, both as places of worship and as the object of worship (Tronchetti 1991; Blake 1997), and oil-lamps have been noted as a recurrent feature of certain Nuragic Iron Age rituals. *Nuraghi* were in fact reused in the Iron Age for a wide range of functions, and housed other kind of rituals as well, as is best shown by the *nuraghe*-shaped altar that was installed in the main tower of *nuraghe* Su Mulinu of Villanovafranca (Ugas and Paderi 1990).

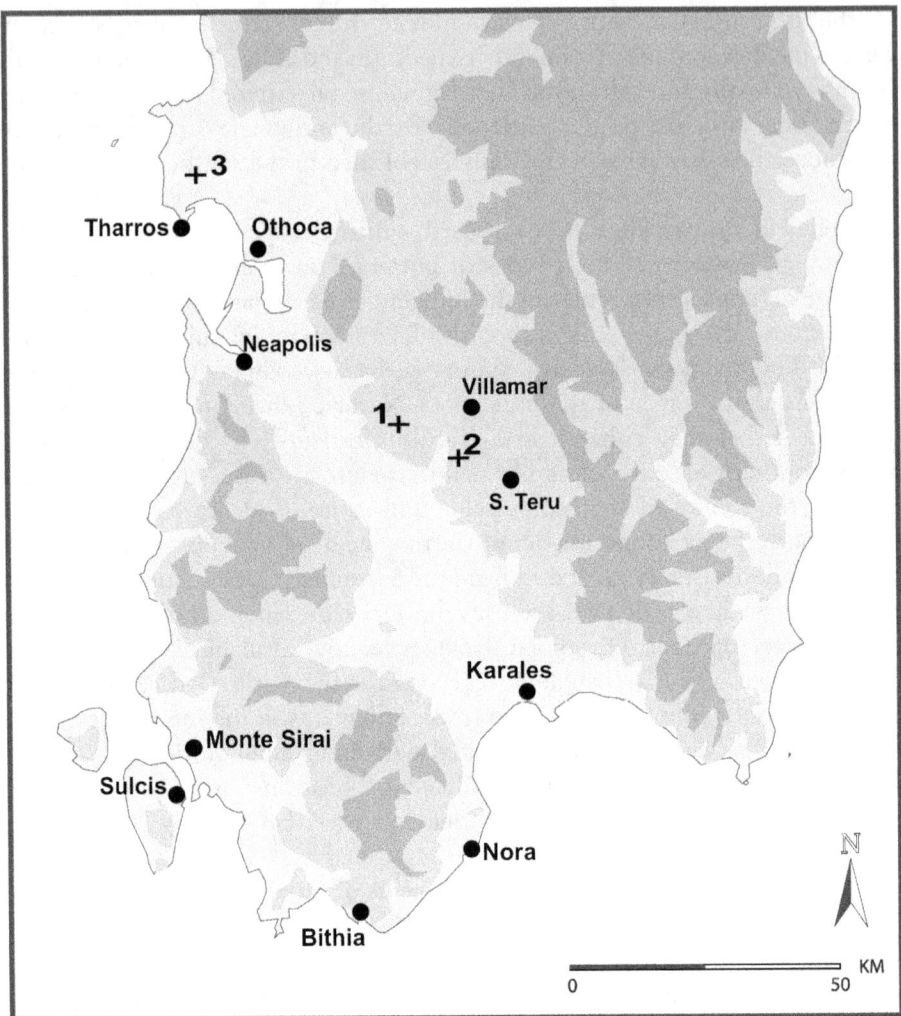

Figure 9.1 Map of southern Sardinia showing the main Phoenician-Punic settlements and other relevant sites mentioned in the text. Legend: 1: Genna Maria—Villanovaforru; 2: Su Mulinu—Villanovafranca; 3: Monte Prama—Cabras.

There are several instances known of *nuraghi*, albeit poorly documented, which were used for rituals involving large numbers of oil-lamps, such as at *nuraghe* Seneri of Pauli Arbarei in the Marmilla hills, which unfortunately remains unexcavated (Locci 2000:30).

The best-known example of the Punic-period shrines is that of *nuraghe* Genna Maria of Villanovaforru in west central Sardinia, where the main courtyard was used as a cult-place from the late 4th century BC onwards. Excavation of the ritual deposits has shown that the lamps offered in the initial phases were exclusively coarsely handmade ones that closely resembled Nuragic Iron Age lamps. These oil-lamps were however soon replaced by more common types of that period such as Black Glaze or Punic Red Slip ones. This underlines that the act of presenting an oil-lamp to the goddess was a key element of the ritual but that the *type* of lamp was of secondary importance. In other words, the choice of the type of lamp was not determined by the ritual and could thus follow contemporary preferences and taste of the area in general (Lilliu 1993; van Dommelen 1997:314–15; Figure 9.2).

While the diverse nature of the Demeter cult in west central Sardinia can readily be characterized as hybrid, the real question is of course what this label means in this context. In particular, how does it contribute to our understanding of these rituals and the adoption of the Demeter cult by the inhabitants of this area?

Tracing the different origins of the features involved in the hybridization process is one aspect but this adds little to our understanding of the cult in local terms. Because the Greek and Punic features of the Demeter cult are both likely to have been regarded as colonial introductions, it is questionable whether they would have been distinguished in the Sardinian countryside. It is indeed far more likely that these elements were more closely associated with major colonial cities as Tharros and Cagliari than with North Africa or Greece. Despite the prominence of the 'indigenous' features—offering of oil-lamps and re-use of the *nuraghe*—the rural shrines similarly cannot be interpreted as a direct relic of the Nuragic past: the simple fact that in all known cases the reused *nuraghe* had been abandoned for several centuries, in the case of Genna Maria since the 7th century BC, simply rules out direct continuity.

Presenting the Sardinian Demeter cults primarily as a process of hybrid integration, in which originally distinct elements were reworked into a new configuration, is nevertheless equally unlikely to add much to our understanding of these cults. Using the term as a mere description of a process in which different cultural elements 'flowed together' in fact only glosses over the specific ways in which these various features were introduced in the local situation. Such a view ignores local connotations and newly constructed meanings of these elements and most of all overlooks the role played by the underlying differential relationships between the various social and economic groups of the colonial situation and the associated power dynamics.

This point is most clearly borne out by the shift in lamp types used in the Sardinian Demeter rituals. Precisely because the type of lamp was of little importance, it follows that it

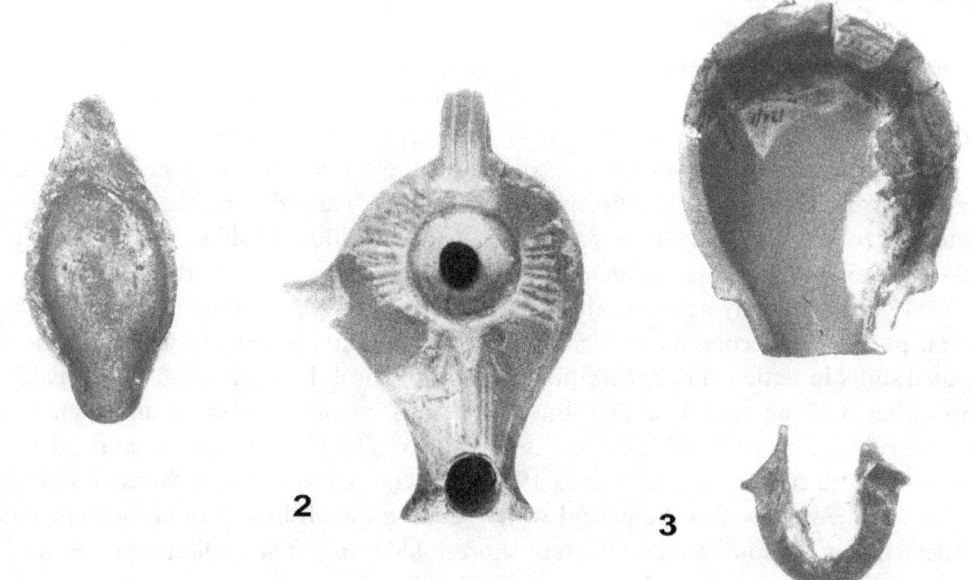

Figure 9.2 Selection of three oil-lamps of Hellenistic date from the ritual deposit at Genna Maria (Villanovaforru). No. 1 is hand-made of the so-called 'boat-shaped' type and nos 2 and 3 are mould-made Black Glaze specimens imported from North Africa (2) and central Italy (3) (after Lilliu 1993: plates I and IV).

was the *practice* of presenting an oil-lamp to the goddess and lighting it in her honour that mattered. The incense-burners, which represent a Punic addition to the Demeter rituals, may well have served as the critical connection between the local custom of lighting oil-lamps and the Punic Demeter cult. This may also have facilitated their introduction and adoption. It most significantly suggests that the introduction of the cult was largely a local affair, if not initiative, of local people drawing on—in their eyes—suitable objects and traditions that were available around them. This not only confirms that the 'originally' Punic and Greek elements were not perceived as colonial impositions at odds with an essentially indigenous ritual but also marries well with the widespread adoption of Punic customs and material culture in southern Sardinia at large, where both settlement and burial contexts were of a largely if not entirely Punic nature. The settlement evidence, at the same time, also supports the view that in certain interior regions of Punic Sardinia people had not simply been assimilated to Carthaginian standards, because in areas like the Marmilla they built their Punic-style farms often in association with an abandoned *nuraghe* (van Dommelen 2000).

While there is no reason to doubt that Carthaginian colonial rule had led, if not forced, the indigenous inhabitants of Sardinia to adopt new ways of building houses and manufacturing pottery, these points make it clear that the degree to which people had changed their lives varied substantially across southern Sardinia. While some communities, notably those in the coastal areas, adhered quite closely to Punic norms in all respects, other people, especially those living further inland, had combined them in various ways with several of their own habits and traditions. As a result, Punic Sardinia was inhabited by a number of distinct communities who related differently to the wider Punic and Classical worlds.

As already argued on theoretical grounds, this supports the point that interpreting the Demeter cults in terms of hybridization or hybrid practice marks the beginning of an investigation of local practices and the construction of local meanings rather than a meaningful conclusion in its own right.

Orientalizing Nuragic Sardinia

The Nuragic Iron Age is a period conventionally defined as covering the last decades of the 9th century BC to the central ones of the 6th century BC. As indicated by the qualification 'Nuragic', it is part of the indigenous Sardinian culture that has been named after the *nuraghi* first constructed in the Middle Bronze Age (c. 1800 BC) and that reached its highpoint in the Late Bronze Age, especially in its 'final' phase (c. 1100–900 BC: Lilliu 1988:355–416; Webster 1996:108–52). While the frequently used label of the 'season of the aristocracies' (Lilliu 1988:418) may or may not be to the point, the Iron Age was no doubt a period of significant social, political and economic changes, which saw a marked increase of social stratification and related shifts in settlement organization. A chronological distinction is usually made between the earlier and the later Iron Age on the basis of decorated pottery and metalwork with respectively 'geometric' and 'Orientalizing' designs. The break is usually situated around the mid to late 8th century BC (Bernardini 1982; Tronchetti 1988:19–39; Webster 1996:155).

The Iron Age was also the period which saw the establishment of permanent Phoenician settlements on the southern and western shores of Sardinia. The earliest one was Sulcis on the south coast, which was founded around the middle of the 8th century BC. It was followed in the later decades of the same century by Tharros on the west coast and by Bithia and Nora on the southeast coast (cf. Figure 9.1). The Iron Age was therefore a period of direct and close contacts between the Sardinians and people and their culture from the East. Although the Nuragic Sardinians had long maintained overseas contacts with regions as far away as Cyprus, the foundation of permanent foreign settlements on the island no doubt signalled a new phase for such relationships (Tronchetti 1988:41–62; Rowland 2001:53–71).

In this context of potentially strong oriental influences, it is hardly surprising that much has been made of the role of the Orientalizing phenomenon in Sardinia, especially in the light of the transformation of late Nuragic society and the resulting distinct appearance of the Iron Age. Orientalization has accordingly not just been used as the chronological indicator for this later phase but it has also been claimed as a 'true cultural climate that ... defined local social development in Sardinia between the 8th and 7th centuries BC' (Bernardini 1992:396). There have similarly been regular and explicit claims that these developments must be ascribed to Oriental influences in Sardinia, although opinion is divided whether these go back to direct contact with the eastern Mediterranean in the precolonial period or must be seen in connection with Orientalization in central Italy. This is borne out most evidently in discussions of the so-called *bronzetti*, the small bronze statuettes of people, animals and boats that are very much the hallmark of the Sardinian Iron Age (Figure 9.3). While some point to Levantine statuary found in Sardinia (Barreca 1986; Bisi 1987), others emphasize Italian connections as evidenced by *bronzetti* found in Etruscan elite burials (Ugas 1986; Contu 1997:760). Others

Figure 9.3   Iron Age bronzetto figurine of a warrior-chief found in Uta (SE Sardinia) (photo Museo Nazionale Cagliari).

still point to the abundant evidence for a largely local genealogy of these artisanal products in both technical and iconographic respects (Bernardini 1992:403; Tronchetti 1997:26–30).

In comparison with other western Mediterranean regions such as central Italy and southern Spain, the Orientalizing phenomenon was not particularly prominent in Nuragic Sardinia. Because local artisanal production did not develop particularly obvious Orientalizing features, it was mostly not very distinctive (Bernardini 1992:407). Although a characteristically Iron Age ceramic production did develop in Sardinia, it already emerged right at the beginning of the Iron Age in the 9th century BC and its characteristically 'geometric' designs such as chevrons and stamped concentric circles, occur not just on pottery but can also be seen on metalwork and even buildings (Figure 9.4). Distinctively Orientalizing features have by contrast proven difficult to identify on local artisanal products; although some features such as the *falsa cordicella* have been singled out as 'typically Orientalizing' (Ugas 1986:41–2), these do not stand out convincingly among the frequent 'geometric' elements that decorate Iron Age pottery in both the earlier and later phase. It is therefore in fact imported items rather than locally manufactured products that most commonly and explicitly denote the Orientalizing period in Sardinia (Webster 1996:156; cf. Ugas 1986; Tronchetti 1988:66–79).

More important, however, is the absence of a close link between these Oriental imports and the newly emerged Iron Age elites and the associated socio-political changes of Nuragic society more generally. While there is no denying that the inhabitants of the Phoenician settlements and the indigenous Sardinians interacted in various ways from the (later) 8th century BC onwards, it is nevertheless *not* possible to ascribe the circulation of these imports simply to 'the introduction of a new [i.e. Phoenician/Orientalizing] value system' (Webster 1996:192).

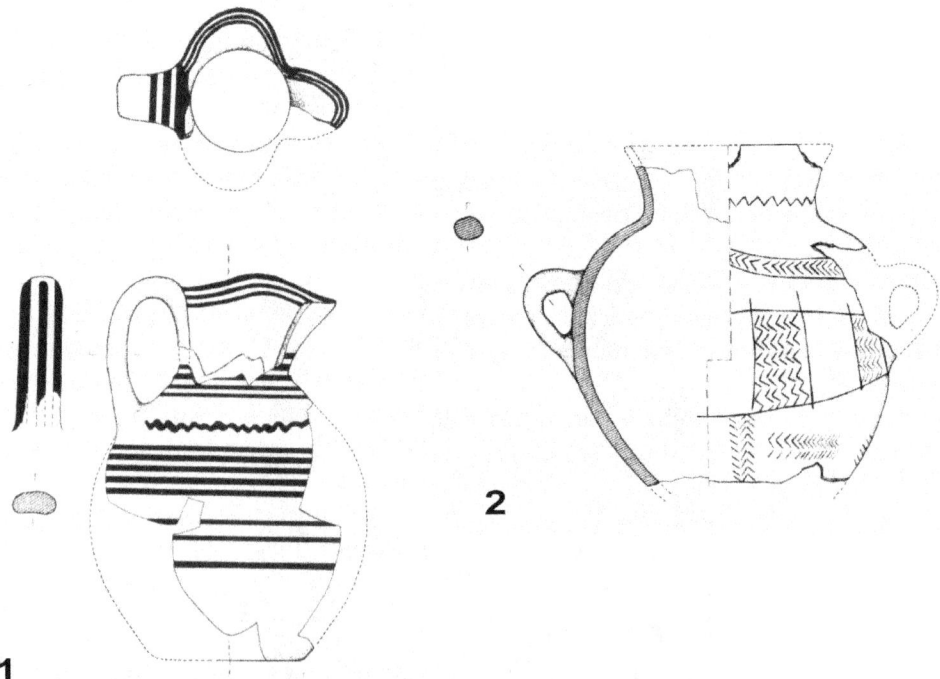

Figure 9.4 Examples of so-called 'geometric' (1) and 'sub-geometric' (2) pottery from early Orientalizing contexts at nuraghe Piscu (Suelli) (after Santoni 1991:figs 7 and 8).

The social transformations of the Nuragic Iron Age can in fact be traced back to at least the beginning of the Iron Age and many elements can already be noted in the Final Bronze Age, that is well *before* the foundation of the Phoenician settlements. While both precolonial contacts and colonial interaction no doubt facilitated the adoption of iconographic and other features of foreign provenance, the archaeological evidence demonstrates quite conclusively that the transformation of Nuragic society during the Iron Age should be regarded as a primarily indigenous development in all respects (Bernardini 1992:396–7, 400; Webster 1996:190–4; Perra 1997:62–6).

Within the mould of the ongoing transformation of Nuragic society, there is yet no shortage of evidence for contacts with and influence of the eastern Mediterranean, the Phoenician colonial settlements and the Villanovan and Etruscan worlds of central Italy. The connection between the already mentioned *bronzetti* and imported bronze figurines of precolonial date is a good case in point, because the dozen or so imported bronzes known have all been found in Nuragic ritual sites, usually a well sanctuary, which was also one of the two typical contexts of indigenous *bronzetti* (see table in van Dommelen 1998:75). While it may well be possible to discern some iconographic influence of these imported bronzes on local production, the more critical point is surely that the imports were apparently categorized alongside the local *bronzetti*: it is thus the imported items that were accepted and treated on Sardinian terms rather than that they introduced a 'new value system' of foreign imprint (van Dommelen 1998:110–12).

Throughout the colonial period, there is similarly ample evidence of contacts between Phoenician settlers and Sardinians, as is perhaps best underscored by the presence of indigenous bronze work, including some *bronzetti,* in Phoenician burials from Tharros and Bithia (Tronchetti 1988:41–62). It is therefore all the more remarkable that foreign, usually Phoenician, items in Sardinian contexts have a highly restricted distribution: they occur primarily in the ritual contexts of large well sanctuaries of regional significance, while only a small number has been found in the largest residential centres. Because this pattern closely matches that of other indigenous status goods such as the *bronzetti* and local fine ware pottery decorated in the geometric style, there is again good reason to interpret these imports as being used on Sardinian terms. When interaction with the Phoenician settlements and the outside world intensified in the 7th century BC, Nuragic elites can in fact be seen to have taken advantage of the opportunity and to have added imported items to an existing range of elite goods, appropriating these imports and incorporating them into indigenous categories, which no doubt were changed in the process as well. On the whole, this confirms the view that the indigenous Sardinians were hardly the passive receivers of foreign imports that they have often been assumed to be, and that these contacts and imports certainly did not introduce a 'new value system' to Sardinian society (van Dommelen 1998:112–13).

This general pattern of appropriation is confirmed by the rare occurrence of hybridization in the Sardinian Iron Age. The most outstanding instance of these is constituted by the sculptures from Monte Prama (Figure 9.1). These are the fragmented remains of at least 25 life-size stone statues as well as a number of stone miniature *nuraghi* that were all found in association with some 30 individual pit burials (Figure 9.5). The statues represent boxers and warriors and are absolutely unique objects, as no parallels have been traced outside the island and all known Sardinian statuary is well below life-size: the *bronzetti* for instance, which constitute the most extensive statuary group, typically measure only 20 to 30 cm (Tronchetti 1986:41–7; Sismondo

Ridgway 1986). Stone is moreover a material that was rarely used in Sardinian statuary, as only miniature *nuraghi* were sometimes produced in stone (Blake 1997:152–3). In iconographic terms, however, the Monte Prama statues match the *bronzetti* very closely in both imagery and stylistic details (Tronchetti 1986:45–6). Chronologically, both the statues and the burials have been dated to the late 7th century BC (Tronchetti 1986:47, 1991:13).

While the Monte Prama burials represent a radical departure from the communal Nuragic burial tradition, they are not entirely without parallel, even if only a few other examples are known. As in Monte Prama, these single burials were consistently associated with both Iron Age elites and ritual contexts. In several of these burials, as in Sardara (Sa Costa, not far from the well sanctuary at S. Anastasia) and Antas, one or more *bronzetti* have moreover been found. Given the presence of the miniature *nuraghi*, it is therefore quite plausible to interpret the Monte Prama as a cemetery-cum-*heroon*, in which local Nuragic elites asserted their prominence and perhaps extolled their contacts with the outside world (Tronchetti 1986:49–50).

Because Monte Prama is only a dozen kilometres or so away from Tharros, and because the larger *nuraghi* in the area north of the Bay of Oristano that have been investigated more intensively (especially S'Uraki of Cabras) have yielded clear evidence of long-standing contacts

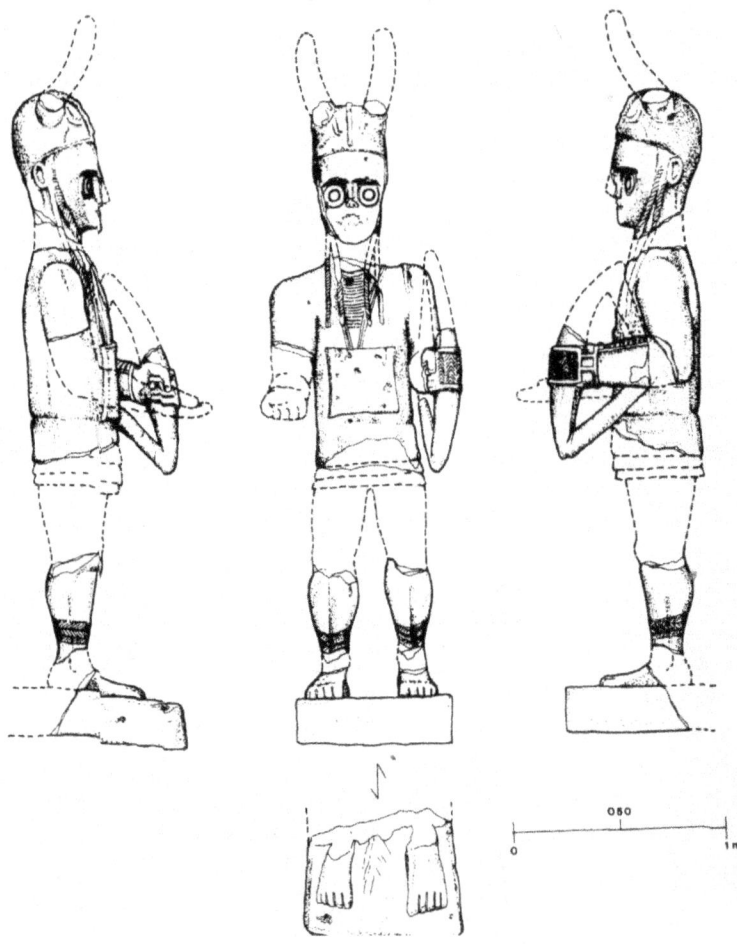

Figure 9.5   Reconstruction of one of the warrior statues from Monte Prama (after Bernardini and Tronchetti 1990: fig. 204).

between local elites and the Phoenician settlers on the Cape San Marco peninsula, it need not cause surprise that at one point some of the local elite families adopted the idea of life-size statues from either Tharros or from travels to the Italian mainland to improve their family burial plot further still. As it is unknown what kind of rituals, if any, were performed at the site, it remains speculative whether the innovative Monte Prama statues entailed a change in the practices carried out at such burials sites. When, however, considered from a local perspective as in the foregoing discussion, the creation of these statues can be understood in terms of both elite practices and elite interactions with Phoenician colonists without invoking grand schemes of cultural encounters.

If the term 'Orientalization' is going to be of any relevance to the Sardinian Iron Age at all, it may clear from the foregoing that it cannot be based on a narrow parallel with central Italy. Precisely because the archaeological evidence flatly contradicts an 'analogous process of formation and development ... between the end of the 8th and the beginning of the 6th centuries BC' as postulated by Ugas (1986:49, note 3), the occurrence of extra-insular contacts and iconographic or stylistic influence must not be conflated with long-term and more profound social and economic developments. If, however, the term 'Orientalizing' can be used 'on Sardinian terms' as simply referring to influences from the eastern Mediterranean in a much wider time-bracket, it can usefully highlight those aspects of foreign extraction that were exchanged and adopted across the colonial divide and thus bring to light the role of cross-cultural contacts in the various communities of (pre)colonial Sardinia.

Contextualizing hybrid practices

The two contexts considered in this paper show a number of substantial differences between Iron Age and classical Sardinia. It is also clear, however, that the two periods shared various features. The most obvious of these is of course that both are contact situations defined by permanent 'colonial' settlements, even if interaction in the Punic period was much more intensive than in the Iron Age.

A major difference between the two contexts is the extent to which existing categories of both colonizers and colonized were transformed in the contact situations: this difference can be captured by the terms 'appropriation' and 'hybridization' for Iron Age and Punic Sardinia respectively. As argued above, I have interpreted the rural sanctuaries of Punic Sardinia in terms of hybrid practices, because *all* cultural elements involved were reworked by the people frequenting the shrines and participating in the cult. These transformations went further than the appropriation process in Iron Age Sardinia, because the norms and values of the Nuragic elite members in contact with Phoenician settlers or traders remained by and large intact. While the addition of imported objects is unlikely to have remained without any consequence at all, the Nuragic categorization of elite goods was not structurally modified. In this case, it was the meaning of the imported items that was changed by their appropriation in the new context and not the context. It is indeed precisely against this background of elite control over and manipulation of colonial contacts that the significance of a rare instance of hybridity as at Monte Prama can be assessed most fruitfully (van Dommelen 1998:110–11).

It is my view that this distinction marks a significant structural difference between the two case studies and that the concept of hybridization should not be stretched to include the Iron

Age context, too. This precludes a straightforward affirmative answer to the question whether Orientalization can be understood in terms of hybridization, because at least in Sardinia this is not the case. Much more important, however, is that the focus on local practices has contributed significantly to understanding the local motives and backgrounds of the developments concerned.

It is also evident that the Sardinian situation was sufficiently different from other regions such as central Italy and southern Spain to leave the question open for those regions. It does nevertheless suggest that the Orientalizing phenomenon was much less uniform than often thought and that its presumed Mediterranean-wide occurrence is perhaps more apparent than real, concealing substantial local differences. This finally confirms the argument to focus on local practices in order to look at and understand apparently supra-regional phenomena such as Orientalization and colonialism.

Acknowledgments

I wish to thank Corinna Riva and Nicholas Vella for inviting me to contribute to their interesting symposium. This paper has benefited from comments during the symposium.

References

Ashcroft, B., G. Griffiths and H. Tiffin (1998) *Key Concepts in Post-Colonial Studies*. London: Routledge.
Barker, G. and T. Rasmussen (1998) *The Etruscans*. (The peoples of Europe). Oxford: Blackwell.
Barreca, F. (1986) Phoenicians in Sardinia: the bronze figurines. In *Studies in Sardinian Archaeology II: Sardinia in the Western Mediterranean*, edited by M. Balmuth. Ann Arbor: University of Michigan Press, pp. 131–44.
Bernardini, P. (1982) Le aristocrazie nuragiche nei secoli VIII e VII a.C. Proposte di lettura. *Parola del passato* 37:81–101.
Bernardini, P. (1992) La facies orientalizzante in Sardegna: problemi di individuazione e di metodologia. In *Sardinia in the Mediterranean Sea: a footprint in the sea*, edited by R. Tykot and T. Andrews. Monographs in Mediterranean Archaeology 3. Sheffield: Sheffield Academic Press, pp. 396–409.
Bernardini, P. and C. Tronchetti (1990) L'effigie, in *La civiltà nuragica* (Catalogo della mostra), Milan: Electa (originally published 1985), pp. 211–28.
Bhabha, H. (1984) Of mimicry and men: the ambivalence of colonial discourse. In *The Location of Culture*, by H. Bhabha. London: Routledge, pp. 85–92.
Bhabha, H. (1985) Signs taken for wonders: questions of ambivalence and authority under a tree outside Dehli, May 1817. In *The Location of Culture*, by H. Bhabha. London: Routledge, pp. 102–22.
Bhabha, H. (1989) The commitment to theory. In *The Location of Culture*, by H. Bhabha. London: Routledge, pp. 19–39.
Bisi, A. (1987) Bronzi vicini-orientali in Sardegna: importazioni ed influssi. In *Studies in Sardinian Archaeology III: Nuragic Sardinia and the Mycenaean World*, edited by M. Balmuth. BAR Int Series 387. Oxford: British Archaeological Report, pp. 225–46.
Blake, E. (1997) Strategic symbolism: miniature nuraghi of Sardinia. *Journal of Mediterranean Archaeology* 10:151–64.
Contu, E. (1997) *La Sardegna preistorica e nuragica 2. La Sardegna dei nuraghi*. (Storia della Sardegna antica e moderna 1.2). Sassari: Chiarella.

Cusick, J. (1998) Historiography of acculturation: an evaluation of concepts and their application in archaeology. In *Studies in Culture Contact: Interaction, Culture Change and Archaeology*, edited by J. Cusick. Centre for archaeological investigations, occasional paper 25. Carbondale: Southern Illinois University, pp. 126–45.

Friedman, J. (1990) Notes on culture and identity in imperial worlds. In *Religion and religious practice in the Seleucid Kingdom*, edited by P. Bilde, T. Engberg-Pedersen, L. Hannestad and J. Zahle. Studies in Hellenistic Civilization 1. Aarhus: Aarhus University Press, pp. 14–39.

Friedman, J. (1995) Global system, globalization and the parameters of modernization. In *Global Modernities*, edited by M. Featherstone, L. Lash and R. Robertson. Theory, culture and society 36. London: Sage, pp. 69–90.

Friedman, J. (1997) Global crises, the struggle for cultural identity and intellectual porkbarrelling: cosmopolitans versus locals, ethnics and nationals in an era of dehegemonisation. In *Debating Cultural Hybridity: multi-cultural identities and the politics of anti-racism*, edited by P. Werbner and T. Modood. Postcolonial encounter. London: Zed Books, pp. 70–89.

Friedman, J. (1999) The hybridization of roots and the abhorrence of the bush. In *Spaces of Culture. City, Nation, World*, edited by M. Featherstone and S. Lash. Theory, culture and society. London: Sage, pp. 230–56.

Jones, S. (1997) *The Archaeology of Ethnicity. Constructing Identities in the Past and Present*. London: Routledge.

Lancel, S. (1995) *Carthage. A History*. Oxford: Blackwell.

Lightfoot, K. (1995) Culture contact studies: redefining the relationship between prehistoric and historical archaeology. *American Antiquity* 60:199–217.

Lilliu, C. (1993) Un culto di età punico-romana al nuraghe Genna Maria di Villanovaforru. In *Genna Maria II,1: il deposito votivo del mastio e del cortile*, by C. Lilliu, C. Campus, F. Giudo, O. Fonzo and J.-D. Vigne. Cagliari: Stef., pp. 11–39.

Lilliu, G. (1988) *La civiltà dei Sardi dal Paleolitico all'età dei nuraghi*. Turin (3rd edition): Nuova ERI.

Locci, M.-C. (2000) Beni archeologici nel territorio del consorzio 'Sa Corona Arrubia'. In *Dentro la Marmilla. Ambiente, storia, cultura*, edited by M. Grimaldi. Lunamatrona: Sa Corona Arrubia, pp. 23–34.

Nederveen Pieterse, J. (1995) Globalization as hybridization. In *Global Modernities*, edited by M. Featherstone, L. Lash and R. Robertson. Theory, culture and society 36. London: Sage, pp. 45–68.

Nederveen Pieterse, J. (2001) Hybridity, so what? The anti-hybridity backlash and the riddles of recognition. *Theory, culture and society* 18:219–45.

Papastergiadis, N. (1997) Tracing hybridity in theory. In *Debating Cultural Hybridity: multi-cultural identities and the politics of anti-racism*, edited by P. Werbner and T. Modood. Postcolonial encounters. London: Zed Books, pp. 257–81.

Parry, B. (1994) Signs of our times. Discussion of Homi Bhabha's *The Location of Culture*. *Third Text* 28–29:5–24.

Perra, M. (1997) From deserted ruins: an interpretation of Nuragic Sardinia. *Europaea* 3:49–76.

Ratnam, N. (1999) Chris Ofili and the limits of hybridity. *New Left Review* 235:153–59.

Rowland Jr., R. (2001) *The Periphery in the Center. Sardinia in the Ancient and Medieval Worlds*. BAR International Series 970. Oxford: Archaeopress.

Santoni, V. (1991) Suelli (Cagliari). Nota preliminare sull'orientalizzante antico-medio della capanna n. 1 del nuraghe Piscu, in *Atti del II congresso internazionale di studi fenici e punici* (Collezione di studi fenici, 30), Rome: CNR, pp. 1233–44.

Sismondo Ridgway, B. (1986) Mediterranean comparanda for the statues from Monte Prama. In *Studies in Sardinian Archaeology II: Sardinia in the Western Mediterranean*, edited by M. Balmuth. Ann Arbor: University of Michigan Press, pp. 61–72.

Tronchetti, C. (1986) Nuragic statuary from Monte Prama. In *Studies in Sardinian Archaeology II: Sardinia in the Western Mediterranean*, edited by M. Balmuth. Ann Arbor: University of Michigan Press, pp. 41–60.

Tronchetti, C. (1988) *I Sardi. Traffici, relazioni, ideologie nella Sardegna arcaica.* (Biblioteca di archeologia 9). Milan: Longanesi.

Tronchetti, C. (1991) Il segno del potere. In *Papers of the Fourth Conference of Italian Archaeology. The Archaeology of Power 2*, edited by E. Herring, R. Whitehouse and J. Wilkins. London: Accordia Research Institute, pp. 207–19.

Tronchetti, C. (1997) I bronzetti 'nuragici': ideologia, iconografia, cronologia. *Annali di archeologia e storia antica* 4 (ns):9–34.

Ugas, G. (1986) La produzione materiale nuragica. Note sull'apporto etrusco e greco. In *Società e cultura in Sardegna nei periodi orientalizzante e arcaico. Rapporti tra Sardegna, Fenici, Etruschi e Greci (Atti del 1 convegno di studi 'Un millennio di relazioni fra la Sardegna e i paesi del Mediterraneo', Selargius-Cagliari, 29–30 novembre, 1 dicembre 1985)*, edited by G. Ugas and G. Lai. Cagliari: Della Torre, pp. 41–53.

Ugas, G. and M.-C. Paderi (1990) Persistenze rituali e cultuali in età punica e romana nel sacello nuragico del vano e della fortezza di Su Mulinu-Villanovafranca (Cagliari). In *L'Africa romana. Atti del VII convegno di studio, Sassari, 15–17 dicembre 1989*, edited by A. Mastino. Sassari: Edizioni Gallizzi, pp. 475–86.

van Dommelen, P. (1997) Colonial constructs: colonialism and archaeology in the Mediterranean. *World Archaeology* 28:305–23.

van Dommelen, P. (1998) *On Colonial Grounds. A Comparative Study of Colonialism and Rural Settlement in 1st Millennium B.C. West Central Sardinia.* Archaeological Studies Leiden University 2. Leiden: Faculty of Archaeology, Leiden University.

van Dommelen, P. (2000) Insediamento rurale in età punica nella Sardegna centro-occidentale. In *Actas del IV Congreso Internacional de Estudios Fenicios e Púnicos, Cádiz, 2–6 Octubre 1995*, edited by M.-E. Aubet and M. Barthélemy. Cádiz: Servicio de publicaciones de la universidad de Cádiz, pp. 1419–28.

van Dommelen, P. (2002) Ambiguous matters: colonialism and local identities in Punic Sardinia. In *The Archaeology of Colonialism*, edited by C. Lyons and J. Papadopoulos. Issues and debates. Los Angeles: Getty Research Institute, pp. 121–47.

Webster, G. (1996) *A Prehistory of Sardinia 2300–500 BC.* Monographs in Mediterranean Archaeology 5. Sheffield: Sheffield Academic Press.

Werbner, P. (1997) Introduction: the dialectics of cultural hybridity. In *Debating Cultural Hybridity: Multi-Cultural Identities and the Politics of Anti-Racism*, edited by P. Werbner and T. Modood. Postcolonial encounters. London: Zed Books, pp. 1–26.

Young, R. (1990) *White Mythologies. Writing History and the West.* London and New York: Routledge.

Young, R. (1995) *Colonial Desire. Hybridity in Theory, Culture and Race.* London and New York: Routledge.

Young, R. (2003) *Postcolonialism. A Very Short Introduction.* (Very short introductions 98). Oxford: Oxford University Press.

10 W(h)ither Orientalization?

Robin Osborne

Issues of culture contact and culture change have long been on the agenda of non-classical archaeologists. During the last 20 years they have made their way onto the agenda not only of classical archaeologists but of classicists of every brand. They have done so because, as has been most particularly clear in the wake of Said's *Orientalism*, the negotiation of culture contact and culture change involves the constitution and manipulation of power relations.

Said himself gave a special place in the formation of Orientalism to Aeschylus' *Persians*, noting that 'the dramatic immediacy of representation in *The Persians* obscures the fact that the audience is watching a highly artificial enactment of what a non-Oriental has made into a symbol for the whole Orient' (Said 1978:21, cf. 56–7). Classicists have come to tell a story in which the Persian invasions of Greece in the first quarter of the 5th century transformed Greek perceptions and representations of the 'Orient'. Up to that time the Greeks had been unprejudiced participants in a wider cultural world which extended east to Lydia and beyond. After that time Persia came to be represented as *the* 'other', Persians treated as the type of the foreign, and Persian culture that against which Greeks carried out their own self-identification (Cartledge 1993: ch.3; Hall 1989). The degree of Greek chauvinism involved in this has become an object of debate (Hall 1989; Harrison 2001), but that 5th-century Athenians were Orientalist, in Said's sense, seems undeniable. Equally undeniable is that 5th-century Athenians continued to import eastern, including Persian, goods and to appropriate them for their own purposes (wearing Persian clothes to distinguish themselves at festivals, for example, Miller 1997). Does that mean that they were Orientalizing as well as Orientalist, or that they were engaged in cultural hybridity or hybridization? Scholars have rarely ventured to use these terms of the 5th century, as if the superiority of west over east involved in Orientalism was incompatible with the superiority of east over west which is generally assumed to be the premise for Orientalizing. But asking ourselves what the Orientalizing debate looks like if we look back from the 5th century has significant advantages.

First among those advantages is that it raises the question as to whether failure previously to class all foreigners together as *barbaroi* really involves there being no Orientalism before the 5th century. As, for example, Gubel's contribution here makes clear, even if the Trojans are not a foreign 'other' in the *Iliad*, there are still type-cast Orientals (Nastes, the Phoenicians) inhabiting Homeric epic. So too the identification, from the first mention in the poetry of Archilochos in the 7th century, of the tyrant, the *tyrannos*, as eastern shows a political Orientalism going on throughout the archaic period. If the terms are to remain useful to us, then 'Orientalizing' must learn to live alongside 'Orientalism', that is, these terms cannot demand simple one-way flows of power relations. But once we recognize that 'Orientalism' and 'Orientalizing' live together, that power relations run both ways, then we come to see that 'Orientalizing' cannot be measured by quantification alone. And this is the second advantage.

Not quantification alone, but if any contact and knowledge of the non-existent 'Orient' is potentially a sign of 'Orientalizing', it remains important to distinguish 'Orientalizing periods' by the quantity of 'Oriental' goods imported, deposited and deployed. It *is* important that we know about the extent and nature of importation of foreign goods, not as an end in itself—to enable us to decide whether or not to award the label 'Orientalizing'—but rather to understand better the dynamics of interaction by being able to see the background against which interaction has occurred. As Oswyn Murray stressed at the symposium, we need to know the cold-spots as well as the hot-spots of activity, in terms of importing material and immaterial 'goods', if we are to create either a history or a geography of culture contact.

The wider and longer the contact, and the more clearly we can document it, the more insistent becomes the question of why reaction to and/or incorporation of and/or building upon what has been come into contact with is so chronologically spotty. Purcell emphasizes rightly the singularity of cultural change, and uses that singularity to argue that no unified cultural change took place. I underline the singularity here not to contrast it with the 'unified' but to contrast it with the general, and to return to the question of power by introducing, as Chris Gosden did at the symposium, the notion of agency (cf. Gosden 2004:24). Eastern artefacts and ideas may be found in large quantities in the Greek world from the Bronze Age on, they may be found in greater quantities in the 8th and 7th centuries than ever before, but it is still not the quantity that constitutes 'Orientalizing', but what Michael Shanks at the symposium called 'the local manipulation of components'.

What happens in the period between, say, 750 and 600 BC in the central Mediterranean that seems to me singular, and worth keeping the term Orientalization for, is the taking up of various ideas, motifs and skills of whose *proximate* eastern origin those taking them up were aware—though they are likely to have had neither knowledge of nor interest in their *ultimate* origins. This taking up involved doing things with these ideas/skills/motifs etc. that were unlike what they, the Orientalizers, had done before, and unlike what those whose ideas were taken up had done with those ideas/skills/motifs, etc. before. What was going on was not a matter of 'straight' imitation (whatever that would be), nor a matter of using exotic goods because their very exoticism was itself enough to lend power (which is perhaps what is going on in LBA Cyprus as described by Knapp, or when we are told the history of a Sidonian bowl in Homeric epic [cf. Gubel above]), but of transformation, transformation of both the ideas/skills/motifs etc. borrowed and of the ways of thought, action, and expression of the borrower.

The debate in this volume has returned on a number of occasions to the origins of the term 'Orientalizing' in art history. The point about Orientalizing in Greek art is not the production of *imitation*: van Dommelen is surely correct in his discussion of hybridization to stress the importance of the cultural elements involved being significantly re-worked. What reworked means is always going to be fuzzy at the edges—using any 'foreign' element in a new context is always going to be re-working to some degree—but the meaning becomes apparent, I think, when the re-worked element does its work in the Orientalizing culture. The re-working is of interest not just for itself but for what it achieves or enables.

But if the transformation of the Orientalizing culture, the notion of re-working what is taken up is central to the art historical use of 'Orientalizing', it is also the reason why I think it is helpful not to put 'Orientalizing' back into the art historian's closet. There is one very simple reason for this: transformation is at the centre not merely of the taking up of artistic motifs and techniques from the east, but of the taking up of cultural goods from the east more generally. For re-working *is* what happens to the alphabet (surely a classic case where Greeks must have been aware of semitic script for a very long time before taking it up and transforming it), re-working *is* what happens to coinage (and why Howgego (1995) is right to insist [*contra* Gubel above] that coinage is a Greek invention), re-working is what happens to law (Harris 2006), as well as being what happens to stone architecture, hard stone sculpture, incision, granulation, filigree, lions attacking deer, and the rest.

It is worth calling this 'Orientalizing', rather than simply 'hybridity' or 'hybridization' for four reasons. First, because, as a matter of fact, as Morris insists above, Greeks did apply this transformation to elements that (they knew that) they acquired from people to their east. Second, because the 'Orient' does not exist—we know that there was no unified Oriental culture, no fixed identity, no fixed address. Third, because for all their rich contacts with the west in the same period, for all the all-too-neglected flow of goods from Etruria to Greece, we cannot point to any comparable transformation of a cultural element come from the west— eventual Athenian imitation of Etruscan pot shapes to serve an Etruscan market is a quite distinct phenomenon. Finally, because 'Orientalizing' points to 'Orientalism'.

Knapp (above) and Kristian Kristiansen at the symposium have emphasised the way in which objects or skills perceived to come from a distance can be a source of power. But it is important to analyse the situation closely here. The world which is explored in this volume is a world in which, in the eastern and central Mediterranean at least (though not in the Iberian peninsula or Sardinia—Aubet and van Dommelen, above, are describing a different world) and in the 8th and 7th centuries BC culture contact occurred outside anything that would normally be called 'colonialism' (where colonizers are alien, external and extract 'food and labour from their subjects. This is colonialism' [Given 2004:3]; I take issue below with the attempt to redefine 'colonialism' by Gosden 2004). We are in a very different situation to Bhabha's colonial hybridity, where the power of the colonizing people is basic to the particular ambivalence. No issue of *colonial* authority arises in relations between eastern cultural features and either Greeks or Etruscans. The absence of Phoenician political ambitions in the Greek world is notable, and Greeks in Etruscan cities did not form even potentially independent political groups. A major part of the interest of the phenomenon of 'Orientalizing' lies precisely here. When it comes to processes like Romanization it would seem bizarre to say that in Romanizing the Romanness of Roman culture was other than essential, but in Orientalizing we find both a known and perceived (non-existent) common origin for the cultural elements that are taken up *and* a rôle for the Orientalizing which relies only minimally on that Oriental origin and not at all upon the presence of directly exercised political power by any 'Oriental' state.

What we face in the Mediterranean in the early Iron Age is culture contact without the extraction of labour or food by one power from another (that would have to await the onset of imperial power, which in the Greek world meant the 6th and 5th centuries). Gosden's recent attempt (Gosden 2004, discussing 'Orientalizing' explicitly at 64–9 and 154–5) to incorporate this sort of cultural contact under the heading of colonialism seems to me to be fundamentally mistaken. Gosden's basic move is to insist that 'Colonialism is not many things, but just one. Colonialism is a process by which things shape people, rather than the reverse. Colonialism exists where material culture moves people, both culturally and physically, leading them to expand geographically, to accept new material forms and to set up power structures around a desire for material culture' (Gosden 2004:153). This startling displacement of a term normally taken to focus on people doing things to other people (cf. Given 2004 quoted above), so as to emphasize instead things shaping people, has the advantage of forcing us to rethink the role of goods in modern colonial arrangements. It takes Marx's view that capitalism controls society through production and exchange of commodities and insists on redirecting attention from what people do to things (produce and exchange them) to what things do to people. But to insist that 'we are constructed by objects' (Gosden 2004:158, but continuing more moderately 'We are constructed as individual subjects *against a background of mass use of* material culture' [my emphasis]) is to let the undoubted agency of objects replace the agency, and obscure the responsibility, of human actors. It is timely to insist on focusing attention on what objects do to us so as better to reveal 'the range of possible shapes power takes' (Gosden 2004:159, part of the final sentence of the book), but to reduce *colonialism* to the process of things shaping people is to rip from it the core of deliberate exploitation of one human being by another, to blank out the oppression, and to set beyond moral judgement.

The rare situation in which people interacted with material and immaterial goods identified as alien *outside* a context of colonial or imperial oppression is what constitutes, in my view, the peculiar interest of culture contact in the eastern and central Mediterranean in the early Iron Age. But the reason for insisting on retaining 'Orientalizing' to describe this phenomenon is to maintain the focus on the play of power involved in this interaction. That 'Oriental' goods carried no colonial baggage, came without accompanying trappings of the forced extraction of food or labour, did not mean that they came with no baggage. Understanding that baggage, which is the baggage of Orientalism, is the most pressing task for future work on Orientalization.

In this context the art historical legacy of 'Orientalizing' is anything but helpful. Poulsen's work, like the vast majority of art history and of classical archaeology until the last third of the 20th century, proceeded by taking the objects which it discussed out of context. If we are to describe what 'Orientalizing' was not just in material but in human terms then we must, as e.g. Morris and Riva do above, see how the material and immaterial goods involved 'shape people' and are shaped by them. Something of the possible contextual dynamics is offered in some of the epic stories of encounter with the Phoenicians which various contributors have referred to above. I take here just one example.

In *Odyssey* 15 Eumaios, the swineherd, tells how he came to be attached to the palace on Ithaka. He had been the son of the ruler of a city which Phoenician traders visited selling geegaws. They did business in particular at the ruler's palace where they met a Phoenician woman who was acting as nurse to the young Eumaios. This woman had been kidnapped by Taphian pirates and sold to Eumaios' father. After a year at the city the Phoenicians left, taking with them the Phoenician woman whom they had agreed to take back home to Phoenicia and who brought as reward for her passage the young Eumaios and a quantity of precious metal vessels from the palace.

This story gives us one, fictional but ancient, context for 'Orientalization' and enables us to see something of the two-way power relations and the embedded 'Orientalism' involved. What the Phoenicians bring may be described as trinkets (*athurmata*, *Odyssey* 15.416), inessential items, but they are nevertheless in demand, and they are in demand in particular at the palace. Low bulk items, their exoticism and their limited supply work together to ensure their high value. But they have that value only because the community to which the Phoenicians bring the items is already marked by hierarchical power relations. That hierarchy enables the ruler to afford these items, and these items reinforce the hierarchy. But the goods' use to the ruler depends not least on the possibility of divorcing the material objects from the people and society which produced them. What the ruler will do with the goods he acquires is independent of what those goods were good for in the society from which they originate. In these circumstances, a high valuation on the goods is completely compatible with a low value on those who produce and exchange them. In this particular case the 'transformation' which the trinkets undergo is trivial, but the process is essentially the same for the adoption of the alphabet, or the idea of law, or of particular techniques of metalworking: all these 'Orientalizing' features can be taken over without requiring any on-going relationship to those who made them available in the first place.

The whole presentation of the Phoenicians here, as elsewhere in the Homeric epics (see Gubel above on uses of 'Phoenician' and of 'Sidonian' in Homeric epic), has a negative tinge. Far from being marked by cultural respect, the treatment of the Phoenicians is marked by claims to cultural superiority—a cultural superiority which such myths as the story of Herakles and Bousiris served to extend to other parts of the 'Orient'. Similarly in the work of the 7th-century poet Archilochos, even in the context of borrowing their term 'tyrannos' the poet will deny that he desires to be part of the Lydian world and its values: 'I don't care about fabulously rich Gyges ... I have no love of great *tyrannis*' (frg. 19 West). 'Orientalism' lies at the very heart of 'Orientalizing'. While taking up ideas and goods from the 'Orient' and deploying them as instruments to reinforce their power at home (by conspicuous consumption of scarce goods, by deploying technologies not generally available, by devising modes of communication which are in important ways arcane, by, most spectacularly, writing laws) Greeks at the same time lay claim not just to independence from but even to superiority over those who bring those goods and ideas as they redeploy them in ways adapted to their own, necessarily (as far as they are concerned) preferable, purposes.

No power without resistance? The power of the colonizer calls forth resistance from the colonized, who are faced with no option but to remake and renegotiate their identities—with one another as well as with the colonizing (cf. Given 2004:164). What we see in 'Orientalizing' is rather different. Here 'Orientalism' constitutes the resistance. Here, indeed, 'things shape people': those who take up 'Oriental' goods and ideas, or who live in a community where others take up 'Oriental' goods and ideas, have to renegotiate their identities to take account of the agency which those things deploy. But by simultaneously deploying the techniques of 'Orientalism' those who take up the 'Oriental' goods at the same time resist the importation of political power from outside along with the imported objects. The agency of the object or idea is appropriated by those who take it up and deflected into local and domestic power relationships. Those power relationships may be comparably oppressive—they may indeed become more oppressive by very virtue of the tools which Orientalizing provides (written law, stone-built temples, new forms of hoarded wealth), but they are independent of the (non-existent) 'Orient' by tapping into which they have been transformed.

Dropping 'Orientalizing', or subsuming it into 'colonialism', should be resisted. Both are strategies by which the exercise of power within communities and in the wider context of the Mediterranean world is obscured rather than clarified. The dynamics of the particular process of taking up and transforming another culture, while maintaining political independence, are distinctly topical matters. To clarify ancient 'Orientalizing', as the papers in this volume have attempted to do, serves more than simply antiquarian purposes.

References

Cartledge, P. A. (1993) *The Greeks: a Portrait of Self and Others*. Oxford: Oxford University Press.
Given, M. (2004) *The Archaeology of the Colonized*. London: Routledge
Gosden, C. (2004) *Archaeology and Colonialism. Culture Contact from 5000 BC to the present*. Cambridge: Cambridge University Press.
Hall, E. (1989) *Inventing the Barbarian*. Oxford: Oxford University Press.
Harris, E. M. (2006) *Democracy and the Rule of Law in Classical Athens*. Cambridge: Cambridge University Press.
Harrison, T. E. H. (2001) *The Emptiness of Asia: Aeschylus'* Persians *and the History of the Fifth Century*. London: Duckworth.
Howgego, C. (1995) *Ancient History from Coins*. London: Routledge.
Miller, M. C. (1997) *Athens and Persia in the Fifth Century B.C. A Study in Cultural Receptivity*. Cambridge: Cambridge University Press.
Said, E. (1978) *Orientalism*. New York: Vintage.

Index

Abdera 94
Abul 106
Abu Simbel 68
Abydos 78
acculturation 49, 50, 135, 136
Achaemenid state 22
Acquarossa 112
Adra 94
Aegean 6, 7, 10–13, 24, 26, 27, 31, 48–54, 56, 58, 59, 60, 68, 69, 72, 75, 78, 87, 89
aegyptiaca 88
Aeschylus 32, 69, 153
Africa 33, 50, 89, 90, 141, 143
Africans
   native 40
agency 60, 155–7
Ancien Régime 33, 35, 36
Akanthos 78
Akkadian 80
Akko 100
alabaster 53, 55, 85, 89
   urns ix, 99
   vessels of 87, 89
Alashiya 52
Alassa *Palaeotaverna* 51, 52, 54, 59
Albion Mareoticus 38
Alboran sea 24
Alcaeus 67, 76
Alexander VI 37
Alexander the Great 22, 39
Alexandria 35, 75
Al Mina 70, 100
Almuñécar ix, 94, 97, 99, 104, 105
alphabet 31, 74, 79, 155, 157
Alyattes 71
Amasis 68, 74, 77
Amathus 6
Amazons 70
amber 70, 117, 124

ambivalence 136, 137, 139, 155
Amenophis III 54, 56
Amenophis IV 54, 56, 59
America 39, 67
Americanalia 44
Americans
   native 40
Ammonites 85
Amphipolis 78
Amphimachos 75
Amphitrite 38
Amrit 87
Amurru 86
Anat-Astarte-Asiti 90
Anatolia 21, 22, 26, 58, 69
Anatolian artefacts 71
   colonists 51
   deities 70
   imports 69
   natives 2, 79
   powers 75
Andalusia 87–90, 94
Antas 148
anthropology 1, 2, 32, 48, 66
Antimenidas 67
anti-Semitism 32
Apasas 70
Aphrodite 76
apoikia 95
Apollo 72, 73, 75, 76, 77
Apophis I ix, 88
Appadurai, Arjun 53, 54, 57
Archilochos 153, 157
Arab 24
Ardys 71
Aramean markets 86
Aramaeans 85
aristocracy 7, 78, 95, 115, 144
art 5, 6, 9, 10, 36–9, 44, 50, 51, 70, 138

INDEX

Cypriot 85
Etruscan 7, 85
Guzana 85
Greek 4, 6, 7, 154
metalwork 7
Mycenaean 6, 7
Orientalizing 6, 7, 89
Phoenician 3, 14, 85
Sidonian 3, 88, 90
Syrian 85
Tanis 59
Tyrian 88
zoomorphic representations 7
art history 1, 4, 7, 22, 23, 26, 31, 53, 110, 154, 156
art historical approach 3, 111, 117, 154, 156
Artemis 70, 71, 76
   statue of 70
   temple of 71
artists 5, 7, 51, 66, 71, 80, 87, 90
Arwad 86
Ashkelon 67
ashlar masonry 99, 102, 106, 112
Asia 2, 22, 24–6, 28, 50, 53, 57, 71, 75
Asia Minor 2, 68, 69, 75, 77, 114
Asios of Samos 75
Assyria 4, 5, 7, 44, 66, 71, 76
Assyrian army 74
   astronomy 69, 77
   campaigns 74
   courts 77
   documents 67, 79
   kings 6, 77
   mathematics 69
   palaces 72
   reliefs 76
   sage 74
   style 5, 6, 24
Assyrians 6, 71, 89
Assyriology 43
Astarte 88, 90
Astarte Hor 88
astronomy 69, 77
Athena 36, 70, 72, 75, 76
Athens 69, 70, 78, 79
Athenians 78, 153
athurmata 156
Atlantic 95, 104
Atum 88, 90

Aubet, Maria Eugenia 1, 3, 155
Australians, native 40

Baal, temple of 102
Baal Horon 90
Babylon 27, 39, 58, 74, 76, 77
Babylonian astronomy 69, 77
   bowl 85
   bronze figures 72
   campaign 67
   courts 77
   geometry 74
   mathematics 69, 74
   monuments 39
   standards 74
Babyloniamania 39
Bahrani, Zeinab 42
Bale, John ix, 38
Banditella, votive deposit at 117, 123, 124
banqueting 12, 111, 112, 114
banquets 13, 90, 121
barbarians 69, 70, 75, 153
Bardus 38
Bardus Junior 38
Barre, J. J. 35
Bast temple 87
Bastet festival, narrative friezes of 87
Batrun 86
Beirut 89
Belgium 36
Bernal, Martin 32, 43, 49
Bernardini Tomb 6, 122
Bernini, Gianlorenzo 37
Bhabha, Homi 136–8, 155
Bisenzio 122
Bithia 99, 142, 144, 147
Black Sea
Blatty, William 43
Bloch, Marc 33
Boas, Franz 40
Boece, Hector 37
Bologna ix, 123–5
Bologna exhibition *Principi Etruschi* 91
Bosco Malenchini 115
Bourdieu, Pierre 118, 139
Botta, Paul-Émile 5
Bousiris 157
bowl/s 4, 7, 55, 87, 90
   art history 4, 5

Bastet festival on 87
Egyptian prototypes 87, 88
from Golgoi 89
from Idalion 5
from Nimrud 5
from Olympia 88
from Palestrina 6, 9, 90
Greek origin 6
iconography 5, 6, 90
inscriptions on Phoenician bowls 88
on Assyrian reliefs 6
Phoenician origin 6
Sidonian 87
tin for bowls 5
Branchidae 75, 76
British Museum 5, 6, 7
Brazil 33
Breughel, Pieter (the Elder) 39
Britain 35, 38
bronze 72, 80, 88, 100, 117, 124
bells 74
bowl/s 5, 73
cauldrons 4, 79
censers 72
daggers 55
ex-votos 102
fan 114, 124
fibulae 71
horse trappings 72, 73, 76, 79, 88, 90
hut urn 120, 123
medallion 35
shields 119
situla 72, 125
statuettes (*bronzetti*) 145, 147
tripod 55, 121
bronzetti 145, 147
Brunn, Heinrich 6
Bubastis 87
Bufolareccia 122
Burkert, Walter 25, 27
Byblos 86, 87, 88

Cadiz 14, 85, 87, 88, 94, 95, 105, 106, 107
Caere ix, 4, 5, 112, 121, 122, 127
Cagliari 143
Cambyses 74
capitalism 42, 156
Carian, graffiti at sites in Thessaloniki 78
weapons 69

Carians 24, 75
mercenaries in Egypt 68, 75
Carthage 9, 26, 85, 98, 100, 140, 141
Casal del Fosso 117, 123
Casale Marittimo 112, 113, 125
Castel di Decima 117
Castelnuovo Berardenga 112
Celtes 38
Cerro del Mar, Phoenician cemetery at 97
Cerro del Villar ix, 94–8, 100, 102, 103, 104, 105, 107
Cerveteri ix, 4, 7, 112, 113, 116, 117, 118
Chalkidike 78
Chalkis 76
Champoillon, Jean-François 36
Chang, K. C. 42
Chares of Teichioussa 75
chariot, accoutrements 88
burials 90, 122–5, 127
representations 5, 54–6, 90, 112, 125, 127
Charles V 39
Charles X 36
Chartier, Robert 28
Chersiphron 71
chiefdoms 41, 66, 95
Childe, V. Gordon 41
China 24, 39, 41, 42
Chinoiserie 25
Chipiez, Charles 6
Chorreras 94, 96–8, 104–6
Cilicia 26, 67, 85
Cimmerians 71
city planning 69
Civita Castellana 123
Clastres, Pierre 33
clan 40, 41
Classical archaeology 156
Clermont-Ganneau, Charles 9
copper 9, 14, 49, 52
coinage 69, 71, 74, 78, 79, 155
colonies 78, 94–7, 100, 102, 104–6
colonialism 29, 96, 136–8, 140, 150, 155–7
colonization 95
Greek 66, 135
Phoenician 88, 94, 99
Colonna, Giovanni 117, 119
Colline Metallifere 113
commodities 2, 50, 53, 57, 58, 67, 100, 156
commodity, Orient as 2, 50

connectivity 11, 21 26, 27, 28
Connerton, Paul 34
consumption 3, 9, 13, 24, 29, 52, 55, 56, 59, 60, 67, 112, 157
Conze, Alexander 4
copper 9, 14, 49, 52
Corinth 6
Corinthians 9
cosmogony 77
cosmology 37, 42
Coulton, Jim 22, 72, 76
craftsmen 5, 9, 86, 104
    itinerant 9, 88, 135
    Greek 135
    Phoenician 7
cremation 89, 112, 113, 116, 117, 119, 120, 123, 125
Crete 6, 71, 86, 88, 89, 90, 106
Croesus 71, 72, 76
cult 72, 141, 149
    Artemis 70
    buildings 102, 106, 142
    centres 116
    Demeter 141, 143, 144
    Eshmun 90
cultural change 21, 23, 26, 48, 49, 135, 138, 140, 153, 154
culture contact 135, 136, 153–6
culture history 1
Cyclades 75
Cypro-Phoenician art 9, 87
Cyprus 2, 5, 6, 9, 10, 12, 14, 25, 48–54, 56–60, 71–3, 86–91, 106, 111, 115, 140, 145, 154
    Anatolian colonists in 51
Cypriot, art 85
    bowls 6
    copper 52
    elites 2, 48–52, 55–7, 59, 60,
    material culture 51, 53, 76
    petal stands 88
    role in contacts 49
    society 51
    statues 79
Cyrus 69, 76

Daidalos 58
Dalley, Stephanie 1
Damascus 73
Danube 37
Dark Age 10, 11, 22, 27, 86
Daskyleion 78
Davy, Georges 39, 41
death 70, 112, 113, 116–21, 123–5, 127, 128
    gender in 120, 123, 127, 128
de Heusch, Luc 41
de Longpérier, Adrien 5, 6
Delphi 72, 74, 76
Della Seta, A. 7
Demaratos 135
Demeter 141, 143, 144
Democedes 74
Dendera 35
despotism 32, 41, 42
Diderot, Denis 39
Didyma 72, 75, 76, 77
diffusionism 7, 8, 9, 13, 23, 24, 29, 110, 111, 114, 115
distance as source of power 49–52, 57, 60, 66, 155
divinity 42, 117
Dodecanese 75
Doña Blanca 95
Druys 38
Ducati, Pericle 7
Dumézil, Georges 41
Dumont, Louis 33
Durkheim, Emile 39, 41

Ebusus 94
Egypt 4, 5, 7, 21, 32, 35–4, 50, 51, 54, 56–8, 66, 68, 69, 71, 72, 74, 75, 76, 86–9
    Nile Delta 25, 26, 51, 86–9
Egyptianizing 36, 55, 80
Egyptology 43
Eion 78
Elea 24
electrum 78
elite/s 2, 12, 33, 38, 50, 55, 59, 67, 77, 107, 111, 112, 114, 115, 149
    burials 36, 55, 57, 145
    gifts 73, 147
    Greek 77, 78
    Hapsburg 39
    horse-riding 90
    in Cyprus 2, 48–53, 55–7, 59–61, 90
    in Etruria 3, 110, 111, 117, 119, 128
    in Sardinia 3, 146, 148, 149

in Spain 3, 14
intellectual 77
interaction 58, 66
motifs 51
Nuragic 147, 148
Ottoman 39
Phoenicians in Spain 99, 101, 104–6, 128
political 33, 117
rulers in Ionia 69
Tartessian 95
emporia 96, 115
Enkomi 49, 51–4, 56, 59, 60
Enlightenment 34
entangled objects 67, 71
equestrian accoutrements ix, 73, 74, 76, 88, 90
Ephesus 2, 69, 70–2, 75, 77
Eretria 73, 76
Eshmun 88, 90
Eshmunya'ad 90
ethnicity 13, 139
Etruria 1, 3, 5, 6, 12, 89, 90, 91, 114–17, 127, 128, 135, 155
   burials in 113, 114, 116, 120, 122, 123
   chamber tombs 4, 113, 121–3
   elite demands in 111
   fossa graves 113, 121
   Hellenic influence on 110
   'lyre-player' seals from 85
   metal bearing 9, 14
   Orientalizing period in 3, 110, 127
   Orientalizing phenomenon in 111, 115, 127, 128
   political authority in 16, 188, 119, 127
   political structures in 112
   status of women in 123
   tumuli graves 114, 115
Etruscans 14, 27, 110, 111, 155
   origins of 111
Euboea 11, 76
Euboeans 9
Eupalinos 74
Euphrates 27
Europe 1, 2, 4, 24, 31–4, 39, 42, 85, 104
ex Oriente lux 50
exotica 2, 57, 59, 67

faience 48, 51–6
Faleri 85
Feldman, Marian 53, 56, 60, 61
Fenkhw 86
Ficana 112
Finley, Moses 10, 58
Fiji 33
Flaubert, Gustave 32
Frankel, D. 51
Frankfort, Henri 33, 42
Frazer, James 40, 41
frescoes 51
Freud, Sigmund 32, 33
funerary symbolism 111, 113, 119, 127, 128
Fustel de Coulanges, N. D. 33

Gades 24, 25
Gadir 94–6, 102, 105, 106
Galassi, Vincenzo 4
Ganges 37
Gardner, Percy 7
Gaul 35, 38
Genna Maria–Villanovaforru ix, 142, 143
geography 77
geometry 74
Gibraltar, Straits of 94
gift exchange 58, 66, 110, 114, 119
Glaukos of Chios 71
gold 4, 48, 52–6, 59, 68, 72, 75, 76, 90, 100, 117
Gordion 79
Gosden, Chris 1, 154, 155
Granate 113
Gravisca 26
Greek 4, 6, 7, 9–14, 22, 27, 28, 31–3, 36, 38, 44, 50, 66–72, 74–80, 85, 95, 115, 135, 140, 153–7
   aristocracry 7
   art 4, 6, 7, 85, 154
   artists 7, 71
   Asian 71
   coinage 155
   colonies 95, 97, 135
   colonization 66, 135
   cosmogony 77
   craftsmen 135
   culture 21, 26, 32, 66, 77, 80
   debt to Egypt 32
   deities 70, 72, 74, 141, 143
   elites 77, 78
   geography 77
   history 10, 22, 70, 76

    interaction with the East 67, 78
    language 23, 25
    megaron 10
    mercenaries 74, 76
    merchants 66
    Orientalizing art 6, 154
    perception of Orient 153
    poetry 77
    pottery 7, 78, 95
    prostitutes 74
    sanctuaries 70, 73
    sculptors 80
    theogeny 80
    trade 2
    tyrants 68
Grifi, Luigi 5
Grotta Gramiccia 117
Gudalhorce valley 105
Gubel, Eric 1, 3, 153
Gula of Isin 72
Gurgum (Maraş) 74
Guzana art of 85
Gyges 71, 78

Hala Sultan Tekke *Vyzakia* 51, 54
Haperin, Baruch 77
Ham 38
Hanfmann, G. 71
harbours 86, 87, 94, 100, 101, 104, 105
Harrison, Jane 9
Hattusas ix, 68, 70
Hawaii 33
Hecateus of Miletus 77
Helbig, Wolfgang 6, 10
Hellenization 26
Helms, Mary 58, 66
Hephaistos 58
Hera, temple of 72, 74, 76, 79
Heracleopolis 88
Herihor 87
Herakles 157
Herodotus 50, 72, 74, 75, 79, 88
Himera 97
Hippias 78
Hiram 87
Histaieus 75
historiography 1, 2, 32, 48, 66
Hittite bowl ix
    texts 80

Hittites 53, 70, 72
Hocart, Arthur 41
Hollywood 43
Homer 6, 32, 75, 77, 80
    Age/epoch 10, 12
    epic poems 7, 11, 12, 114, 153, 154, 157
    Heroic age 10
    portrayal of Phoenicians 75, 157
    world of 9, 10
Homeric tradition 79, 86
Homerists 10
Horden, Peregrine 29
horns of consecration 55
house, as element of funerary symbolism in Etruria 119–25, 127, 128
Huelva 88–90, 106
Humber 38
hut urns 120, 121, 123
hybrid cultures 138, 139
hybridity 3, 136–140, 149, 153, 155
hybridization 3, 153–5

Iberia 3, 9, 11–14, 94–7, 100, 104, 106, 107, 112, 155
Iberians 27
Ibiza 106
    Punic cemetery at 97
iconography 7, 9, 48, 50, 56, 57, 110, 114, 124, 146, 147, 148, 149
iconographic exchange systems 60
iconographic *koine* 56, 58, 60
iconographic motifs/themes 3, 154
    bull 5, 48, 55, 56
    chariot 5, 54, 55, 125, 127
    fan 114, 124
    griffin 4, 5, 6, 9, 48, 53, 55, 56, 59, 76, 79
    hunting theme 7, 48, 53, 55, 56
    lion 4, 5, 48, 56, 85
    palmette 5
    Paradise Flower 87, 88, 114
    pothnia theroon 90
    sacred tree 90
    sphinx 55, 76
    warriors 48, 55, 147
Idaean Cave 6, 90
Idalion 5
ideas, transfer of 2, 7, 26, 27, 51, 60, 61, 111, 114, 140, 154, 157

incense burners 117, 141, 144
India 35, 41
inhumation 112, 113, 116, 121, 122, 127
Innocent X 37
International Style 53, 56, 59
Ionia 2, 68–71, 74–9, 114
    Greeks of 71
    hotbed of intellectual disciplines 77
Ionian 67
    epic 75
    mercenaries in Egypt 68
Iron 74, 100, 105, 117
Isis 38
Isis-Athena 36
Italy 4, 5, 7, 12, 13, 27, 36, 48, 86, 90, 110, 112, 135, 143, 145–7, 149, 150
Ittobaal I 86
ivory 48, 52–6, 68, 79, 90, 124
    Enkomi ivory 65
    Nimrud 9
    North Syrian 85
    Tyro-Sidonian 88
    Tysckiewicz sceptre 85

Japhet 38
Jardín, Punic cemetery at 97
Jerusalem 67, 88
jewellery 4, 5, 51, 55, 87
    Aegean 51
    Cypriot 51
    Egyptian 87
    Levantine 51

Kadmeia grammata 79
Kadmos 79, 80
Kalabaktepe 76
Kalavasos *Ayios Dhimitrios* 51, 52, 54, 55, 59
Kantorowicz, Ernst H. 33
Karalas 142
Kavala 78
Keftiu/Kptr 58
Keswani, Priscilla 51–5, 60, 61
Khaldeh 87, 89, 90
Kilian-Dirlmeier, Imma 71
King Arthur 38
kingship 34, 41
    divine 41
    Egyptian 33, 41, 42
    Etruscan 111, 115, 117
    ideology of 49, 53
    Mesopotamian 33, 42
    Near Eastern 49, 53, 55
    political institution 33, 34, 40
    sacerdotal 33
    sacred 32, 34
Kircher, Athanasius 37
Kition *Bamboula* 56
Kition *Kathari*, Phoenician temple at 106
Kition *Chrysopolitissa* 56
Knapp, A. Bernard 1, 2, 154, 155
Knossos 70
Kommos 106
Kopytoff, Igor 53
Kothar-wa-Hasis 58
Kristiansen, Kristian 1, 2, 155
kula 57, 58
Kyme 71
Kypselids 68
Kyrielis, H. 72

Laconians 72
Laghetto 122
Lagos 97, 99
Lamberg-Karlovsky, K. 42
Lanfranchi, Giovanni 67
Latins 27
Latium 111, 120
law 155, 157
Laurita 97
Layard, Austen Henry 5, 6, 9
Lebanon 9
Lefkandi 10, 11, 70
Lelantine War 76
Lesbos 67, 72
Lévi-Strauss, Claude 41
Libyan pharaohs 87, 88
Ligurians 27
Linear B 10
literacy 111, 123
lituus 117, 118
Livorno-Stagno 116
Lixus 94, 106
London 139
Longho 38
Louvre 5, 36
Lucus 38
Lundquist, J. M. 39
Luni sul Mignone 115, 116

Lursitan 89
luxury objects 9, 49, 41, 53, 55–7, 59, 60
Lycians 53, 75
Lydia 69, 77, 79, 153

Macedonia 78
magic, Egyptian 50, 72
Magnus of Smyrna 75
Magus 38
Mainake 94
Málaga ix, 89, 94, 97, 103, 105
Malagrotta 122
Malaka 94, 95, 103
Malkin, Irad 29
Malta 89, 106
manners and customs 2, 4, 10, 12, 13, 111
maps 9, 77
Maroni *Vournes* 54
Marsiliana d'Albenga 90, 123, 124
Marx, Karl 41, 156
mathematics 69, 74
Matthäus, Helmut 87
measurement, systems of 74, 100
Melanesia 57, 58
Melqart, temple of 102, 106
Memphis 88
mercenaries 66–8, 74, 75, 76
Mesopotamia 40, 42, 46, 69, 89
metalwork 4, 5, 9, 23, 51, 144, 146
metalworking 54, 100, 103, 157
Metropolitan Museum of Art 7
Michelet, Jules 36
Midas 71
Miletus 2, 66, 69–71, 73, 75–8, 80
Millawanda 75
Miltiades 78
Minoan artists, craftspeople 51
    occupation at Miletus 51
    pottery 75
    wall paintings 51
Minoanizing pottery 75
Mobile
    people 2, 69
    populations 67
mobility 11, 26
Mogador 106
Molinello 113
Montañez, Phoenician cemetery at 97
Monte Abatone 122

Monte Cetona 116
Monte Michele 122, 123
Monte Prama ix, 142, 147–9
Monte Rovello 115, 116
Monte Sirai 85, 142
Moret, Alexandre 39
Morgan, Lewis Henry 40
Morris, Sarah 1, 2, 3, 29, 31, 32, 58, 155, 156
Morro de Mezquitilla ix, 94–8, 103–5
Moscati, Sabatino 85
Mosul 5
Motya 99
Murlo 112
Murray, Oswyn 1, 32, 154
Mursilis II 72
Musée Charles-X ix, 37
Musée Napoleon 5, 35, 36, 38
Museo Gregoriano Etrusco 4
Museum Central des Arts 36
Mut 72
Mycenae 6, 7
Mycenaean
    art 6, 7
    elites 60
    palaces 7
    period 140
    pottery 54, 55, 70
    ruler 59
    thalassocracy 85
    tombs 7
mythology 9, 40
    Indo-European 41
myths, Bantu 42
    Heracles and Bousiris 157

Nabonidus of Babylon 74
naiskoi 87
Napoleon Bonaparte 35, 36
Napoleon III 6
Narce 90, 123
Naso, Alessandro 1
Nastes 153
Naukratis 75
Necho 77
Neo-Assyrian kings 27
Neo-Babylonian kings 27
Neolithic 31
Neptunus Heliconius 38
Nerval, Gérard de 32

Newton, Charles 7
Niemeyer, Hans-Georg 9
Nikoria 10
Nimrod 39
Nimrud 5–7, 9, 87
Niniveh 6, 7, 10
Nora 25, 87, 142, 144
North Africa ix, 90, 140, 141, 143
nuraghi 141, 142, 144, 147, 148

Oceania 42
Odysseus 10
Ofili, Chris 138
Olbia 24
olive oil 52, 67, 103
Olympiad 10
Ophion 80
Oran 106
Oriental Institute, Chicago 42
Orientalizing phenomenon 1, 3, 12, 51, 95, 110, 111, 114, 115, 127, 128, 135, 136, 140, 145, 146, 150, 155, 156
Orvieto 123
Osborne, Robin 1, 3
Osiris 37, 38
Osorkon II 87
ostrich eggs 89
Othoca 142
Ottoman Empire 35, 39

Pacific 66, 67
Padania 85
palaces 7, 12, 72, 100, 115
Palestine 27
Palma di Cesnola, Luigi 6
palmette iconographic motif 5, 88
Pallottino, Massimo ix, 8, 12, 111
Papua New Guinea 58
Peabody Museum 42
Pedon 68, 75, 76
Peisistratids 78
Peltenburg, Edgar 52, 55
Perachora 72
periodization 4, 7, 10, 13, 21, 22, 27, 29
Peroni, Renato 117
Perrot, Georges 6
Persia 69, 71, 76–8, 153
Persian Wars 32, 39, 77
Pherekydes of Syros 80

Philo of Byblos 80
philosophy 77
Philistine coastal strip 26
Phoenicia 6, 7, 25, 90, 91, 156
Phoenician
   art 3, 14, 85
   artists 5
   bowls 16, 88, 90
   colonies ix, 94–7, 100, 102, 104–6
   colonization 88, 94, 99
   commercial amphorae for cat burials in Egypt 89
   craftsmen 7, 9, 86, 88, 104
   domestic architecture 97
   ethnicity 13
   expansion 85, 86, 88, 89, 95
   industrial installations 103
   luxury items 7
   maritime culture 3, 25
   merchants 3, 86, 100, 105
   political ambitions 155
   public buildings 100
   script 5, 100
   settlements 3, 14, 27, 94, 96, 135, 140, 144, 146, 147
   settlers in Andalucia 89
   settlers in Sardinia 3, 147, 149
   traders 7, 88, 90, 149, 156
Phoenicianizing 3, 79, 80
Phoenicians, as construction of modern scholarship 25
   at Ephesus 71
   Northern 86, 89, 90
   Southern 86
Phokaians 24
Phrygia 71, 72, 89
Phyrgian iconographic style 71
   textiles 71
   transmission of alphabet to Greece 79
   votives 76
Phrygian
Phrynichus 69, 78
Piazza Navona 37
Piranesi, Giovanni Battista 36
Pisa 113
Piscu, Suelli nuraghe ix, 146
Pithekoussai (Ischia) 14, 85, 97
Plutarch 36, 37
Poggio alle Fate 115

Poggio Buco 112, 116
Poggio del Molino 113
political organization 96, 106, 116
Polykrates 68, 72, 74
Pontecagnano 13, 123
Populonia 113, 116, 123, 124
ports 26, 71, 105, 106
Portugal 94, 106
Postcolonial theory 136–40
potlatch 41
Poulsen, Fredrick 7, 100, 156
Praeneste 6, 89, 122
prehistory 41, 48, 49, 70, 75, 115
Priene 68, 75
princely burial 12, 13, 117, 119, 120
princely culture 3, 13, 110, 112, 115, 120
production 3, 5, 9, 36, 49, 52, 54, 56, 57, 60, 66, 86, 87, 91, 103, 104, 106, 107, 125, 146, 147, 154, 156
Propontis 78
prostitution 68
Psammetichos 68, 75
Puente de Noy 97, 99
Purcell, Nicholas 1, 2, 3, 11, 69, 154
Pythagoras of Samos 74, 77
Pythagorean theorem 74

Radicofani 116
radiocarbon dating 95
Raoul-Rochette, D. 5, 6
Ras el-Bassit 70
Red Sea 89
Regolini, Alessandro 4
Regolini-Galassi Tomb 4–6, 122
Renaissance 32, 36–9, 44, 70
Renan, Ernest 6
Reshef 87, 90
revolutions, American 34
    French 34
    Russian 34
Rhodes 8, 9
Rhodopis 68, 74
Rhoikos 72
Richter, Gisela 7
Riegl, Alois 7
Río de la Plata 37
Rio Tinto/Sierra Morena 87
Riserva del Bagno 122
ritual knowledge 111

Riva, Corinna 156
Robertson Smith, William 40
Romanization 26, 155
Rome 6, 33, 42, 43
Roselle 112

S. Anastasia, Sardara 148
Sahlins, Marshall 33, 42
Said, Edward 2, 31, 32, 35, 39, 42, 49, 153
Sais 36, 89
Salamis 75
Samos ix, 2, 26, 66, 70–4, 76, 78
    slave trader from 68
    temple of Hera 72, 76, 79
Samothes 38
San Cerbone 124
sanctuaries 2, 70–3, 75, 76, 79, 100, 102, 106, 147–9
Sanchuniathon 80
San Giovenale 115
Sardinia ix, 1, 3, 136, 142, 146, 149, 155
    Carthaginian occupation of 140, 141
    contacts with Etruria 113
    Demeter cult in 143
    Levantine statuary found in 145
    Nuragic 113, 144, 146
    Orientalizing period in 144
    Orientalizing phenomenon in 145
    Phoenician settlements in 144
    Phoenician tombs in 6
    Punic 3, 141, 144, 149
Sardis 24, 70, 71, 76
Sargon II 67
Sarron 38
satraps 78
Schama, Simon 37
Schliemann, Heinrich 6, 7
Sciacca 87
Scota 38
Scotland 38
Scythians 24, 27
Sea Peoples 53
seals, cylinder 54, 59
    Israelite 85
    scarab 90
Selbstdarstellung 112
Selçuk 70
Sesto Fiorentino 90
Seville 88

Sexi 94
Shaffer, Lynda 24
Shalmaneser III 87
Shanks, Michael 1, 3, 154
Shefton, Brian 87
Shem 38
Sherratt, Andrew 1, 28, 50, 80
Sherratt, Susan 1, 28, 50, 80
Sheshi-Maaibre 88
Sicily 74, 87, 97, 135
Sidon 27, 87, 88
    in Homer 86, 157
    sack of 89
Sidonian art 3, 88, 90
    deities 88, 90
    expansion 89
    interests abroad 88
    impact on Orientalizating art 89
    kingdom 90
    metalwork 5, 87
    naiskoi 90
    origin of bowls 67, 88, 154
    royal storerooms 89
    territory 87
silver 4, 5, 6, 9, 54–6, 59, 78, 100, 104, 106, 107, 123, 141
smelting 52, 100, 104
Smith, A. H. 7
Smyrna 71
social organization 40, 42, 96, 106, 116
Sorgenti della Nova 115, 116
southernization 24
Spain 7, 12, 48, 146, 150
Spano, Giovanni 6
state formation 51
St John's College, Oxford 1, 14, 61
Steiner, Franz 42
Stoker, Bram 43
Su Mulinu–Villanovafranca ix, 141, 142
Sulcis 14, 142, 144
Süleyman the Magnificent ix, 39
S'Uraki, Cabras 148
symposion 23, 31
Syracuse 26, 27
Syria 71, 72, 76, 86, 89, 115

Tabbat al-Hammam 86
Tanis 86, 87, 88, 89
Tarquinia ix, 112, 113, 116–19, 121, 122, 127

Tarshish 87
Tartessos 94, 95, 105, 106
Tas-Silg, Phoenician temple at 106
Tel Kabri 51
Tel Sukas 70
Tell ed Dab'a 51
Tell Kazel/Sumur 86
temples 71, 77, 78, 102, 157
textiles 67, 71, 86, 125
Thales of Miletus 71, 75
Tharros 90, 142–4, 147–9
Thebes 27, 59
Theodorus of Samos 71, 72, 74
theology 80
Therme 78
Thermaic Gulf 78
Thessaloniki 78
Thomas, Nicholas 66, 67
Thouin, André 36
Thrace 78
Thracians 27
Tigris 27
Tiglath-Pileser III 67
Timotheus 69, 78
tin 5
Tiy 54, 56, 59
Tomb of the Statues, Ceri 117
Tomba del Guerriero, Tarquinia 117
torch holders 88
Torelli, Mario 125
Torone 78
Toscanos ix, 94, 96–101, 103, 105, 107
totem 40, 41
Triadcna squamosa shells 89
trade 2, 10, 24, 35, 49–52, 57, 67, 74, 85, 86, 87, 96, 100, 104–7, 115
    colonies 95, 96
    routes 89
Tragana 74
Trayamar 89, 97, 99, 104, 105
tribes 39, 41, 135
Trigger, Bruce 41, 42
Trojans 75, 153
Troodos mines 52
Troy 69
Tubinamba Indians (Brazil) 33
Tuna el-Gebel/Hermiopolis 87
Tuscania 112
Tutugi 85

Tylor, Edward 40
tyrants 68, 69, 72, 74, 78, 153
Tyre 5, 25, 26, 86, 89, 100, 106
    art 88
    cemeteries 90
Tyro-Sidonian kingdom 86, 88, 89
Tyrrhenian 24

Ugarit 53, 56
Uhhaziti 70
Umqi 73
Urartu 89
urbanization 51
Uta ix, 145

Vaccareccia 123
Val d'Arno 113
van Dommelen, Peter 1, 3, 154, 155
Veii 117, 120–3, 127
Vella, Nicholas 22
Verucchio 123
Verucchio throne ix, 125–8
Vetulonia 116, 120
Vico, Giambattista 34
Villanovan 116, 117, 119, 120, 123, 147
Villaricos, Punic cemetery at
von Eles, Patrizia 125, 128
Vulci 85, 90, 116, 117, 120–2

Walz, C. A. 49
Warkat-ili 86
warrior graves 9, 113, 117, 119, 125, 127
warriors 41, 48, 55, 68, 75, 90, 120–4, 145, 147
Wedgwood, Josiah 36
well sanctuary 147, 148
Wenamon 86
Wengrow, David 1, 2, 115
West, Martin 23
Willey, G. 42
wine 87, 103
    commodity 67
    drinking 12, 13, 111, 112, 114, 115
Winter, Irene 75
Whitehouse, Helen 38
world system 31
writing, alphabetic 24, 79

Xerxes 78

Yaba 87

Zemarites 85
Zeus 70
Zeytintepe 76

www.ingramcontent.com/pod-product-compliance
Lightning Source LLC
Chambersburg PA
CBHW080736300426
44114CB00019B/2610